Signal Crimes

Signal Crimes

Social Reactions to Crime, Disorder, and Control

Martin Innes

OXFORD
UNIVERSITY PRESS

OXFORD

UNIVERSITY PRESS

Great Clarendon Street, Oxford, OX2 6DP,
United Kingdom

Oxford University Press is a department of the University of Oxford.
It furthers the University's objective of excellence in research, scholarship,
and education by publishing worldwide. Oxford is a registered trade mark of
Oxford University Press in the UK and in certain other countries

Published in the United States of America by Oxford University Press
198 Madison Avenue, New York, NY 10016, United States of America

British Library Cataloguing in Publication Data

Data available

Library of Congress Control Number: 2014931560

ISBN 978–0–19–968446–5 (Hbk.)
ISBN 978–0–19–968447–2 (Pbk.)

Printed and bound by
CPI Group (UK) Ltd, Croydon, CR0 4YY

Links to third party websites are provided by Oxford in good faith and
for information only. Oxford disclaims any responsibility for the materials
contained in any third party website referenced in this work.

For
Bernard, Oscar and Kieron Innes
As one story ends, others begin.

Preface

The essays in this book all derive from a single simple premise—that some crimes and disorders are especially influential in shaping how we think, feel, and act in relation to our security. We attend to these signal crimes and signal disorders because of how they act as indicators about the distribution of risks and threats across social space. They organize social reactions, functioning like lightning rods, channelling public attention and sentiments in particular directions— towards some issues and concerns, whilst away from others. The aim of what follows is to re-frame our understanding of how we think about crime and disorder to properly take account of these events. To explain this intent, we should begin at the beginning.

'Has there been another murder?' It is November 2003. My research team and I are being shown round the Brunswick Estate by several police officers prior to starting a period of intensive fieldwork. The disconcerting question asked by our interlocutor, as she stepped out of the tower block lift, was her way of making sense of the apparently unusual sight of several police in the area. Entering the lift, the officers stated confidently that there had been a cluster of suicides recently but no murders. It was, they said, journalists generating headlines about suspicious deaths that reflected Brunswick's public reputation as a place where bad things happen.

Stepping inside the lift one officer pressed the button with the end of his pencil. We should do the same he advised, as the local drug users had taken to breaking off their 'sharps' in the buttons. Contact risked all kinds of blood infections. But not using the lifts meant, as we would subsequently discover, navigating stairwells reeking of urine and faeces (not all of which appeared to be animal), graffiti and encounters with aggressive young men.

The Brunswick Estate is situated behind the fading glamour of Blackpool seafront. In November a biting wind whips in from the sea, tossing litter and detritus around the crevices of the tower blocks. With concrete grey edifices stretching towards an overcast sky, the overall colour palette was pallid. There was also a strange absence of people. It was like they had retreated from all unnecessary public display and interaction. Amongst those who were to be seen, an unusual number walked with a limp or used a walking stick, even relatively young people. It was as if the creeping destruction of the physical environment was leeching into their bodies. Over in the play park, groups of young men, accompanied by their status dogs were a far more regular presence than any children.

As we started interviewing residents, it became clear that their stories and concerns were not the same as those of the police. The latter were focused on the reductions in recorded crime that had been achieved. Contrastingly, residents' anxieties gravitated around the messages conveyed to them by a stream of disorders. It was 'a nervous, nervous place' as one interviewee described. A recurrent concern was arson. It seems that local youths had taken to recreational fire-setting around the rubbish chutes in the flats—when fire engines turned up they could throw stones at them and their personnel. But in a large tower block, the threat of fire taking hold and the difficulties of evacuation played on the minds of many residents.

The salience of this signal was reinforced by the fact that some months earlier a neighbouring school had been destroyed by arson. The burnt out hulk of the building could be directly seen from many windows in the flats; a constant visible signifier of risk. Similarly, many people talked about the impact repeated vandalism of local bus stops and phone boxes had upon them. The significance of such destructive acts is acutely meaningful in a highly deprived area where people had few other assets. Indeed, in a number of flats where we conducted interviews there was little in the way of furniture. It had been sold either to feed chronic drug and alcohol addictions, or sometimes, just to make ends meet.

This sense of fragility was compounded by the ways 'private' conflicts and violence 'leaked' out into the other spaces within the flats. Thin walls and heating ducts threaded through the building meant private troubles were routinely public knowledge. Residents talked also about burglaries that were never reported to the police because of fears of reprisals and intimidation.

The purpose of the research was to understand how incidents of different kinds, framed by different situations, impact upon sensations of neighbourhood security, and to feed the findings to local agencies. Over a period of time, police and their partners managed to 'bend' some of their procedures and assets to become more focused upon the problems prioritized by the residents. I have not been back to Brunswick for several years now. I do not know whether the improvements have been sustained. But for a little while at least, the well-being of a vulnerable community was supported by better understanding the detrimental impacts crime and disorder has.

That there are signal events that achieve disproportionate impacts relative to other similar incidents is something we both intuitively recognize and elide in public and political talk about crime. For instance, there is an annual ritual when national crime statistics are released, involving vociferous media debate about the extent to which the aggregate level of criminality can be asserted to have gone up or down. Depending upon whether the figures have risen or fallen, government policy is celebrated or lambasted. There is an assumed public interest attached to such reporting and commentary, on the grounds that crime statistics act as an index of societal security in some fashion.

This is a symptom of how a veritable industry has grown up around trying to make sense of the crime problem. Governments expend considerable effort and resource upon gauging and measuring increases and decreases in the total amount of crime. Journalists regale us with stories about notable incidents.

Police and criminal justice institutions, through the implementation of the auspices of criminal law, seek to lead a societal response to such incidents. But each of these institutional responses frames the crime problem in ways that are partial and misleading. An alternative point of departure for an enquiry into how publics interpret and make sense of crime could pose a counterfactual question such as 'What if aggregate national crime rates have little to do with how safe people perceive themselves to be?' Might it be more insightful to assume that peoples' sense of security, pivots around a blend of a few exceptional high profile crimes and what they encounter more locally?

This way of thinking has additional purchase in a historical moment of over two decades of year-on-year reductions in crime in a number of Western countries and cities. Whilst we cannot be sure whether this is a temporary abatement in rising crime levels, it appears less certain than when Garland (2001: 106) was writing, that high crime rates are an incontrovertible and irreversible 'normal social fact'. Indeed, it is precisely because crime has been reducing that the role and salience of signal crimes has become easier to discern. For set against a backdrop of less crime, it has been possible to clarify that public sentiments and perceptions are not a simple correlate of overall crime levels. The thesis propounded in the following pages is that instead, individual and collective security is significantly influenced by illegal and disorderly acts, and control responses to these, that send signals to people about the distribution of risks and threats.

From time-to-time there are, of course, crimes so horrific and unusual that they transcend local interest. Listing names such as Stephen Lawrence, Amanda Dowler, and Sarah Payne almost intuitively captures how particular incidents possess significant legacies in shaping thinking about crime as a category of social problems. The harm visited in such cases is clear and present. But in seeking to make sense of public reactions to crime, it is important that we do not focus solely upon such incidents, neglecting the less visible occurrences.

Indeed, over recent years there has been growing recognition of the significance of a range of anti-social behaviours in terms of influencing perceptions of neighbourhood security. Many of these are not proscribed in law, and thus defined as crimes, but nevertheless have corrosive impacts upon social cohesion and perceptions of local safety. In part, this might reflect how the institution of law struggles to deal adequately with forms of harm that are collectively rather than individually based.

The argument developed in the essays comprising this book is that there is a generic social reaction process to how we perceive and interpret incidents of crime and disorder, as well as the organized social control responses to these. Empirical warrants for this claim are now available via a number of studies that have drawn upon the earlier articles where the signal crime construct was originally worked out (Innes and Fielding, 2002; Innes, 2004). Notably, Tony Bottoms (2012) has located it within the purview of socio-spatial criminology, emphasizing the insights it affords into how local micro-cultures shape what disorder and anti-social conduct come to be defined as matters of collective concern. In his discussion of why 'white collar crimes and criminals' tend to attract so little public attention despite involving considerable social harm, Levi (2008) invokes signalling processes to explain the absence of a defined public problem, where perhaps there should be one given the increasing prevalence and impacts of this form of illegality.

A perspective is a way of seeing. It affords a particular field of vision by bringing some items to the foreground, whilst others are rendered more obscure.[1] The point of perspective is that precisely what is perceived depends upon how and where one is positioned. In the following pages this central conceit is explored and configured, to disinter the processes through which individuals and collectives perceive, interpret, and make sense of crime and disorder. Across the essays a key theme that emerges is that how events are reacted to depends on whose perspective one is talking about. Individuals and institutions may frame the same incident very differently, depending upon the social, physical, and material positions they occupy. Consequently, different communities and neighbourhoods may view similar problems in markedly different ways.

Crime signals occur in two principal registers—the everyday and the catastrophic. The former refers to mundane, 'normal' crimes (Sudnow, 1965), the latter covers far less frequent, but high public profile incidents. Whilst there are obvious differences in the prevalence and intensity of these everyday and catastrophic forms of signal event, and the extent their effects 'travel', they share important elements in terms of how they are interpreted and influence patterns of social order. The key assertion of this book is that some crimes and disorders matter more than others in shaping and influencing our feelings and beliefs about security.

Extending this way of thinking about processes of social reaction, it is suggested that similar modes of interpretation and sense-making are applied to acts of social control. Just as signal crimes and disorders are generative of an array of cognitive, affective, and behavioural reactions, similar effects can be detected in relation to the presence of 'control signals'. This latter concept is important in opening up the communicative properties of much social control work, offering the potential for a richer and more supple analysis of how it functions across varied forms and situations. It enables us to see how acts designed to regulate troublesome or problematic behaviours routinely seek to send messages to a number of audiences.

It has become commonplace in talk about contemporary technological innovations to refer to 'disruptive technologies' that alter patterns of behaviour and social ordering. Analogous to this, the triad of key concepts introduced via the essays in this book, which are all species of signal event, can be thought of as

---

[1] There is a deliberate connection here to Kenneth Burke's (1954) instruction that 'a way of seeing is also a way of not seeing'.

'disruptive concepts'. They are intended to reconfigure the ways we understand the social impacts and consequences of crime and disorder, and our responses to such occurrences. They are insurgent ideas that challenge aspects of the public understanding of crime.

The essays have been crafted to be standalone but connected. They are designed to throw contrasting shafts of light on to processes of social reaction to crime, disorder and control. As 'etiolations', each illuminates slightly different aspects of how we individually and collectively react to particular kinds of public problem. Overall, the intended effect is a 'theme and variations' approach. As such, they can be read in different orders, but by viewing them together a more complete understanding of the particular insights that are gained by seeing the world through a 'signal events' lens can be achieved.

To comprehend how the parts of the whole 'hang together' it is potentially insightful to clarify some of the key elements featuring in the book's title. The focus throughout is upon individual and collective reactions. These reactions encompass perceptions and interpretations, emotions and subjective feelings, and acts and behaviours. They are 'socially organized' reactions in the sense that there are discernible base patterns to their respective causes and consequences. Finally, the individual contributions are presented as essays in the sense of the etymological roots of this form of writing that lie with the French word 'essaier' or 'to try'. That is, they are attempts to work out the consequences of a fairly radical theoretical position that attends to events and their impacts, and in the process move beyond more orthodox approaches already available in the research literature.

The opening essay in the collection sets out the principles of the analytic schema through which a signal can be detected by listening to how people talk about crime. Betraying an influence from a symbolic interactionist sociology that has appropriated some conceptual tools from pragmatist semiotics, it is defined that all signals comprise three principal components: an expression; content; and effect. The main conceptual innovation is to connect particular events to the discrete and distinct effects that they trigger and induce. These arise in different combinations, but gravitate around three main effect types: thought and cognition; affect and emotion; behaviour and action. An important aspect of the ensuing discussion is showing how application of this conceptual scaffolding leads down different paths from some more established theories about the impact of crime and disorder upon social life. As is asserted in the essay itself, it is an approach that provides a unique perspective to the empirical and theoretical study of social reaction. Informed by interview data where people are talking about crime in their neighbourhoods, the discussion sets out the main precepts of a signal crimes perspective (SCP).

Attention turns in the second essay, to focus more exclusively upon the notion of the signal disorder. How an incident is defined via the auspices of criminal law, is found to be of only marginal influence in terms of its power to shape public perceptions and sentiments. The social visibility of disorder is shown to have a vital role in terms of its capacity to signal a sense of risk or threat to on-looking audiences. The key contribution this makes to the SCP overall, is evidencing that the capacity of a signal to alter thought, emotion, and action, is dependent upon aspects of the social context in which it arises. Recognizing this situational influence is an important refinement to understanding the social dynamics of signal events.

The next essay alights upon a crime that is very much the property of the criminal justice system—criminal homicide. Starting with the question 'how does fear travel in the aftermath of fatal violence?' the essay maps out how thinking about signals and their effects inclines one to new ways of framing public reactions to crime. Pivoting around a critique of the ways the concept of fear of crime has been formulated and operationalized, and informed by a series of field studies designed to measure the community impacts of several high profile murders, the alternative notion of the harm footprint is laid out. This is progressively broken down to delineate three prototypical harm footprints—private, parochial, and public.

In the fourth essay the focus is upon how rumours of crime events are sometimes sufficient to generate similar effects and reaction patterns to those where incidents actually did occur. A careful and detailed analysis of the causes and consequences of a number of crime rumours, uncovers 'phantom' signal crimes that, although they were never there, were nevertheless consequential in shaping public perceptions and concerns. This sense of a presence in absence reflects how crime rumours are often deployed as 'soft facts' filling in knowledge gaps when people are seeking information about events, but authoritative sources are unavailable.

The penultimate contribution moves away from the public and their reactions to consider the effects of signal crimes upon social institutions. Just as the thoughts, emotions, and actions of individuals and groups are shaped by the occurrence of signal crimes and disorders, similar reaction patterns pertain to institutions. This is an idea of some import for the signal crimes perspective overall. In a chain of events initially set in motion by the attacks of 9/11 in the United States of America, and subsequently propelled by a series of other terrorist incursions, the institutional structures and processes of counter-terrorism policing have been re-thought and re-made in many Western states. Through a case study of the ways counter-terrorism policing policy and practice has been revised in the UK in particular, this essay considers how significant institutional reform is frequently a consequence of signal events.

The final essay explores the communicative properties of acts of social control. It is argued that communication is fundamental to how social control works and is a dimension neglected by previous contributions to the scholarly literature. An important distinction is made between: 'signals of control' that emanate from, or are transmitted by acts or interventions effecting social control; and, 'signals to control' involving targeted and intentional attempts to persuade, instruct, regulate, or coerce people to think and/or behave in particular ways. In an era of public sector austerity, the value of this approach is in understanding the wider potentials and ramifications of social control interventions.

Whilst each essay has been written to work as a separate and individuated entity, there are meta-narratives that span across them in terms of recurrent themes and concerns. The first of these is the presence of a generic process of reaction that is transcendent of any substantive issues that trigger concern, whereby the principal interpretations and effects obser. ed across individuals, collectives, and institutions maintain similar forms and functions.

A second cross-cutting theme is that culture and situation matter. The tenor and tone of any reaction is shaped by the social setting in which the signalling event is itself located. Local cultures and their moral orders play a crucial role in selecting which events function as focal concerns for a particular community and which are deemed less salient.

The third meta-narrative concerns the ways some signals fade and decay, but others are amplified over time. Such legacy effects are important in labelling particular places and people as sources of trouble. Past signals establish frames influencing the interpretation of subsequent happenings. This is a particular variant of a wider challenge relating to how to capture the cumulative impacts of different signals. In any everyday situation there are a multitude of items signalling the presence of potential risks and threats, alongside multiple indicators of social control. How and why are some of these attended to, but others are not?

That the essays in this collection span from anti-social behaviour through to terrorism and homicide, and encompass both contemporary and historical examples, showcases the extent to which signalling processes are integral to the ways we collectively process and make sense of these issues. This diversity reflects also how the empirical materials are derived from a ten-year programme of field studies designed to investigate in different ways and from different vantage points the problem of understanding individual, collective, and institutional processes of reacting to crime, disorder, and social control.

Given the extensive research base that underpins these essays, a final afterword is included reflecting upon matters of method and methodology. For although the individual essays exhibit different substantive concerns, they share a common methodological base—a blend of systematic and unsystematic social observation. That is, a more creative and less structured phase of conceptual innovation and initial development, followed by more rigorous and systematic testing and refinement of these ideas through exposure to detailed empirical data. At a moment where academic disciplines across the social sciences are seemingly increasingly attracted to being 'scientific' in their orienting dispositions, it is important that we do not neglect the importance of creativity and intuitive insight. For want of a better label, it is argued that a form of 'gonzo research' may be helpful in this endeavour, particularly for more 'naturalistic' (as opposed to experimental) research. Rigorous empirical testing is important, but good research involves both skilled craft and science. The purpose of this short-ish afterword is to lodge the notion that by combining gonzo research's unsystematic approach, with more structured empirical studies it has been possible to uncover some generic properties of how we collectively ascribe meaning to crime, disorder, and control. This book then, is more about our reactions than the events that stimulate these reactions. For it is in the processes of how we react and make sense of occurrences that trouble us or disturb the patterned rituals and routines of social order, that we find out so much about who we collectively are.

Acknowledgements

This book has taken me far longer to complete than I ever originally envisaged it would. It is probably the better for this, but a series of events have interceded along the way and subtly influenced its contents.

Around the time that I started working out my thinking about signalling processes and how certain moments change the ways people think, feel or act, several things happened that impacted upon how this book came to be. First, my father fell ill and after a prolonged struggle with his illness died. A short while later, my wife and I experienced the excitement of our first son being born. This was then followed by the birth of our second boy. Births and deaths are events that impact upon our individual thoughts and feelings like nothing else can. And whilst such occurrences conform more to what C. Wright Mills dubbed 'private troubles' than the public issues that are the focus of the following essays, in a book on reactions to significant events, these biographical moments are of some consequence.

The lengthy process associated with the research that underpins the different essays in this book has benefitted from the contributions of a large number of people. Some of my initial ideas about signal crimes were developed in conversation with Nigel Fielding at the University of Surrey. We published an early piece deriving from these conversations in 2002. Ever since that point, Nigel has provided invaluable help in thinking about how this approach should blend the conceptual and empirical. He is an outstanding methodologist and sociologist. I benefited greatly from the detailed comments he provided on several of the essays in this collection. A second colleague from my time at Surrey, Alan Clarke, was an important collaborator in investigating the legacy effects of major crimes and establishing the notion of 'retroactive social control'.

The extensive fieldwork and in-depth interviews that underpin several of the essays was originally conducted as part of the National Reassurance Policing Programme, that I was involved in between 2003–5. Meeting the demanding schedule for collecting and analysing data to inform a pioneering and rapidly developing policy initiative involved a dedicated team of researchers working in often quite difficult conditions. So I would like to record my thanks to Sophie Langan, Sinead Hayden, Laurence Abbott, Philip Murray and Helen Mackenzie for their contributions in conducting and rigorously analysing such a large number of interviews. As part of the wider project team, Carl Crathern, Gavin Stephens and Tim Godwin provided invaluable support and help at several critical junctures, ensuring that the work got done. A special mention in all this must go to Sir Denis O'Connor who identified initial potential in the nascent signal crimes work, and secured the resources to underpin the extensive fieldwork that enabled it to grow and develop. In subsequent years, he supported several projects that have informed the work reported herein.

Since moving from Surrey to Cardiff University I have been fortunate to work with several excellent colleagues. Mike Levi has been especially supportive and provided insightful comments on drafts of two of the essays herein. Trevor Jones, Amanda Robinson and Fiona Brookman have all helped me, in different ways, to make sense of the Welsh criminal justice 'landscape'. At Cardiff I have been working on a number of research projects that have sought to extend and work through the implications of the signal crimes concept. In these efforts I have been aided by: Nicola Weston, Charlotte Leigh, Daniel Grinnell, and Sarah Tucker.

Several of the essays in this collection draw upon data from the applied research studies that have been conducted by the Universities' Police Science Institute team. Essay II reworks material originating in two projects funded by Her Majesty's Inspectorate of Constabulary. The first of these was co-authored with Nicola Weston and the second with Helen Innes, and I have made use of analyses conducted by them. Essay V draws on material originally published in a report for the Association of Chief Police Officers on Prevent policing that I undertook with Colin Roberts, Helen Innes, and Trudy Lowe. In addition to which, some of the concepts used to document the emergence of the co-production of counter-terrorism were a product of activities undertaken under the auspices of an ESRC grant on the co-production of social control, and more latterly the Productive Margins programme funded by the AHRC and ESRC. The parts of this essay discussing policy analysis were first presented as part of a lecture at the Australian National University in 2011, during my time as a Visiting Fellow at the Centre of Excellence for Policing and Security. Some of the empirical material reported in Essay III originated in a study funded by the National Policing Improvement Agency and was collected by Trudy Lowe and Colin Roberts.

In addition to those who have been directly involved in the fieldwork effort, Sir Anthony Bottoms, Rod Morgan and Patrick Carr have, at critical junctures, encouraged me to develop my thinking about signal crimes, signal disorders, and control signals in a number of important ways. In preparing the book I have been fortunate to work with a great team at Oxford University Press, in particular, Peter Daniell, Matthew Humphrys and Lucy Alexander.

A special note of thanks goes to Trudy Lowe and Colin Roberts. They both started working with me in the early days of the Reassurance Policing initiative and have stuck with it, in what has turned out to be a decade long effort to understand what the implications of thinking in terms of signal events might be. They have endured a succession of temporary contracts and funding uncertainties, but in the process have developed into two of the most professional and accomplished fieldworkers I have ever had the pleasure to work with. Trudy has played an important role in developing the ongoing practical utility of the ideas we have formulated. Colin's influence has been especially important in terms of how I have come to think about counter-terrorism and how this can be conducted.

They have both made a significant contribution to the issues and ideas pursued in the following essays.

My final words are for my family. Over the past few years Helen has started to work at the Institute, where her quantitative analysis skills have been put to good use. Her analysis features in several of the essays in this respect. But it has meant that she has become more closely involved in the writing of this book than either of us imagined. She proofread and commented on the essays, and helped to improve them. She has also had to put up with at least eight years of regular moaning about not having enough time to write 'my' book, and periods of grumpiness and withdrawal when I did actually get around to doing some writing.

This book is dedicated to the memory of my father and to my two boys. Each of them has made me a better person for knowing them.

Martin Innes
Cardiff
May 2014

Contents

Contents

Abbreviations

ASB	anti-social behaviour
BCS	British Crime Survey
BIT	Behavioural Insights Team
CCRs	cold case reviews
GCHQ	Government Communications Headquarters
NRPP	The National Reassurance Policing Programme
NSA	US National Security Agency
PCSO	Police Community Support Officer
PIRA	Provisional IRA
QCA	Qualitative Comparative Analysis
SCP	signal crimes perspective
SOCA	Serious Organised Crime Agency
UK	United Kingdom
US	United States of America

A Signal Crimes Perspective

A signal is a sign that has an effect. Signals are present when, in moving information from a transmitter to a receiver, some change is induced in the state of the latter. Conceptualized in this way, the notion that some crimes act as signals focuses upon how they communicate information about the prevalence and distribution of risks and threats across social space. They conduct and channel processes of social reaction towards some issues, and away from others.

These signalling processes can be observed in public reactions to a large number of crimes over the years. For example, when the deceased body of Rachel Nickell was found on Wimbledon Common in South West London, it rapidly acquired the properties of a powerful signal crime. Intense media and public interest in the murder was triggered by a confluence of factors. First there was the uniquely harrowing circumstances in which she was found, with her two year old son found clinging to his mother's blood soaked body saying 'wake up mummy'. This was augmented by the fact that the victim was extremely photogenic, which provided the tabloid and broadcast media in particular, with an iconic image that could be repeatedly attached to their reporting. In this sense, it was an archetypal signal crime. It was eminently visualizable, with the capacity to connotatively depict the presence of danger, invoking consequences for how many people thought and felt about their safety.

But as the police investigation and subsequent court case progressed a second, very different 'signal' emerged. Very early on in their enquiries police had identified Colin Stagg as a potential suspect and he was prosecuted and convicted on the basis of the evidence that they generated. However, following 14 months in custody, after which his conviction was overturned upon appeal because of serious doubts about the integrity of aspects of the police investigation and its evidence, a negative control signal was triggered, causing damage to public trust and confidence in the police. It was not until 16 years after the original murder that Robert Napper was convicted of manslaughter on the grounds of diminished responsibility.

Each year there are a small number of serious crimes that achieve the kinds of intensive and widespread impact upon public understandings of crime that resulted from the *Nickell* case. For instance, in the UK: the murders committed by Peter Sutcliffe across the North of England in the 1970s; the racist murder of Stephen Lawrence in London and the abduction and murder of James Bulger, both in 1993; the disappearance of Madeleine McCann; and the more recent abduction and murder of April Jones in Wales, all display the dramaturgic capacity of certain moments of criminality to elicit profound collective reactions. Similarly, in the United States: the murders committed by Islamist jihadist terrorists on 9/11/2001; the assassination of President John F. Kennedy in Dallas, 1963; the killing in Perugia, Italy of student Meredith Kercher and the subsequent trial of Amanda Knox and her boyfriend Raffaele Sollecito; and the mass shooting of 27 people in 2012 when Adam Lanza broke into the Sandy Hook elementary school in Newtown Conn., amongst many other similar cases, all exemplify the traits of signal crimes. Each of these crimes signalled and communicated slightly different messages, depending upon the precise circumstances involved. But of broader significance is that they all resulted in impacts and effects upon public sentiments and views far beyond those felt by people directly connected to the crimes. Equally, in both countries, there are a multitude of other occurrences that have acted as signal crimes and could have been referenced in this way. Indeed, every country and every culture has its own similar litany of acts and events.

The ability of particular crime events to send signals to people is not restricted to high profile major incidents though. Similar processes of interpretation and sense-making can also be found in how people react to local crime and disorder. The 'reach' of these crimes in terms of the extent that their impacts 'travel' within and across different social groups may be more limited, but fundamentally there is a generic process of social reaction. The initial event cues particular patterns of thought, behaviour, and emotion connected to the management of safety and security.

As a conceptual model, this is broadly coherent with the position worked out by Erving Goffman (1972) in his essay on the significance of a veneer of surface impressions for sustaining fragile urban social orders. For he identified that the articulation of signals in human communicative interaction is heavily dependent on social convention, defining a signal as,

> ...a conventional sign, which, by prearrangement, has been arbitrarily established for this purpose—the purpose of announcing that there is something about which to be alarmed. (Goffman, 1972: 247)

This broadly interactionist take on signalling processes can be further enhanced and elaborated by appropriating aspects of Umberto Eco's (1976) pragmatist semiotic theory. For Eco also discusses the importance of signals, noting that the basic signalling function applies both to human-to-human communication, and the 'physical' and automated informational processes involved in machine based communications where humans are absent.

Although they are both attending to processes of signification, Goffman and Eco's theoretical predispositions lead them to accent different aspects of signals and signalling. Their positions are not necessarily incompatible however. From Goffman, there is a sense of how the act of interpretation is performed and the wider situational influences upon it, together with the behavioural consequences. Eco is more attuned to the presence of pre-existing categories framing peoples' perceptual fields and the interpretations they assemble to render meaningful the information derived from their sensory apparatus. What locating semiotic concepts within an interactionist framework supplies, therefore, is a diagnostic method for taking apart peoples' speech acts as they construct representations of their reactions to instances of crime, disorder, and social control.[1]

By blending aspects of these two approaches to understanding signalling processes, it is possible to arrive at the position that a signal is a sign that has an effect. It can be suggested that all signals are possessed of three component parts: the 'expression'—that is the signifier or denotative aspect; the 'content'—what is connotatively signified; and an 'effect'—the change induced from the connecting of a content to an expression. These elements all feature in the following extract from a person talking about how they had been affected by a burglar breaking into a neighbour's house:

> There had been a burglary, either it was that night or the night before...I was very anxious then...and it was the first time in eight years I actually did not feel one hundred per cent safe. (Ash214)

In this example, the 'burglary' functions as the expression, the effect of which is that the respondent felt 'anxious'. The content of the signal can be connoted from the phrase 'I actually did not feel...safe', wherein the interviewee is identifying how she interpreted the occurrence of this crime as representing a risk to her own personal security. From this account it can be seen how an event that has not happened to the person directly has nonetheless caused them to alter their perceptions of their own safety—it had functioned as a signal to them.

Goffman's (1972) formulation, in particular, accents the role of signals in portending danger. This reflects his view that, along with all social animals, humans are both 'hard-wired' as a result of evolutionary processes and 'soft-wired' through socialization and culture, to attend to indicators of potential threat or risk in their environments. In human group life, one commonly encountered species of risk and threat are those acts and forms of conduct generically labelled as crimes through the classificatory and definitional power of the state's criminal law apparatus. But as has been shown by a growing number of studies, it is not just those acts codified as crimes that give rise to alarm and trepidation. Much concern about security in public places gravitates around the presence of sub-legal incivilities and disorderly conduct (Taylor, 2001; Bottoms, 2006; Skogan, 2006). This reflects

---

[1] This melding of symbolic interactionist sociology with semiotics has precedent in the work of Manning (1987), Denzin (1987), and Morris (1964), amongst others.

how, in terms of the ways that they are interpreted within the flows of everyday life, many types of crime and disorder are not possessed of clearly demarcated ontological distinctions. The suggestion that they are is an artifice of juridical discourse and practice (Harcourt, 2001). This is consequential for a signal crimes perspective in that how criminal law and its attendant institutions and processes categorize different forms of offence, may not be equivalent to the harm and impact that particular incidents have upon collective perceptions of neighbourhood security and safety.

The notion that both disorder and crime can perform a signalling function has been previously identified, albeit in a perfunctory fashion, in both Wilson and Kelling's (1982) broken windows thesis and Ferraro's (1995) theorization of fear of crime. For the former,

> ...vandalism can occur anywhere once communal barriers—the sense of mutual regard and the obligations of civility—are lowered by actions that seem to signal that 'no one cares.' (Wilson and Kelling: 270)

Thus for Wilson and Kelling, crime and disorder functions as an expressive index of the state of the local social order. A not dissimilar approach can be found in Ferraro's (1995: 51) risk interpretation account of fear of crime:

> Signs of social and physical incivility such as disruptive neighbors, unsupervised youth, vacant houses and unkept lots are generally associated with higher perceived crime risk. These phenomena are signals to residents that more vigilance is needed to avoid crime in their daily activities.

Both of these formulations reference the fact that under certain conditions, and located in particular settings, the presence of crime and disorder acquires communicative properties, influencing how people appraise their situated environments. However, neither dissects the signalling process itself and how specific crime and disorder incidents are perceived, interpreted, and invested with meaning by those members of the public who attend to them. Moreover, little consideration is given to why some incidents trigger alarm, but others do not. This essay sets out to provide a more thorough analysis of how and why crime and disorder may function as signals of risk to people, and some of the insights and consequences that flow from the adoption of such a conceptual framework.

The discussion, informed principally by an analysis of 333 in-depth interviews with members of the public living in different neighbourhoods distributed throughout England, starts by mapping the contours of a conceptual framework for understanding how and why certain acts, and the material traces of these acts, function as significations that generate particular reactions in those people aware of their presence.[2] This involves working out the position of a signal crimes based approach in relation to other, prior, contributions to understanding reactions to

---

[2] A more detailed description of the research design, data, and methods is provided in the afterword to this volume.

crime. Then, developing this position, the issue of how certain 'signal crimes', 'signal disorders' and 'control signals' relate to the prevalence and distribution of a range of cognitive, affective, and behavioural reactions is considered. Having established this framework, the focus shifts to illustrate how it can be applied to an analysis of collective perceptions of security and insecurity across different neighbourhoods. This serves to emphasize that the particular strength of the approach outlined is that it affords a coherent approach for studying processes of social reaction to both routine and everyday troubles, and less frequent, more spectacular, catastrophic events. These insights are developed to explore how experiences of crimes or disorders performing a signalling function in the past can exert a potent influence upon how people think about who they are and the levels of safety afforded to them in the present.

The Public Understanding of Crime

The study of social reactions to crime has gravitated, to a significant extent, around two principal and quite different positions: studies of the fear of crime; and, work on moral panics. What sociological criminology has lacked is a disciplinary equivalent of the 'public understanding of science'. This is an approach that occupies a unique space in the social studies of science literature, looking at the array of influences that shape public attitudes and perceptions of new scientific innovations, technologies, and risks. Whilst a direct parallel for the study of crime perceptions and attitudes is probably not appropriate, adopting a more holistic and comprehensive effort to document and interpret the varied array of factors feeding into the formation of public views, would have considerable merit. In this sense, the predilections of a signal crimes-type approach to studying social reactions to public problems, would be positioned within the broader ambit of this public understanding of crime agenda.

The particular contribution of the signal crimes perspective to this is clarified somewhat by counter-pointing it with aspects of the extant literature on fear of crime. The concept of fear of crime is an idea that continues to exert a centrifugal pull on work in the area of public perceptions and attitudes. This is despite growing recognition of significant conceptual limitations with how it tends to be formulated (Jackson, 2004; Farrall et al., 2009). Importantly, a mounting number of empirical studies document that crime incidents trigger fear reactions only comparatively rarely (Ditton et al., 1999). Likewise, some of the most routinely cited 'causes' of negative affective reactions are not criminal acts, but forms of social and physical disorder (Farrall et al., 2009; Ferraro, 1995).

Broadly speaking, studies in this tradition can be distinguished on the basis of whether they see the key explanatory factor for the prevalence and distribution of crime fear as being related to 'people', 'places', or 'problems'. 'People' based studies are grounded in the socio-demographics of the individuals and groups encountering crime. Thus age, gender, and ethnicity all become positioned as critical variables in accounting for how, when, and why negative reactions to crime and disorder incidents arise (Hale, 1996). A privileging of place is to be found in the literature on socio-economic deprivation, inequality, and neighbourhood effects, where local or structural contextual conditions are attributed causal primacy in terms of crime concern (Sampson, 2011; Taylor, 2001). Thirdly, within the fear of crime canon are 'problem' based accounts, that attempt to document the capacity of different incident types to elicit negative responses and reactions.

Moral panics

The second key position in the literature on social reactions to crime has pivoted around the concept of moral panic. In his original formulation, infused as it was by the radical politics of the 1960s, Cohen (1966/2002) sought to describe how societies are periodically subject to episodic convulsions of collective panic, as they respond to particular problematic or troublesome occurrences. Under such conditions the agendas of governmental, social, and cultural institutions coalesce to translate private issues into public problems, about which there is a collective sense that something must be done.[3] In turn, this facilitates the onset of a moralization campaign that helps to separate out, in the words of Mary Douglas (1966), 'the pure' from the 'dangerous'. Applying this approach, periods of acute social panic have been identified and traced out in relation to a variety of issues and problems, including delinquent youth subcultures, drug use, and child abuse. What moral panic theory supplies, especially in Cohen's initial formulation, is a structured approach to disaggregating the ways in which processes of collective reaction to resonant events unfold and evolve through a sequence of phases.

In a new foreword to the third edition of his book *Folk Devils and Moral Panics* published before his death, Cohen (2002) re-engaged with the social mechanics and dynamics of moral panics, how they arise, are sustained, and abate. The twenty-first century is, after all, a societal order much changed from when he was originally formulating his ideas. Several of his reflections on this theme are directly relevant to the task of delineating the distinctive space occupied by the 'signal crimes perspective' when compared with the concept of moral panic.

Of particular interest, are his ruminations upon why some crimes trigger full-blown moral panics, whilst other ostensibly similar incidents do not. Comparing reactions to the killings of James Bulger and Stephen Lawrence, his analysis has implications for comprehending the importance of the intersection between culture and politics in shaping collective reactions. For as he notes, where the *Bulger* case created a sharp collective paroxysm of anxiety and morally

---

[3] On this point Cohen was directly influenced by the work of Leslie Wilkins (1964) on deviance amplification. Picking up on this connection, the importance of amplificatory processes, especially in relation to series of signal events, is developed subsequently in this essay.

freighted concern, the tenor and tone of social reactions in the *Stephen Lawrence* case were markedly different.

That such differences arise he uses to argue against a tendency to suggest that we are entering a period of 'perpetual panic', affirming instead that panics are short episodes, rather than more underlying and sustained sensations of anxiety. Second, he cautions against the overuse of the moral panic frame. He explicitly recognizes that some issues trigger moral panics, but other ostensibly similar events incur no such consequences. The different trajectories depending in part both upon 'the raw' ingredients of the problem itself, but also the extent to which these align with pre-existing sensations of concern or alarm in the enveloping culture and politics. To these, Garland (2008) adds a third point about there being a new politics of panic. He contends that the very popularity of the moral panic concept has served to shift the conditions of its operation, suggesting a greater reflexivity by political actors in terms of them understanding how their actions and interventions can actively induce or mitigate collective 'panic'.

Taken together these points assist in clarifying the unique contribution that an analysis pivoting around the signal crime construct can make. For whilst signal crimes can be the catalyst for the kinds of moral panic process to which Cohen and others attend, more often than not, they do not induce these wider and deeper processes of reaction. Specifically, the kinds of moralization campaign and moral entrepreneurship that are intrinsic to processes of panic are not required for a crime to act as a signal. Neither do they necessitate the involvement of institutions to produce their impacts. Signal crimes can be very limited in terms of their reach and influence, with their effects resonating in quite a constrained fashion across social and geographic spaces.

In this sense, the signal crime concept can be seen to occupy an important intermediate space between fully-blown 'moral panics' and 'normal' crimes. Signal crimes can have deeply penetrating effects upon how publics conceive and perceive their safety. Equally, their effects can be relatively limited in their reach and significance. But where analyses guided by moral panic theory focus upon explicating wider processes of political and cultural change and reform, a signal crimes approach is more concerned with how and why certain incidents come to be interpreted as indicators for individual and collective concern in the first place. This is reflected in its preeminent concern with understanding processes of social reaction in terms of how specific cognitive, affective, and behavioural effects are induced by particular crime and disorder events.

Patterns of perception

Understanding how and why collective reactions to major crime events follow the kinds of patterned sequences that Cohen and others label as moral panics has been recently enriched by studies in the social psychology of risk perception. Work in this field shines a light upon the neural bio-mechanics of individual perceptions, as well as how these are inflected by more social and cultural influences.

Underpinning this approach is the base contention that evolutionary processes have weighted our patterns of perception and cognition towards bad news and threat. Within the human brain, the amygdala performs a specific 'threat centre' role, ensuring we react almost automatically and instantly to both actual and symbolic threats (Taylor, 2004; Kahneman, 2011). This editing of perception, in terms of steering what is attended to and consequently 'sensed', induces a number of interpretative dispositions and heuristics into the ways in which people see the world around them, and the judgements and decisions they consequently make (Rose and Abi-Rached, 2013). Many of these have been well documented in the now voluminous literature on risk perception. Slovic (2000) for instance, has produced compelling evidence from studies across a range of substantive issues and problems, about how people are predisposed to focus upon low frequency, highly visible, and impactive issues in terms of making judgements about their own levels of safety and security. Associated with which, they tend to downplay and ignore longer term, less visible, and potentially more corrosive forms of harm to concentrate instead upon those that can be easily recalled and recollected. Especially when our senses are 'loaded up' or under threat, these base patterns of thought and action tend to override any higher level cognitive functioning to play a vital role in governing how we interpret and react to situations.

These individual level procedures, in terms of how we process information about the situations in which we are located, should not be divorced from other social influences. For there is a growing body of experimental evidence documenting that in addition to environmental and experiential influences moulding neural pathways in the brain, there is also a social aspect to perception. It turns out that our interpretations, judgements, and decisions are highly malleable, and easily influenced by the emotions, utterances, and judgements of others. When individuals are co-present with others, patterns of group-think and collective perception can emerge (Taylor, 2004). Equally, emotions are infectious and we are all susceptible to being influenced by the prevalent public mood in any given setting (Cialdini, 2001).

These patterns in perception that arise are freighted with political consequences too. As Hutter and Lloyd-Bostock (2013) document, they act to steer political attention and effort towards certain issues, whilst at the same time neglecting other matters. When framed as a particular kind of risk, it is clear that the politics of crime and disorder tends to follow these same pathways. Indeed, in his early studies of crime risk perceptions, Mark Warr (1980, 1982) found that members of the public were actually fairly accurate in their beliefs about the frequency with which different crimes occurred, albeit they over-estimated more serious and under-estimated less serious crimes. This is consistent with how many other risks are interpreted.

Collectively what these various studies of social reactions point to is the role crime has as a boundary marker in the ordering of reality. The unique contribution that a signal crimes-based analysis makes to this effort is in taking

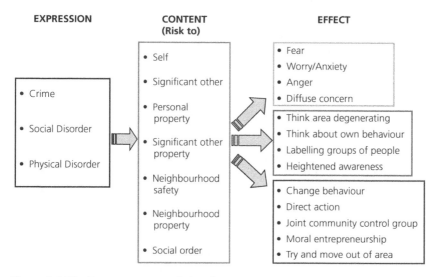

Figure 1.1 The Key components of signal events
Source: Derived from qualitative interviews conducted by the author

a systematic and structured approach to understanding how certain crimes induce particular cognitive, affective, and behavioural impacts, and why some events rather than others are imbued with attributes that render them suitable vehicles for such processes of reaction.

The overarching framework for diagnosing the presence of signal crimes and disorders that has been distilled from the analysis of the extensive empirical data collected is represented in Figure 1.1.

The left hand column of the diagram sets out the key expressions. The right hand column lists the most prevalent types of effect that were observed to have been triggered, sub-divided according to whether they are cognitive, affective, or behavioural. In between these two points are positioned the 'contents' which capture to whom a sense of risk or threat is attributed. In the next section, each of these elements are addressed in a bit more detail.

Three Species of Signal Event

There are several different ways in which crime and disorder incidents impact upon and come to function as signals for people. One important influence is whether the focal incident is experienced directly or indirectly. The interview extract used in the introduction to this essay (Ash214) was deliberately selected because of how it demonstrated the ways that incidents that happen to others can generate wider collective effects upon perceptions of safety and security. But importantly, from the point of view of this essay, direct victimization experiences

9

appear to be similarly structured in terms of specific effects being induced by the occurrence of crime events. For example, in the next quotation, a clear set of behavioural effects are described, reflecting a perceived risk to the respondent's safety:

> On New Year's Eve there was a massive fight outside on my landing and there was blood everywhere and the police were called it was a domestic violence issue which was incredibly scary…I shut my door and hope that nothing touches me. (NW057)

As recounted, this was a domestic violence incident that had 'leaked' out into the more public spaces of the flats. For the interviewee, although the violence itself was not targeted at her, she had introduced particular behavioural responses to try and sequester herself from the presenting risks. As previously, it is clearly evident how the intertwined affective and behavioural responses reported were understood as being directly connected to the violent event.

Located in a very different neighbourhood context, another interviewee discussed the emotions they had felt when reports of a gun crime incident were received:

> There was an incident a few weeks back with someone shooting a rifle in the street and a helicopter was brought over straight away and people were alerted to stay in their houses…They came off the canal path and walked down Dunbar with it shooting it…it really affected me. It made me worried about my own area around my house. It made me very scared…(Ing135)

In this account all three components of a signal crime are present. The 'shooting' that triggers the effects that are mentioned is the signal expression. When the respondent recalls that, as a result, she 'worried about my own area', she is identifying that the 'content' of the signal involves the connotation of a collective sense of risk to those in her neighbourhood. This is additional to her sense of personal risk clearly specified. The references to being 'worried' and 'scared' locate the reactions in an affective register. Looking across the interview data more generally, it is clear that signal crimes can generate a varied range of effects, from clear behavioural modification through to more subtle changes in perception and attitude. People get angry, frightened, and invoke a range of other emotional states in terms of how they gauge and account for the ways they react when encountering different forms of crime. Others utilize particular behavioural strategies to reduce their exposure to potential concerns. Moving from describing these reactions to a more analytic view, these varied signal effects can be grouped together according to whether they are primarily cognitive, affective, or behavioural. This conceptual modelling clarifies that a defining quality of a signal crime is that it changes how people, think, feel, or act in respect of their security.

If the 'effect' element of a signal crime captures what changes, the 'content' relates to how people interpret the incident concerned and ascribe it meaning. Crimes and disorders impact upon individuals and groups not just because of any personal risk or threat they communicate, but also where they send signals about issues for people that others are concerned about. This is clearly present in the following, where the anxiety gravitated around how a recent crime signified the presence of a threat to the respondent's daughters:

> We have had a rape recently in the town... I mean I've got three daughters so obviously two of them are sort of out and about... so yeah it is worrying. (Gre184)

This sense of vicarious concern and worry, is an important aspect of the collective reactions that signal crimes are able to elicit.

By way of summary, it can be seen that the principal risks communicated by the presence of signal crimes are either 'personal' (where a problem is interpreted as a direct threat to a person's safety or property), or they can be perceived as directed at someone's 'significant others' (for example, parents often invoked concern about the safety of their children, and adults of their partners). Intriguingly though, analysis of the empirical data also identified a form of collective risk perception encoded in how the interviewees talked about their responses to incidents. So for example, they would talk about matters 'that were a problem for everyone living in the area', or 'disturbed everyone on the street'. In so doing, they were explicitly recognizing that the fates of neighbours co-present in a space are intertwined to a significant extent. The occurrence of a burglary for example, in addition to the direct material consequences on the primary victim, is likely to cause their neighbours to raise the security thresholds for their properties.[4] This collective dimension to risk perception was especially prevalent in how people talked about their responses to incivilities and disorder.

In the following extract, the acquisition of knowledge or at least plausible rumours about recent occurrences elicited a behavioural effect:

> I go running. I have heard reports recently of men attacking women, one was down by the train station and one of my routes does go past the train station. It worried me and I actually changed my route so I suppose that caused me a problem; a minor one, but it did affect me. (Ash213)

For this woman, her behaviour modification was connected to adaptations in the ways in which she perceived and thought about the distribution of risk locally as a result of learning about a particular crime. This multi-dimensionality to social reactions, wherein affective, behavioural, and cognitive responses are nested within one another is a common feature of how people react to, and interpret, troublesome and problematic incidents. This is a quality that extant positions on the public understanding of crime and disorder struggle to capture.

---

[4] It is worth stating explicitly that in the case of burglary this constitutes a reasonable response in that research evidence on patterns of repeat victimization clearly demonstrates that in the period following the occurrence of one incident, the targeted property and those neighbouring it have an escalated chance of being attacked again.

Careful examination of how respondents talked about crime problems in their neighbourhoods makes evident that a lot of the incidents that they were aware of had no discernible effect upon them. However, there were a more limited number where specific cognitive, affective, or behavioural effects were attributed to the incidents. This suggests that a significant amount of crime features as little more than the 'buzzing static' of the background 'noise' to everyday life in urban areas. However, some incidents assume more salience to people shaping how they think, feel, or act in relation to their perceptions of security. They are attended to because of how they function as signifiers about the levels of security afforded by the local social order.

Signal disorders

The expression component of a signal event refers to the problematic or trouble-some occurrence that is responsible for triggering specific effects and reactions. The interviews clearly show that negative reactions are not just attached to those acts formally defined as crimes, but are key features of how people respond to and interpret disorderly conduct of all kinds. This reflects how most people, most of the time, do not ordinarily distinguish between crimes and disorders in the ways that criminal justice institutions do.

Anti-social behaviour and the material traces of such forms of problematic, but not necessarily criminal, conduct routinely elicit strong public reactions:

> The phone box on the corner being vandalised, yes it's always getting vandal-ised that phone box on the corner, always...I suppose annoyed really, very annoyed. It brings the area down, the community you're living in really. (F&W084)

In a very similar manner to that observed in relation to the previous interview extracts, in this account the interviewee is attributing two specific effects to the act of vandalism. There is an affective impact of 'annoyance', blended with a more cognitive change in perceptions of the state of local social order. In refer-ring explicitly to the local 'community' they are also providing a clear sense of who they see as baring the risks of this kind of activity. It is an issue that has an effect upon them as an individual because of the perceived collective ramifica-tions for their community.

Signal disorders of this kind were actually more numerous in the interview accounts than signal crimes in terms of how people sought to navigate their sense of neighbourhood security. This is in keeping with large-scale public opinion and attitude surveys on crime and anti-social behaviour, where concerns about phys-ical and social disorder are consistently rated as uppermost in the public's com-munity safety priorities.

It was clear from the interview data that peoples' cognitive maps of their neigh-bourhoods and areas, together with the ways that they thought about disorder more broadly, were structured by an understanding that there are particular places, spaces, and times where disorders coagulate and concentrate. Some of the most potent signal events in this regard were tied to activities in the night-time economy:

> Very, very, occasionally I go and have a drink at night, and I have been in my local...and fights have broken out. So I tend not to go there at night, but yeah, I was concerned for my safety. It was a couple of times you know in the last year. (NW063).

A second interviewee living in the same area, expressed very similar views when they said:

> During the day it's a normal town centre, people going shopping and up the pub...But by 7 o'clock in the evening you've got a completely different environment...it's not a very nice place to go. So you just don't go. (NW064)

Both of these respondents describe the local town centre as an area to be avoided because of the levels of physical and social disorder occurring there. Indeed, they both report similar effects inasmuch as they actively avoid the area. These were not concerns restricted to older people. Many of the younger respondents also described a high concentration of disorder problems in these spaces and places. However, for many in this latter group, these were risks that had to be negotiated in order to participate in important leisure and social activities with their friends. In the next account for example, the young interviewee describes an effect of having being 'scared', but there is no suggestion that he feels able to adopt the kinds of avoidance strategy that featured in the previous two quotations:

> On a night, if you are coming home from the pictures and stuff, if you want to go to McDonalds you can't cos there's loads of people...they start doing loads of violence and being aggressive...just scared really. Once I was with my mates and we got chased for about half and hour. (W157)

Analysis of the interview data clearly evidences that incidents labelled as disorders rather than crimes, possess a capacity to generate reactions just as varied and intense as those involving an infraction of criminal law. Moreover, signal disorders are especially consequential in terms of the labelling of places:

> For about the last three years I've not even been down that road because of what I've been hearing. I just think everyone in the area says [it] is one of the worst roads to live on. (Ing135)

People rely upon signal events in terms of the impressions they form of an area, especially when it is unfamiliar to them. However, it is equally important to recognize that signals are not interpreted in isolation from each other. Indeed, a cumulative process of signal amplification often occurs, whereby perceiving one signal attunes peoples' perceptual radar for other indicators of risk or threat. This process of signal amplification is clearly present in the following story:

> I did go to North London six months ago, we were trying to find Camden Market, but got lost actually and ended up somewhere near Highbury...walked

down this road treading on broken glass all the way, this is where we were shocked, so we're not naive, but there were people openly smoking joints, just generally openly smoking joints...but the most surprising thing was the amount of people selling kind of smuggled cigarettes...so you can go any Sunday and see this, the mixture of this, the broken glass and walking along this road where so many cars had their windows smashed, all along the gutter was broken glass, every bus shelter...every one was smashed, every single one along this great long high road. So if you imagine this environment with all this glass with people just smoking joints openly...well kids mainly, quite young, not old enough to smoke let alone joints, but no fear, you know just openly and then again you know the Eastern European appearance males, openly selling cigarettes there was police cars driving past...we felt a bit uncomfortable there, we couldn't leave quick enough....We went into MacDonalds and had to go and ask them to unlock the loo you know, on a Sunday afternoon! It's all these things in one area together. (S4)

What this detailed description captures is how, although there were a number of individually 'weak' signal disorders encountered within the setting, it was their concentrated accumulation and co-occurrence that served to amplify the overall impact upon how the person concerned viewed the area more generally.

Physical and social disorder in a neighbourhood often functioned as a visible index of the local social order. It was interpreted as an indicator from which could be read some sense of the degree of safety afforded in that locality. In this sense, the incident itself may or may not involve the enactment of a direct harm or offence. Rather, it is ascribed salience because of the message it encodes about the likely presence of other risks and threats, and the capacity of local formal and informal social control to afford protection from these.

Control signals

So far the analysis has explicitly concentrated upon documenting the range of ways that crime and disorder acts upon and influences peoples' perceptual field. It has been shown that various events in particular contexts function as warning signals to people, directly altering how they think, feel, or act. Indeed, it is this explicit connecting of specific events with specific effects that distinguishes a signal crimes analysis from many other contributions to the literature on the public understanding of crime.

What is missing from this account is whether social control interventions performed by police and other criminal justice agencies who are tasked with managing these kinds of social problem work in similar ways. To engage with this issue, a third species of signal event needs to be introduced—the 'control signal'.

Applying a similar conceptual framework to public perceptions and experiences of social control interventions involves attributing particular effects and impacts to acts that proactively or reactively tackle crime, disorder, and other problematic behaviours. In the interviews that provide the empirical base for this essay, there was a particular focus upon seeking to gauge perceptions and public attitudes to increases in police foot patrol. Where this occurred, the following type of reaction was fairly common:

> Now you see the police walking round...So therefore, you've got the confidence of the people seeing it happen, so therefore the ball rolls onwards and they start cleaning up their own mess as well. (BrunsFG1)

Given that this is a more positive form of intervention in the social order than acts of crime and disorder, it is unsurprising to note that a different set of reactions is recorded by the author of these comments. They describe how the increased police presence induced a greater sense of community confidence. Importantly though, this respondent also articulates how the control signals deriving from the formal social control activities of the police had a supplementary effect in terms of bolstering levels of resilience and informal social control.

Positive control signals of this kind were also detected in the data on occasions where police engaged in more assertive forms of social control. For instance, in a neighbourhood in Birmingham, police undertook an operation against a local drug market. Many people voiced similar sentiments to the following participant in a focus group that was conducted to try and gauge the community impacts of the interventions:

> And this couple of weeks have been fantastic, because they raided like a dozen houses in Aston and they're doing a very good job. (Astfg1)

As can be seen in relation to these last two quotations, control signals tend to induce rather different forms of perceptual, attitudinal, and behavioural effects than crimes and disorders. They can result in improved public confidence in the criminal justice process, or enhanced satisfaction with a particular agency, and a greater willingness of communities to solve their own problems. But equally, it is clear from the interviews that just as there can be positive control signals, so there can be negative ones:

> You never see a bobby on the streets anymore. You never see them walking around or any kind of presence...What does it say to me? It says the police are not doing anything. I get really angry about them. They're not worth having as far as I am concerned, they don't do anything for this community. They just seem to pass us by and when you want them, they're just not there, ever. (StH132)[5]

The kinds of negative effects spelled out here are similar to those recorded in relation to signal crimes and disorders. It is suggestive of how poor or inadequate criminal justice responses to signal crimes and disorders amplifies the power of the negative effects that individuals and communities experience. Negative

---

[5] It is worth noting that these are perceptions and interpretations, rather than objective records of police activity. It may be that police were present in that area but just not at times that coincided with when the respondent was there.

control signals act as 'semaphores' in terms of distributing and propagating a sense of insecurity.

Thinking in these terms raises the prospect of interaction effects between signal crimes and control signal-based counter measures. For where a criminal or disorderly act is clearly functioning as an indicator of harm, agents of social control frequently seek to manufacture control signals that will mitigate or over-ride the negative perceptual consequences. When this occurs something akin to a signification contest arises.

Some of the complex ways in which such signal and counter-signal processes act upon the make-up of the prevalent order of reality are captured in the following recounting of a local policing initiative:

> It's all bravado, oh let's get stuck in, let's clear this area up, blah,blah,blah...It's all very well the police turning round saying we are putting 1.6 million into this, we're going to get this, we're going to get that we're putting more police on the streets. But if they've just spent 1.6 million and you've still got shootings, you've still got car crime and everything else. Excuse me, where's the reassurance? (ASstFG2)

This slightly cynical and sceptical reading is helpful in teasing out how public interpretations of policing action are frequently finely balanced. The capacity of good police work to reassure and imbue a greater sense of community confidence can easily be overturned by the occurrence of a high profile signal crime.

Of more consequence in terms of the overarching interests of this essay is that these passages establish that a conceptually coherent framework can be applied to acts of crime, disorder, and control, in terms of how these communicate messages to people, and how they are interpreted by different social audiences. This is important methodologically because it affords a systematic and structured approach for the analysis of individual and collective reactions to social problems and their responses. In contrast to previous studies of the symbolic meanings of crime and social control that have tended to be rather abstract in their approach, what a signal crimes analysis seeks to establish is the connection between specific events and specific reactions.

Collective Reactions

To this point, the discussion has focused upon analysis of signal effects at an individual level. Across the different neighbourhoods where the field research was conducted, however, there was often a fairly high degree of agreement among people questioned about what the most pressing local issues and problem were. Analysis of the data reveals that, very often, individuals who were not known to each other were referencing the same specific incidents or areas as animators of their concerns. Where this occurs the signal event can be said to possess high 'coherency' in that a significant proportion of those interviewed made reference to it.

By aggregating the data collected from all the individuals in the field site areas together, it is possible to start to test whether issues and localities were exhibiting high signal coherency. To give a sense of this, in Table 1.1 the top five 'most coherent' signal crimes and disorders have been listed in rank order, covering five very different sites from different parts of the country.

Presenting these data in this way helps tease out the commonalities and differences in terms of what the most coherent signal events were across these neighbourhoods. It can be seen for instance, that anti-social behaviour associated with young people and drug-related crime and disorder have a fairly dominant position in terms of shaping how people perceive levels of neighbourhood security. However, it is equally noticeable and important that there is variation across the different areas in terms of what occurrences local people were attending to. This points to the significant role of local culture and norms in determining what is and is not viewed as acceptable conduct. More generally, it is striking that these reported signal crimes and disorders are largely problems associated with public spaces. With a few exceptions, they are not 'private' crimes.

What has started to be traced out is that there are certain incidents around which peoples' perceptions of safety and insecurity gravitate. These signal events assume significance because of how they trigger a range of effects, owing to the wider sense of risk encoded via their presence. These effects can be categorized according to whether they are 'cognitively', 'affectively', or 'behaviourally' oriented. The most prevalent emotional effects include: 'fear'—when a respondent says they are afraid; 'worry'—when worry or anxiety is reported; and 'anger'. Cognitive effects capture when someone states that knowledge of an incident has altered how they think about themselves, other individuals or groups, or their environment in some fashion. So this might refer to 'labelling' groups of people or places as problematic or troublesome, or relatedly, when it leads to thinking that an area is degenerating in some fashion. Behavioural effects are concerned with the adaptive acts that people perform in response to a signalled risk or threat. These regularly include: 'avoidance behaviours', where an individual deliberately orients their conduct in such a way as to avoid coming

Table 1.1 Top five signals across five research sites

Rank	Area 1	Area 2	Area 3	Area 4	Area 5
1	Youths	Drugs	Drugs	Drugs	Youths
2	Graffiti	Burglary	Guns	Youths	Drugs
3	Litter	Mugging	Litter	Drinking	Mugging
4	Damage	Theft	Youths	Anti-social neighbours	Violence
5	Mugging	Assault	Mugging	Damage	Damage

into contact with particular people, places, or events; a more pronounced version of this is where the effect of a crime causes someone to 'move out of a neighbourhood'; 'direct action'—is when someone decides to engage directly with a problematic situation to try to resolve it, or mitigate its effects; 'joining a community control group'—involves participation in some collective problem-solving effort, either in partnership with, or independent of, formal social control agencies; and engaging in 'moral entrepreneurship'—where the campaign is aimed at changing rules or laws.

Processes of signal identification and detection not only illuminate those events and issues that trigger and cue collective anxiety and concern in neighbourhoods, they also point to those crimes and disorders that do not induce these effects. It is clear that in some areas quite a lot of disorder was deemed tolerable and featured as little more than background 'noise' to social life. But of course, not all neighbourhoods demonstrated equal levels of tolerance. Indeed, in every area where interviews were conducted the respondents demarcated particular social and physical disorder problems, and crime incidents, as signal events. Especially where such problems were encountered regularly, these incidents distinctively shaped their perceptions. Goffman (1972: 241) provides insight into how and why this might be:

> ...the minor civilities of everyday life can function as an early warning system; conventional courtesies are seen as mere convention, but non-performance can cause alarm.

Monitoring the environments in which they are situated is part of how people make judgements about their security. Manifestations of social and physical disorder are important as risks that connote other risks. People attend to the presence of such problems as indicators about the state and resilience of the local social order, and the levels of safety afforded to them.

The Everyday and the Catastrophic

Individual and collective security is not just shaped by signal crimes and disorders at the neighbourhood level. As noted in the introduction to this essay, high profile incidents involving extreme violence against 'pure' victims, routinely emerge as signal crimes, changing how the public think, feel and act (Innes, 2003a). Moreover, the performance of criminal justice agencies in dealing with such occurrences is frequently construed as a powerful control signal, condensing and encoding wider public sentiments about the state's competence. By way of illustration, recalling the spectacle of planes crashing into the World Trade Centre and Pentagon on 9/11 serves as a compelling exemplification of how such incidents can signal the presence of new security risks. The physical and symbolic violence enacted in these attacks focused the attention of governments in the United States and across Europe on a new threat and source of risk.

It caused them to adopt a new national security posture, altering at an institutional level how security and policing agencies across the globe thought, felt, and acted subsequently.

High profile signal crimes often possess particular signal strength and coherency. This reflects how the harm they involve is unambiguous. They frequently embody qualities making them comparatively easy to recall and recollect. Whereas forms of neighbourhood disorder routinely rely on accumulation and amplificatory processes to influence public sentiments and perceptions, high profile crimes do not need these forms of scaffolding. They display a particular sense of definition in terms of their ability to reach across different communities and groups to shape public perceptions and attitudes, certainly when compared with the more nebulous effects of weaker signals.

A particular strength of the signal crimes perspective is that it provides a coherent framework for analysing and understanding individual and social reactions to both everyday encounters with crime and disorder, and more unusual catastrophic events that occur from time to time. In so doing, it circumvents some of the problems found in the extant literature on social reactions to crime. These accounts typically focus upon co-present and direct experiences (Hale, 1996), or the role of mass mediated communication in shaping levels of fear (Altheide, 2002). Few studies have successfully integrated these two dimensions of experience. According to a signal crimes analysis, typically what changes between the everyday and catastrophic is the channel of communication, as well as the extent to which cognitive, affective, and behavioural effects travel across different social groups. The base processes of perception, interpretation, and reaction are understood to be fairly generic though. Most knowledge of these major events is mediated, rather than based upon direct experience. But reactions to information gleaned from a variety of sources can be understood as involving similar interpretative processes in terms of how meaning is ascribed to and invested in disorderly events.

In the immediate aftermath of their occurrence, many major crimes function to signal the presence of threat—a process amplified via mediated reportage, although the intensity of the induced effects decay over time. However, some incidents do sustain a more diffuse and subtle form of 'signal resonance' over an extended period. They demonstrate a particular capacity to resonate in terms of leaving a legacy of shock and trauma within the life of a community. This can remain lodged in the collective memory having 'real' effects upon a situation long after the empirical warrant for the problem has been removed.

When this does occur, the legacy effects can be simultaneously subtle, pervasive, and profound. Scenes of notorious incidents, for instance, frequently retain an aura and association with the crime. The locations become labelled as 'dangerous places', with residents persisting in avoiding them, which in turn confirms the sense of insecurity imputed. A perpetuating signal resonance that is often associated with major crimes can result in particular locations acquiring what Fine (2001) dubs 'sticky reputations'. Such places become popularly known as locales where troubles aggregate, and very often these reputations persist in a nebulous form in the collective memory for long periods, bedevilling attempts to alter them. Places that are collectively conceived of as 'dangerous' become ciphers for wider concerns. At a more theoretical level, this gestures to the role that signal crimes and disorders have in shaping the symbolic construction of social spaces.

The Symbolic Legacies of Signal Crimes

When accounting for their perceptions of risk and threat in their neighbourhoods and elsewhere, people regularly reference past experiences and events that they feel have had a significant impact upon their outlook. These signal events are immersed in the eddies and flows of unfolding local histories, shaping how individuals conceive of their self and social identities as these past crimes and disorders emit echoes over an extended period of time.

Past signal crimes were routinely cited as grounds for current and ongoing concerns of various kinds, as in the following interview with a burglary victim, who clearly spells out the profound behavioural effects that the crime had upon them:

> I've had an alarm fitted and we don't go on holiday, we do not go on holiday together, me and my husband. I wouldn't want to leave the house. I wouldn't want to leave it empty. (SM287)

As conveyed by this respondent, signal crimes can be invoked as markers of important fractures and turning points in terms of how people construct and narrate their lives to themselves and others. A second respondent, talking about the sense of vulnerability induced by a burglary some months earlier, described the longer term emotional effects this had on her in terms of what happened once her sense of security had been destabilized:

> This was the only place I felt at peace and when they broke in it was like they took all of that from me. I had to change the wardrobes, I felt dirty, my whole house felt dirty. I've repainted now and it's starting to feel like mine again...for weeks I was just sleeping in the sitting room waiting for these people...I slept in the sitting room and when I was at work I was stressed. (Upe177)

In terms of constructing a general theoretical position on social reactions to crime, it is clear from the empirical data that interpreting and invoking past events did not just pertain to individual victims. They were equally significant and present in the sense-making of groups and communities, where aspects of the crime or the response to it were seared into the collective memory. Thus it is possible to state with some confidence that, at both the individual and collective levels, past experiences of crime and disorder, where the presence of risk and threat are clearly demarcated, can play an important role in foreshadowing how individuals and groups react to new occurrences. Most signals fade and decay with the passing of time, but some display a capacity for an ongoing influence upon perceptions and experiences of safety and security.

During the interviews, people were asked to recall and describe in as much detail as possible 'any events that they had experienced directly or heard about from other sources that had made them concerned about their safety over the past twelve months.' Repeatedly though, when responding to this question, a number of respondents made reference to incidents outside of this time-frame. It was apparent that in making sense of their current levels of safety and security, a number of past events were afforded particular significance by them. In the process of re-interviewing some of these individuals 12 months later, an important dimension to this phenomenon was revealed. It became apparent that when describing these past events they invoked 'scripted' accounts. Their stories at times one and two (12 months later) were strikingly similar. For example:

> **Year 1:** A friend of ours in [street name] was clearing out a room in his house, walked down the stairs, left his front door open, went to the garage, put some stuff in the garage only to find someone running out of his front door, he chased after them but he couldn't catch them and it turned out that they had stolen his wallet and money and other stuff from the house I don't know I didn't go into detail. That was a particular incident that I know of.

And then, when they were re-interviewed a year later this person said:

> **Year 2:** R - Um well as I say its only just one chappy that's a friend of ours. He was putting some stuff in his car from his house, err put the stuff in the car and when he came out he just caught someone going out. He had lost his, quite a bit of jewellery and his money.
> I - So he'd been loading the car up outside the house?
> R - Yes, no inside the garage.
> I - Oh inside the oh right.
> R - The garage and cause naturally he walked out the front door, left the door open and went into the garage and this opportunist was in and out like a yoyo. (F&W80)

Aside from the methodological implications this has for victimization surveys that typically frame their questions in terms of events that have happened to respondents in the past 12 months, the finding that people assemble stories about such incidents and draw upon them as a consistent resource in accounting for their security perceptions and attitudes, reveals some important aspects about how such matters are assimilated into constructions of self and social identity.

The framing effect of past events is a long standing theme across the social and human sciences, and is something that has been addressed by a number of learned scholars. Over 50 years ago now, W. Lloyd Warner summarized the principal issues as follows:

> Every interpretative act is but one momentary event in an infinite series... Tomorrow's meanings are prepared by those of today; those of the present are firmly founded on the meaning of yesterday. The meaning of an interpretative

act must always be sought in the present, as the past is momentarily caught, rushing into a previously structured future. (Warner, 1959: 476)

That this is so is immensely consequential for any theoretical account of signal crimes and disorders. It points to the temporal aspect of how signal events influence public views and sentiments. Not only do we need to be alert to how their effects travel across different communities and neighbourhoods, but also how they reach across spans of time. The 'afterglow' of crimes past can be seen to play an important role in attuning and sensitizing local public opinion towards some problems and issues in particular.

Nowhere were these echoes emitted by past signal crimes more pronounced than in St. Mary's ward in Oldham, the scene of race riots in 2001. In this area, the interviews captured evident tensions between the white working class and Pakistani-Asian communities. Feeding these tensions were collective memories maintained by the two ethnically and geo-spatially divided groups about past incidents: especially the riots; but also a sequence of homicides and violent assaults that were repeatedly invoked as evidence of the problems in the area. In terms of how these past incidents were constructed and reconstructed, they possessed the features of signal crimes. Specific incidents were mentioned by a significant proportion of those spoken to across both communities that had had particular effects upon people because of how they signalled the presence of risk to the collective safety of their community. These historic signals had become integrated into the interpretative framework within which any newly occurring incidents were assessed. Consequently, what in other situations would be construed as comparatively trivial occurrences, assumed a much greater significance against this backdrop, as a result of processes of signal amplification. So a number of seemingly minor events acquired the potency and influence associated with signal crimes, signal disorders, and negative control signals because of how they 'reheated' extant insecurities and uncertainties.

Conclusion

A perspective is a 'way of seeing'. The signal crimes perspective provides an optic for viewing social reactions to crime, disorder, and control, and how public perceptions and reactions gravitate around particular incidents. Stated simply, it maintains that some events matter more than others in terms of their impact upon individual and collective security because of how they symbolize wider social problems. Relative to other ostensibly similar incidents, these signal crimes and disorders acquire a disproportionate impact upon how people think, feel, and act about their safety and security because they are interpreted as indicators of other risks and threats. The research described has outlined both a conceptual apparatus and set of analytic methods designed to locate the presence of such signal events and to distinguish them from other crime and disorder incidents that occur without impacting upon collective security. In sum, the signal crimes perspective suggests a generic social process for how individuals and collectives interpret and make sense of both serious high profile incidents, but also the kinds of disorder problems that occur with greater regularity in some neighbourhoods. What separates 'signals' from 'noise' is whether a defined cognitive, affective, or behavioural reaction is elicited.

Accenting the role of disorder and incivilities in how people construct perceptions of their environments, there are surface affinities with the more established 'broken windows' approach. But there are significant differences and important empirical refinements also. Broken windows theory casts disorder as criminogenic, with untreated disorder ultimately generative of higher crime rates. On the other hand, the signal crimes perspective maintains that there are certain crime and disorder events that signal the presence of risks, but other ostensibly similar transgressions that do not induce insecurity. Some disorders exhibit influence because of how they signal the presence of risk, but others do not.

In accordance with such a logic, this perspective suggests important differences between neighbourhoods and their communities in terms of what incidents do, and do not, act as indicators for concern. Although somewhat tentative at this time, it does appear that there is a relationship between an area's signal profile and several key factors. First is the issue of 'sensitization': if people have attended to certain kinds of issues as signals in the past, then their 'cognitive radar' is likely to be attuned to similar matters in the present and future. Culture also plays an important role here. It is clear that different crimes and disorders work as signals for different social groups. The make-up of these groups must change as population turns over, which in turn, exerts a set of 'push and pull' influences on what kinds of events are likely to be functioning as signals to them. As such, it becomes important to ask 'what becomes a signal for whom and when?'

The integration of culture as a pivotal variable in explaining the observed patterns helps to differentiate a signal crimes approach to the public understanding of crime from those accounts that have gravitated around the concept of fear of crime. For what these lack is an appreciation of the densely interwoven ways in which the cognitive, affective, and behavioural dimensions of reacting to crime refract and entwine one another. Thus, in seeking greater definition and precision in understanding the ways that people perceive and respond to disorderly conduct, the signal crimes perspective casts fear as one quite defined effect that crime and disorder can have upon a social order.

Different crimes, disorders, and control-based counter-measures, located in different settings induce variegated effects and impacts at both individual and group levels. Sometimes these initial effects recursively fold back upon themselves, sensitizing public attention, amplifying the reaction to encourage the identification of other problems and issues as signal events. A continual stream of events arise as the focus for public concern and anxiety. But each new signal crime, signal disorder, or control signal is both framed by what has come before it, and alters the frame for anything coming after.

The signal crimes perspective is intended to change the ways in which we think about how people view crime, disorder, and social control. It is calibrated in such a way as to explicate both how and why, under certain conditions and when located in particular circumstances, there are incidents that profoundly influence how people appraise their security. It is designed to capture the ways in which the collective impacts of criminal and disorderly conduct can extend beyond the directly victimized, with a single incident becoming imbricated into patterns of thought, feeling, and action, altering how individuals and groups symbolically construct social spaces and their orders of reality.

Why Disorder Matters
Reading Urban Situations

Graffiti is the thing that sort of bothers me more because it is in my face every day. I mean obviously rape and murder are more horrendous crimes, but it is graffiti that I see.

This lay disquisition on the intertwined salience and ironies of physical disorder comes from an interviewee talking about life in her neighbourhood. In attending carefully to incidence of disorder and interpreting them as indexical expressions of levels of local safety and security, she is not alone. Large-scale surveys of public opinions about crime have repeatedly documented that anti-social behaviour problems are routinely uppermost in peoples' minds when they are asked about what worries them or has detrimental impacts upon their neighbourhood quality of life (Hale, 1996; Ferraro, 1995; Farrall et al., 2009). Such incidents often take precedence over those acts formally labelled and defined as crimes that are the principal focus of the criminal justice process. The interview extract is intriguing though, for it draws attention to two particular qualities that shape the impact and influence of disorder. The first is its visual nature. The second, the repeated encounters involved in seeing it 'every day'.

In discussions of urban social order, there is a long history of considering the significance of what can be visually sensed. In his seminal essay 'Urbanism as a Way of Life' Louis Wirth (1938) famously discussed what he saw as the defining quality of urban living—encounters and contacts that routinely intermingle physical proximity and social distance—concluding 'The urban world puts a premium on visual recognition' (Wirth, 1938: 14). He attributed this to the fact that a far greater proportion of our social relationships in urban formations are superficial, anonymous, and transitory than is the case under other arrangements. This sense of precariousness to urban living and that there are complexities to how people negotiate meaning to their experiences, has remained an abiding preoccupation of studies positioned at the intersection of urban order and disorder.

Wirth's concern with the contingent ways people interpret urban experiences can be traced back to the work of Georg Simmel. Writing in 1908, he talked of a 'rush' of stimuli as a characteristic of urban living that provides it with a sense of frisson and edge. He describes how, as a consequence:

> Social life in the large city as compared with the town shows a great preponder-ance of occasions to see rather than to hear people...Modern social life increases in ever growing degree the role of the mere visual impression which always characterizes the preponderant part of all sense relationships between man and man, and must place social attitudes and feelings upon an entirely changed basis. (Simmel, 1908, in Park and Burgess, 1925: 360)

These are all themes that resonate with more contemporary accounts. For Lofland (1985), urban environments are 'worlds of strangers', where travellers through these worlds have to be especially attentive to the surface signs visible to them in order to negotiate the risks and opportunities that are presented. Sennett's (1990) account attends to the aesthetic dimensions of urbanity and the ways in which physical forms encode deeper cultural themes. As far as he is concerned, urban patterns and forms subtly evince a 'fear of exposure' embedded within Western culture and its psyche, with the built environment increasingly adapted as a mechanism for the economically and socially included sections of society to physically attenuate themselves from difference and difficulty.

Although such accounts differ in terms of their themes and approaches, what they share, albeit implicitly, is a conception that urban situations are typically possessed of a high informational load. That is, the bringing together of large numbers of people into limited geographic and social spaces intensifies and com-presses the amount of data available to be processed. Under such conditions, a key issue becomes 'how do the human inhabitants cope with the large volumes of information that are present in many of the urban situations routinely encoun-tered in everyday life?' The potential to be cognitively overwhelmed by the volume of stimuli is ever present, and thus the sense-making processes by which meaning is constructed become vitally important in understanding how individ-uals and groups negotiate these situations on a routine basis. It is against this backdrop that the meaning of disorder, in terms of how people read and interpret their environment, can start to be illuminated.

In order to manage their experiences people do not attempt to process all the information potentially available to them when situated in urban environ-ments. A lot is screened out. People attend only to those facets of any situation that biographical and cultural experience has taught them may be potentially relevant, interesting, or necessary. In effect then, a separation is made between 'signals' and 'noise'. Signals are the important information required to success-fully negotiate a situation, and are qualitatively different from the unimportant and meaningless information, that can be effectively ignored and treated as mere background noise to the conduct of everyday life. The process is an almost unconscious and effortless one of reducing complexity by seeking out those units of information needed to act in a manner coherent with a particular situation.

Signal disorders are important in all of this because of how they are interpreted as conveying a sense of the distribution of risks across social space. They provide perceptible indicators about the state of a locality for people. So, for example, where there is a clustering of visualizable problems this can be taken as a cue about the underlying condition of the social order, as illustrated in the following extract from an interview conducted in South London:

> I mean the streets aren't clean. There's always paper and rubbish and it looks like a ghetto. It's starting to look like a ghetto. (StH107)

The key element articulated in this brief account concerns how the overall volume of physical detritus in key public spaces framed the impressions that the interviewee had of the area and how they had come to define it as a 'ghetto', a term freighted with both descriptive and normative connotations. Individually, the instances of physical disorder may not have been that consequential, but their repetition and cumulative presence served to 'amplify' their power as signals about the state of the local social order.

In what follows, refinement and elaboration of these initial ideas will be informed by two sets of empirical data. The first comprises 333 in-depth qualitative interviews with members of the public living in 18 wards throughout England.[1] During the interviews respondents were asked a range of questions about their experiences of crime, disorder, policing, and social control in their neighbourhoods and further afield. For the purposes of this discussion, the focus will be upon their accounts and narratives about experiences and perceptions of disorder. These interview data are supplemented and augmented by analysis of a large-scale telephone survey conducted by Ipsos-MORI with 9311 victims of anti-social behaviour across England and Wales who had contacted the police in September 2011. These survey data are used to develop and test the generalizability of some of the insights derived from the qualitative interviews.

To orient analysis of this combination of qualitative and quantitative data, throughout this essay, reference is made to how disorder is 'read'. This is intended to focus upon the processes by which people scan their environments, identify and interpret aspects of these that need to be attended to, and ascribe meaning to them. For it is the meanings attributed to disorder that render it consequential in influencing patterns of neighbourhood development.

The remainder of the essay continues with an overview of the key concepts and ideas employed to frame discussions of disorder and its salience and significance

---

[1] The data were originally collected as part of the National Reassurance Policing Programme research, as detailed in the Afterword.

to the conduct of social life. This leads to a discussion of the importance of repeated exposure in shaping levels of impact and harm for people residing in an area, but also those passing through. To develop these insights and to start to identify patterns in individual and collective reactions to forms of disorder, a differentiation between personal, situational, and incidental vulnerabilities is introduced. These concepts are positioned as part of an attempt to unpick how various qualities of the social setting and situation in which disorder occurs frame the problem, and the meaning and salience it is attributed by those attending to it. The concluding sections of the essay return to consider some of the broader implications of thinking about disorder that have started to be outlined here.

Disorder as a Signal

A signal disorder is distinct from a signal crime inasmuch as the latter requires an infraction of the criminal law to have occurred. In contrast, a disorder covers any breach of prevalent norms and conventions that is disturbing or troubling. Across the research literature a range of terms are used to describe this category of troubles. In North America the preferred label has often been incivilities, whilst in the United Kingdom the notion of anti-social behaviour has become increasingly commonplace. Whilst these terms can be used largely interchangeably, herein the discussion will make reference to disorder. This is because the established distinction between physical disorder and social disorder is analytically helpful in the context of understanding the signal value of particular occurrences and different forms of disorder.

Physical disorder refers to the material detritus of anti-social behaviour and incivilities. Vandalism, graffiti, litter, and all deliberate forms of damage to the physical environment can be classified as forms of physical disorder. Its importance resides in the sense of visual or aesthetic impairment it introduces to an object, place, or area. Distinguishing these layers of impact is important inasmuch as the effect of a physical disorder signal routinely transcends the immediate damage. Rather they are read as sending a more general message about the setting or situation in which they are located, exhibiting a wider influence upon perceptions of safety and security. By way of illustrating how physical disorder can function as a signal, in the following interview, the respondent from Leicester was discussing how the rubbish and general levels of physical degradation impacted upon their perceptions:

> It's deteriorated at such an alarming rate. We thought it was bad when people
> ɔ the area and didn't bother with things like gardens. Then we got
> tipping and dumping rubbish anywhere they wanted. (Newp123)

> unt the 'fly-tipping' and the 'dumping of rubbish' are acting as the
> for the signal, the effect of which is to induce the person concerned

to perceive that the area is 'deteriorating' at an 'alarming rate'. An inference can be drawn that the physical disorder is serving as an indicator of a permeating decline and aura of degradation.

Similar sentiments were evident during interviews in Aston, Birmingham, where many people talked about the general impressions of visual disrepair that shaped residents' views of their area:

> There's things like cookers and settees left in front of peoples' houses and you walk past and it just looks like one big rubbish tip...it does make the area look quite run down. (Ast234)

This was not an isolated view. Many of the residents spoken to in the area voiced similar concerns about the prevalence of physical disrepair.

Physical disorder signals can also serve as signifiers of, and the products of, criminal conduct. For example:

> My husband went out the other day...and pushed the bath back over there...and there was a needle and syringe...[name] upstairs, he found 8 needles outside his front door a couple of weeks ago...it's got worse in the last 2 years since we've been here and in the last six months it's escalated. (Brun085)

In this case, the discarded drugs needles provided an index of the scale of the illegal drugs use taking place on and around the estate. This induced the effect of a perceived accelerating trajectory of neighbourhood decline.

These kinds of consequences are not just found in relation to how people interpret and make sense of encountering physical signal disorders. Indeed, if anything such effects are even more prevalent in relation to forms of social disorder. Conceptually, this term tends to refer to troubling or problematic, but not illegal, conduct. What is conveyed very clearly in the following account is just how acute the effects of such behaviour can be:

> I was frightened when they was outside the end. That lad was jumping around screaming 'I want to break windows, I want to break windows' and the others was dragging him away. I was frightened to death. (FwW137)

The respondent here clearly articulates the fear that was generated by this anti-social behaviour even though, in this particular case, no actual damage was committed. The significance in terms of understanding social reactions is that members of the public do not construct hard and fast distinctions between those issues definable as crimes, and other forms of disturbing or disruptive behaviour.

This explicit connecting of individual disorder events to specific interpretative reactions, directs the analytic gaze in very different ways to other influential approaches. For example, Sampson and Raudenbusch's (1999) application of systematic social observation method enables them to make important claims about associations between particular neighbourhood conditions and the prevalence and distribution of key forms of disorder. But what this method cannot engage with is whether such patterns are especially meaningful in terms of impacting upon peoples' perceptions of safety because of the meaning that any disorder acquires for residents and others who encounter it. Very few people, if any, even in high disorder neighbourhoods, seek to systematically audit the prevalence and distribution of disorder in the ways utilized by Sampson and his colleagues. Rather, people tend to focus upon and react to visible incidents that they encounter, directly, vicariously, or through mass media reporting.

The rowdy behaviour of young people is an oft-mentioned social disorder because it flouts the shared conventions that people often have about appropriate modes of conduct in public spaces. Similarly, drinking alcohol in public places, shouting, and aggressive behaviour are also forms of social disorder that feature regularly in the list of top public concerns. These kinds of problem are often seen as linked and co-related:

> Just gangs sitting on walls drinking, abusive…You just feel very intimidated when they are all sitting on walls drinking cans and shouting abuse, you do. (Ing097)

As with the previous examples, this is clearly an example of a signal disorder. Several 'expressions' are cited and identified as causing an intimidatory effect. This account of the impact of visible disorders on residents' perceptions and quality of life is drawn from Ingol ward in Lancashire where these kinds of issues featured in many of the interviews conducted, thus capturing how signal disorders exert collective influence upon peoples' views. Another resident from Ingol, for example, talked about how reading the kinds of problems highlighted earlier induced specific avoidance behaviour:

> For about the last three years I've not even been down that road…They spend most of the day staying in the house either taking drugs or drinking or stuff. (Ing135)

Insights into just why social disorders of this kind are so influential and consequential can be gleaned from Duneier and Molotch's (1999) dissection of 'interactional vandalism'. They use this term to explore what happens when people deliberately 'crash' the rituals and conventions of the interaction order. Through a high resolution examination of instances of verbal harassment on the streets of American cities, they document how even seemingly trivial contraventions of cultural expectations about how to behave in social encounters can prove profoundly troubling and unsettling for those exposed to them. From this we might extrapolate that other forms of disorder and indeed the physical traces of anti-social behaviour might induce similar social-psychological effects. The presence of social and physical disorders are together read as signals about the condition of a local social order, and the levels of safety and security it can be anticipated to afford. Duneier and Molotch also note that whilst Jane Jacobs's (1961) emphasis upon the choreography of the street as a source of reassurance may have held true for earlier generations, the construction of urban situations has changed. They are now riven with more danger and imbued with a perpetual potential for risk.

The eyes and ears of strangers that previously afforded a sense of reassurance are now seen as precursors of predation and threat.

To provide a 'richer' sense of some of the subtle judgements and interpretations invoked in how people read social disorder, the following account from an interviewee living in Oldham is illustrative:

> The gangs that roam about are pretty intimidating and it's not just in this particular part of Failsworth, it's all over Failsworth, you'll see gangs roaming about. They're intimidating in so far as the fact that a type of uniform as I would call it that they wear, with the hoods, the baseball jackets the baseball caps and the long coats and things. They look intimidating, they act intimidating and they're pretty scary to people, to most people and they're quite a big worry to everyone I think that lives in Failsworth. (FwW316)

The compelling thing about this description is how it starts to unpack some of the linked effects that arise in relation to issues with a higher signal value. In this case, it is not just the behaviour of the young people that is at issue but their appearance. This confirms the importance of the visual register. Equally importantly though, the respondent describes several effects arising out of this situation. There is mention of how they personally feel a sense of intimidation. But at the same time there is a clear indication about how exposure to these issues has led to them labelling most of the youths in the area as trouble.

A sizeable majority of the residents interviewed in Failsworth made repeated reference to the anti-social activities of groups of youths in the area as signalling the presence of risk and threat. As connoted by the reference to these groups being scary to 'most people' there is a clear steer that there is a collective dimension to these perceptions and reactions. The negative consequences are not confined to those directly harmed by the activities, but rather all those exposed to the levels of social disorder. The account clearly conveys how social disorders can function as signals in urban environments.

Such perceptions and concerns were not just found amongst adults. In this area of Oldham, the concerns voiced could not be reduced to, or dismissed as, the product of inter-generational tensions. When other young people were questioned about their perceptions and experiences of neighbourhood security they too talked at length about the threats and risks posed to them by groups of youths in the area. A strikingly similar pattern was evident amongst interviewees in North London. One young person elaborated just why their concern was focused in this way:

> I have known a lot of people, youngsters in the main, that have been attacked, have been mugged for their mobile phones, for what they have got in their pockets. (UppeE178)

This analysis keys directly into an important difference between perceived disorder and experienced disorder. For many young people, their interpretation of other groups of youngsters as signalling a potential risk was grounded in personal experience. Confirming this, during fieldwork in St. Helens in Merseyside, a young man aged about 16 told how:

> There's nowhere to go sometimes, cos you've got parks where loads of people hang around from Thatto Heath and everyone is scared of them cos they do bad things. (WstP157)

In this area, many of the young people tended to 'hang out' in groups in order to foster a degree of protection from other groups of young people whom they perceived as threatening. But in so doing, their activities were interpreted as a 'threat posture' by other older groups of residents. More conceptually, this captures a sequence of actions and reactions that together form a 'signal disorder chain'. These occur where the behavioural adaptations to an original signal event, are themselves interpreted as markers of risk by a wider audience, triggering a further set of cognitive, affective, or behavioural responses.

Youth related disorder consistently features as a form of social disorder about which publics express considerable concern. Indeed, in nine of the 16 neighbourhoods where face-to-face interviews were conducted, youth related disorder was the most coherent signal disorder for the people interviewed. An intriguing difference was detected between the attitudes of the adult and younger respondents interviewed. A sizeable proportion of adults, when they talked about the risks posed by young people, identified them as a risk to their personal safety. But when asked about their actual experiences of, or knowledge about, young people causing problems, with a couple of exceptions, they all talked about damage to property. In contrast to which, when young people were interviewed, they often identified other groups of youngsters as signalling a risk to their safety, and their actual experiences were frequently of direct threats and violence. This hints at how concerns about anti-social behaviour, can easily slip into more categorical forms of worry, where the focus shifts from the behaviour to the people themselves.

To extrapolate more detail on the risks signalled by the anti-social behaviour of youths a technique called semiotic cluster analysis (derived from the work of Peter Manning (1987)) can be applied to some of the interview data. This involves trying to tease out the various interpretations and connotations that become attached to a problem in a structured way. The results from this analytic manoeuvre are displayed in Figure 2.1. They show that the high signal value attributed to youth related disorder is an artefact of them engaging in a range of problematic behaviours that are interpreted rather differently by a range of audiences. So although individual community members may well be expressing concerns about different youths and behaviours, a veneer of homogeneity is provided by blaming these diverse activities on 'young people' as a categorical group. Indeed, it is precisely this process of attributing blame to a group with a defined social identity that is an important general effect for the signal crimes perspective overall.

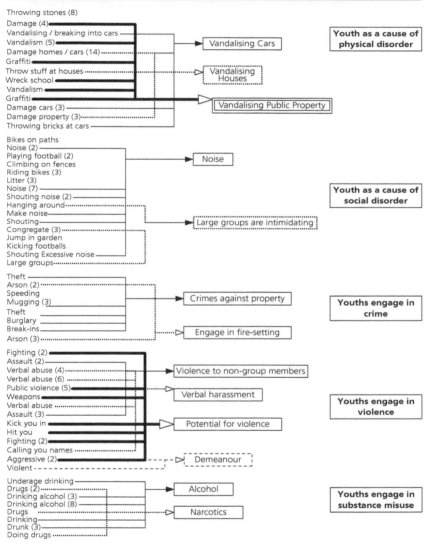

Figure 2.1 Semiotic cluster analysis of 'youth disorder'

Source: Derived from qualitative interviews conducted by the author

The results of the semiotic cluster analysis of data extracted from five research sites teases out how the actual concerns that people had about groups of youths were diverse in nature. Youths were identified as a problem because of their involvement in: physical disorder; social disorder; crime; violence; and substance abuse. The left-hand column of the diagram lists a range of issues and problems that the interview respondents identified as being particularly caused by young people. The fact that specific problems are repeated in the list simply reflects that these are occurring in more than one research site. Where a number in brackets is included after an issue, this denotes the number of times it was separately mentioned by individuals in that site. The middle column is a first level analytic interpretation seeking common elements across the list of issues in the left-hand column. The column on the right-hand side of the page is the second level interpretation, which at a further level of abstraction seeks to identify any unifying thematics identified as being present during the first level interpretation. In effect, the diagram moves from left to right mapping out two interpretative steps via which the 'deeper' connotative themes underlying public concerns about youth disorder can be extracted.

This sense that there can be very different 'readings' of disorder risks and threats is the centrepiece of Girling, Loader and Sparks's (2000) discussion of young people in Macclesfield, where they uncovered layers of nuance in terms of how markedly different threat constructions were generated by various groups. However, one concern with their analysis is that they seem to cast some reactions as more legitimate than others, in terms of being more closely aligned to the 'real' level of local problems. In contrast to which, the orienting proposition for a signal crimes perspective analysis of reactions to disorder is that the key analytic task is to determine how and why perceptions of risk arise. This might require very different explanatory accounts for those situations where public perceptions of disorder reflect levels of prevalence, and those where perceptions are significantly in excess of the actual situation. Within the signal crimes perspective's analytic framework the 'content' of the signal plays a vital role in this regard, steering attention towards what or whom is regarded as being 'a risk' or 'at risk' by virtue of the presence of the signal event. The former refers to inferred causes, the latter consequences.

Across the different neighbourhoods where the empirical fieldwork was conducted, this gap between perceived and actual levels of disorder was occasionally detected. Notably, in a small number of areas, levels of perceived disorder amongst local residents were significantly higher than might be anticipated on the basis of the number of incidents recorded by police. These disjunctions appeared to reflect the presence of relatively powerful physical and social disorder signals, that were influencing collective perceptions of safety and security in the area. At a neighbourhood level this reproduces a pattern that can be observed amongst individuals, namely, that some people worry more or less about some things, than do others who are similarly positioned. One especially intriguing variant of this is that the ASB victims survey data suggest women, on average, attend more carefully to physical disorder signals, whereas male attention is focused more upon social disorders.

Fundamentally, people 'read' the presence of disorder as an indicator about the state of a local social order, the efficacy of neighbourhood governance mechanisms, and the condition of social control. In so doing, subtle but important differences are detected between readings of social and physical disorder. When discussing physical degradation and a disorderly built environment, people did not often talk about there being an explicit risk to their personal safety. Rather, they tended to couch their comments in terms of a perceived risk to the local social order. In so doing, there was a significant social and collective dimension to their concerns and an appreciation that, to a degree, the fates of the members of a neighbourhood are intertwined.

Collective reactions to physical and social disorder involve impacts and effects similar in scope and scale to those triggered by incidents defined as crimes in criminal law. Beyond the direct harm caused to any primary victims, the impacts upon the perceptions of a wider audience can be equally profound whether an incident is definable as a crime or 'merely' an instance of disorder. The implication being that whilst legal epistemologies may be profoundly consequential in determining what are deemed appropriate issues for criminal justice agencies to formally engage with, such imperatives are less influential for the tenor and tone of public reactions. To put it another way, the capacity of an event to function as a signal for collective concern depends upon factors other than how it is legally categorized.

Such considerations become especially consequential when used to reflect upon the make up of some of the principal positions on the nature and role of disorder in social life. For example, in one of the most influential criminological accounts of all time, Wilson and Kelling's (1982) broken windows theory, the occurrence of untreated disorder was posited to be criminogenic. They hypothesized a basic causal relationship whereby untreated disorder is generative of fear of crime amongst people because it acts as an indicator of the fragility of local social control. In turn, this leads to a withdrawal from public space by individuals and groups who would otherwise engage in informal surveillance and acts of guardianship. Over time, this establishes the area concerned as a conducive environment for the commission of more, and more serious, crimes.

This causal sequencing was originally formulated in a somewhat abstract and general form. It subsequently received a degree of empirical support from the work of Skogan (1990) who traced out, in some detail, the dynamics involved where areas and neighbourhoods tip into high crime situations. More focused, yet quite compelling evidence of this causal chaining of events was provided by Keizer's (2008) injunctive and descriptive norm alignment experiment. In this he described how the initial breaching of a no-littering norm resulted in other people engaging in anti-social conduct when exposed to it. The implication being that an area with an emergent graffiti problem is likely to experience an accumulation not just of more graffiti, but other social problems as well.[2] This keys us into a second way in which signal disorders can work in terms of having an effect upon the wider environment. Not only do they act as signals about the social distribution of risks, they also signal to potential authors of anti-social acts that such misconduct might be possible and permissible here.

This notion that disorder acts as a magnet for other social problems is pivotal to the explanatory power of the broken windows theory. Others, though, have contested this logic in important ways (Harcourt, 2001). Notably, Taylor (2001) suggests that disorder is less a cause of subsequent problems than a consequence of them. Based upon longitudinal data in Baltimore, he concluded that neighbourhood areas with high levels of disorder were some years previously identifiable as highly deprived and crime ridden. A connection can be made in this respect to Sampson's (2011) detailed work in Chicago wherein he describes the reproduction of problems in specific troubled neighbourhoods over time. According to his analysis, comparatively few neighbourhoods change their trajectories to tip from disorderly to orderly, or vice versa.

Despite such empirical equivocations, policy applications deriving from the logic of the broken windows approach have acquired considerable traction. These kinds of ideas have been used to promote a variety of different intervention programmes that have collectively contributed to the 'soft' securitization of our cities, whereby a plethora of disorder counter-measures have been designed into the urban fabric (Harcourt, 2001). But these measures seem to have been introduced without any thought that some anti-social behaviours and their material traces, albeit ostensibly similar in form, may be more harmful than others. It is precisely this issue that a focus upon signal disorders keys into.

Repetition

Broken windows theory's causal chain accents the importance of untreated disorder, stating that it is the failure to repair or interdict issues that creates the impression of a permissive environment where other problematic behaviours can be 'acted out'. In so doing, however, it rather elides the significance of a difference between 'general' and 'specific' repetition. The recurrence of disorder is held to be pivotal in triggering a retreat from public spaces, rendering more disorder possible in terms of both quantity and quality. But what this neglects is how it matters whether the repetition involved pivots around the same problem recurring, and/or the same individuals being exposed to it.

At an individual level, repeated exposure to disorderly incidents is important in driving an accumulative sense of harm and negative impact. Elements of this are captured in Figure 2.2, which compares and contrasts data from the British

---

[2] For Keizer an injunctive norm instructs people about what to do, whereas a descriptive norm provides information on common behaviour patterns in a given situation.

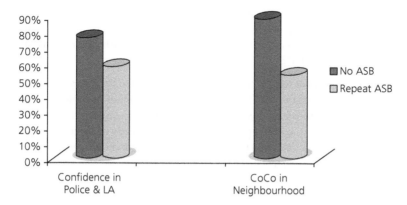

Figure 2.2 The effects of repeat ASB victimization
Source: BCS 2008/09

Crime Survey on the attitudes of repeat anti-social behaviour (ASB) victims with non-victims across two measures. It can clearly be seen that members of the public who have encountered four or more incidents of ASB over the past 12 months have significantly lower community cohesion, and lower confidence in the police and local authority, compared with people who have no direct experience of ASB. Similar patterns are evident across a number of other measures.

The occurrence of these kinds of effect are supported by the narrative data. When physical disorder occurs in isolation, then the majority of people are unlikely to interpret it as a signal that levels of risk have changed. However, when physical disorder co-occurs either with other signs of physical degradation, or with social disorders or crimes that they seem to trigger, a process of signal amplification can be instigated. This co-occurring signal amplification quality is exemplified in the following:

> Damage, where do I start? The roof, the house next door with the wall down, the lady across the road had her window broken in ... and a house with windows broken in further down on Cresswell ... next to a burnt house on Creswell and a car parked opposite in a driveway, they've had their window broken in and paint splashed all over it. Further down there's a phone box that's always being targeted. (Ing137)

From the point of view of the residents exposed to these differing forms of disorder, they are not seen as being separate and isolated. Rather they are collectively read as being connected to each other and mutually conditioning, and consequently a picture of an increasingly threatening and ominous environment is articulated.

A similar amplification effect, but triggered by a slightly different problem profile was also observed in St Helens:

The bus stop is regularly smashed, how they smash it I don't know. They must go out with a hammer, they must, because it's special glass. But that's regularly done, and the telephone box up there. There is not a month goes by when it is not smashed up. (StH131)

Several interviewees described examples of where particular places and/or amenities were the repeated targets of vandalism. What is evident in these descriptions is how a 'destruction-repair-destruction' cycle served to amplify the overall resonance of the signal disorder represented by the physically damaged objects. The pattern of destruction followed by repair leading to further damage came to symbolize not just the disorderly intentions of some people, but also the inability of the authorities to prevent such behaviour and protect public property from it.

The two preceding examples illustrate different ways in which repeated disorder impacts upon communities. The first is a more general repetition. The second, a more focused recurrence of more specific types of problem. There is a third variant where a sense of harm accumulates rapidly. This tends to arise when an individual victim feels they are being personally and repeatedly targeted.

Being more explicit about the significance of repeated instances of disorder in shaping collective perceptions and reactions is important in terms of being able to understand how and why disorder matters in shaping public perspectives of urban environments. This notwithstanding though, there is a counterpoint to this and allied positions, asserting that fundamentally they share a tendency to over-state and over-inflate the import of social and physical disorder.

There are a variety of inflections of this critique, many of which trace a lineage back to Jane Jacobs' *The Death and Life of Great American Cities*. In particular, there is an oft quoted passage where she describes an elegant street ballet as those co-present in a space choreograph their actions to craft a spontaneous and evolving sense of social order. This passage is frequently deployed to imply that more recently policy architects have become liable to over-estimate the social impacts of disorder, and to under-estimate the capacity of community resilience to negotiate any potentially harmful effects.

Jacobs' concern was with the importance of diversity and tolerance in urban environments. Her critique of attempts to regulate disorder was grounded in how such interventions frequently impede the informal interactions and spontaneous social ordering that she sees as so vital for urban living. For Jacobs, and those who have subsequently appropriated aspects of her work, practical attempts to deal with disorder routinely elide the distinction between problems and people. As a consequence of which, such initiatives tend to end up targeting marginal individuals and groups, rather than anti-social behaviour (Duneier, 1999). It is a tendency evident in the interview quotation included previously from Failsworth where the interviewee rapidly shifted from concern about anti-social behaviour to the intimidatory appearance of groups of hooded youths.

Whilst recognizing that there is a certain element of truth in this view, there is an equal danger with this position, namely, that we fail to recognize just how salient and influential the presence of disorder is in shaping how people view urban environments. As Valverde (2012) contends, the 'Jacobian' view suffers from an idealized understanding of contemporary urban forms. Specifically, she concludes, that Jacobs' vision of cities constituted out of a series of urban villages would struggle to accommodate the levels of inequality and diversity that are features of most urban environments today (see also Duneier, 1999).

In this regard, an analysis of signal disorders is concerned not so much with whether public perceptions are right or accurate, but rather, with explaining how and why people read and interpret disorder in particular ways. Only once it is understood why these readings are patterned in certain ways is it possible to move to the second order question of whether they are 'correct' or not.

This is not to say that protecting diversity and promoting tolerance are not important, nor that achieving these aims is unproblematic. For instance, Richard Florida (2002) has argued persuasively that, for what he labels 'the creative class', diversity is explicitly valued. As he describes it, an urban aesthetic that might prove unsettling to some, is celebrated by others as a series of positive cues about the kinds of people living and working in an area. Similar sentiments to these were prefigured in the work of Sennett (1970). He too sought to illuminate the uses of disorder in the rituals and routines of social life. But he recognized how, in policy terms, there were tensions that had to be reconciled because of the ways more affluent groups in society were increasingly seeking physical sequestration from environments that they found too troubling or unsettling.

To help negotiate and navigate these subtleties in terms of how differently situated individuals and groups in society read various kinds of disorder, it is potentially helpful to distinguish between signals of diversity and difference, and signal disorders. The former are displays of identity and character, whilst the latter provoke negative and harmful responses. As such, a differentiation can be made between those things that are not to everyone's taste, and those that elicit a perception of risk and thus negative cognitive, affective, or behavioural effects.

Three Forms of Vulnerability

Analysis of the survey data of ASB victims clearly shows how repeated exposure to problems of disorder increases the negative sentiments and perceptions that such people display. Compared with individuals who have not been victims of ASB and single incident victims, the repeatedly victimized are significantly more likely to say that: environmental issues; road safety; noise; public drinking; rowdy behaviour; and problem neighbours have a negative impact upon their quality of life.

From a signalling perspective, this is because of how the occurrence dent 'tunes' the attention of those exposed to the presence of other indicators of risk and threat in the environment. The nature of the matters in this respect. The empirical survey data make clear that where an ASB incident is viewed as being personally targeted at the victim concerned, then pronounced negative effects can be induced. For example, hate motivated ASB where the victim is targeted because of their skin colour, sexuality, or because of a disability, frequently has a profound negative impact. Taken together, these forms of repeated victimization and personal targeting involve a form of 'incidental vulnerability' where the overall effects are amplified due to the particular qualities of the disorder incident itself.

To extend this insight we can analyse data from the British Crime Survey 2009/10 to model which kinds of ASB are more likely to induce a sense of incidental vulnerability. The starting point for this approach was to separate out the prevalence of exposure to the different problem types (labelled the scale of the problem) from the intensity of the effects elicited. The results of this are plotted in Figure 2.3.

Differentiating between the intensity of effect (x-axis) and the scale of its reach starts to unpick how some ASB issues are generative of particular perceptual and material harms because of the nature of the incident, whereas others are important because of the numbers of people that encounter them. The intensity measure for each ASB type was derived by combining the indicators contained in the survey on 'confidence in the police', 'fear of crime', 'social cohesion', and 'quality of life'. Across each of the four measures an average score was then independently established for all respondents reporting

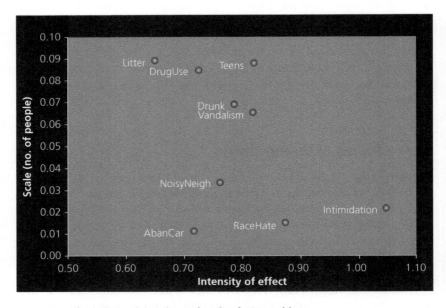

Figure 2.3 The Relative intensity and scale of ASB problems
Source: BCS 2009/10

no ASB exposure and deployed as a baseline measure. A similar score was then constructed, for each ASB type, for respondents who indicated that the issue was a problem for them. The intensity value was calculated by subtracting the value for those identifying the problem from the mean value for no-problems, creating a difference score. It is this difference score that is represented in Figure 2.3.

The details of this analytic procedure can be illustrated by examining 'intimidation and pestering'. Baseline figures for each outcome are displayed in the first column of Table 2.1. Intensity scores were then calculated for each individual outcome measure from the respondents stating intimidation is a problem for them. The intensity effect is calculated by subtracting the score for that problem from the baseline, as displayed in the third column. To derive the overall harm intensity measure these differences are averaged across all four effects (final line last column).

Pursuing this approach, litter emerges as a form of environmental disorder impacting upon a lot of people, but fairly diffusely. Contrastingly, being 'intimidated and pestered' is not something many people encounter, but those who do are intensely affected by it. Youth disorder, which as noted previously tends to dominate public debates about social disorder, achieves a high profile because it is something encountered by a sizeable proportion of people, and can generate fairly intense reactions. Further shape to the overall patterns of reaction stem also from the personal characteristics of who is involved, as well as the situational context.

The interplay between such factors is clarified by the survey of 9311 ASB victims across England and Wales. The percentages of victims who say their quality of life is 'very bad' divided by the three types of ASB used to categorize incidents by police are presented in Table 2.2.

The top row of the table shows only three per cent of people who self-identified their quality of life as 'very bad' had not experienced any ASB, compared with seven per cent who said they had experienced personal disorder. In turn the latter figure rises to 18 per cent for those who had called police ten or more times about such problems—confirming the importance of repetition identified previously. There was also a significant increase in the impact of personal ASB amongst people who stated they were in poor health. Equally important are the data in the

Table 2.1 Calculating the intensity effect of intimidation and pestering

	Baseline	Intimidation	Intensity effect
Fear of crime	1.58	2.31	.73
Confidence	2.61	3.28	.67
Quality of life	1.28	2.8	1.52
Social cohesion	2.13	3.41	1.28
Average			1.05

Table 2.2 Variations in ASB exposure

	ASB call type (by respondent)			
	Personal	Nuisance	Environment	None
All	7	3	3	3
Age 55+	8	3	3	5
BMEG	10	4	4	0*
Health (long-term illness or disability)	11	4	4	5
Repeat caller (3+)	11	4	3	3
Repeat caller (10+)	18	7	4	3
Disagree close knit community	14	7	6	6
Reject belonging to local community	18	10	9	13

* Base number less than 50 cases

bottom two rows in the table, showing a lack of community cohesion is associated with disorder incidents having marked consequences in terms of quality of life, particularly for victims of ASB.

One limitation of Jacobs' (1961) notion of the role of spontaneous social orders in urban social life, is that little reference is made to how potential participants in or onlookers to these may not be similarly positioned. In urban environments where people are not necessarily known to each other, some people may be more worried and concerned by particular types of encounter than others. Individually or collectively they may display less resilience when exposed to troubling issues. The presence of this 'personal vulnerability' effect in terms of how people respond to disorderly behaviour is confirmed by the survey data. Victims of anti-social behaviour who had existing longstanding health problems were found to be significantly more intensely concerned by the occurrence of incidents than those individuals without these vulnerability factors.

In effect then, aspects of a victim's identity and biography shape their propensity to be negatively affected by particular experiences of disorder, and for an incident to acquire the properties of a signal disorder for them. These same qualities can also shape wider collective reactions to disorder. Where a victim is personally vulnerable in some sense, this sometimes increases wider awareness and concern about an incident.

A third quality that alters the power of a signal disorder to influence popular concern relates to elements of the situation in which the incident occurs. Situational vulnerability is present where the impact of physical or social disorder is amplified by aspects of the context in which it arises. For instance, neighbourhoods that are economically stressed frequently have fewer material and social resources with which to overcome the occurrence of new problems. This is a conditioning factor that has been discussed most prominently by Sampson and

Raudenbusch (2004) in their discussion of 'collective efficacy' and how the capacity to tolerate different quantities and qualities of disorder is structured by the make-up of a community, together with its history and situation. If the amount and distribution of collective efficacy affords a degree of resilience, its absence induces vulnerability to the prevalence and effects of disorder.

Personal, incidental, and situational vulnerabilities are not, of course, mutually exclusive. They can and frequently do intersect and overlap. When this occurs the power of social signal disorders and physical signal disorders to trigger negative behavioural, cognitive, and affective responses is significantly heightened. When ASB repeats, is personally targeted towards victims, and occurs in settings lacking community efficacy, the consequences for perceptions and attitudes tend to be severe.

Experiences of racialized graffiti clearly capture these social dynamics. In the following two accounts it can be seen how personal experience of such issues, and then reading the experiences of others, act as signals about the condition of the local social order:

> We had all our window sprayed once, National Front, all up front window. (StM287)

> It's on the first lot of houses here somebody's wrote. Well I don't like to say it because I don't like swearing, but somebody's wrote 'Paki shit' on the house door up here. (StM299)

In an area with a history of racial tension, the presence of such graffiti was a visual indicator of the more entrenched social issues. As captured in the second quotation in particular, people did not need to be direct victims of such incidents to tune into them and read them as signalling insecurity.

The three forms of vulnerability sketched out in the previous paragraphs, all recognize that some people and communities are more liable to being negatively impacted by the occurrence of physical and social disorder, often because they lack social, economic, and psychological resilience to withstand the negative effects associated with such experiences. The introduction of such considerations is important because they tend to have been neglected in a number of influential accounts of urban life. It is not a feature of broken windows theory, nor is it sufficiently acknowledged by Jacobs. Moreover, the identification of the three different forms of vulnerability—personal, situational, and incidental—opens up the potentially vital issue for understanding signal disorders (and signal crimes more generally) that the overarching impact or effect of a signal event does not just inhere in the qualities of the incident itself, but is structured also by the situation in which it occurs.

Segmented and Laminated Social Orders

Signal disorders work differently across different settings. The amplitude of the perceptual effects generated by individual and series of disorders, and their capacity to resonate more widely, is reciprocally shaped by the situation. There are two particular types of situation that are consequential in this regard: 'segmented'; and 'laminated' social orders. The complexity of contemporary urban environments is vital in understanding how and why certain disorder events come to act as signals of the distribution of risk and threat across social spaces. But as has been rehearsed previously, one of the unique challenges posed by disorder in urban environments is that negative cognitive, affective, or behavioural effects are dependent, at least partly, upon the viewpoint of the person concerned. What for one individual is disorderly, for another may be simply part of the urban milieux, providing local colour and frisson.

Such permutations become particularly pronounced where diverse communities are co-habiting the same geographic spaces. Traditionally, communities living in particular areas frequently tended towards a degree of homogeneity, however, in some (but by no means all) contemporary British neighbourhoods such spatial patternings are breaking down. Driven by a diverse assemblage of social forces that interact with and rub up against each other, including: patterns of immigration and settlement; a neo-liberal, post-fordist economy emphasizing flexibility of production; a dynamic housing market; increasing job insecurity; and a general emphasis upon geo-spatial mobility, some urban communities now exist in a state of constant flux and change (Young, 1999). The residential population in such areas is continually altering as groups of people move in and move on, reflecting the macro-structural 'pushes' and 'pulls' of the economy and society.

Studying 1960s Chicago, Gerald Suttles (1970) could talk of 'segmented social orders' with geographically distinct communities constructing and operating different norms and conventions according to their backgrounds across fairly distinct territories. There are certainly examples of this within the data and accounts of how the boundaries between communities become areas where disorders are routinely read for their signal value. The clearest example of this was in Oldham, an area with a well-known history of inter-community tensions. Set against this backdrop, many residents discussed their concerns about the racialized graffiti and how it was read as a signal of wider and deeper tension:

> There's another problem we have, graffiti... It's on the walls 'whites keep out'.
> They have it up here 'Pakis keep out'. (StM278)

As this interviewee identifies, this problem was especially prevalent at the geographic border between the deprived white working class community and the adjacent neighbourhood where most of the residents were Pakistani-Asians. Importantly though, this graffiti that was placed by youngsters from both communities, did not exist in isolation. It was one component in a series of overlapping signal disorders. For instance, field observations conducted in the area also identified a number of other visual signifiers being used to send signals across the communities. For example, a number of 'George Cross' flags were displayed prominently in the 'white area', which added extra resonance to the graffiti.

Interviews with representatives from the white communities in these parts of Oldham revealed clear perceptions of there being 'no go areas for whites.' Likewise, members of the Asian community expressed similar sentiments about there being places where it was not safe for them to venture. The physical disorders, in terms of how they were read and interpreted by local residents, were overlaid on collective memories of a history of violence between the two groups. But such problems had been accentuated by changing socio-economic and demographic profiles in the area. The two main housing estates had been getting progressively less integrated and mixed over time. Where previously a limited degree of inter-community mixing had existed, the working class white residents had increasingly sought housing only in the 'white area'. Likewise, Asian residents had tended to move into property in the Asian area. In effect, the divisions and tensions had been hardening.[3]

To a significant extent then, the array of social and physical incidents that occurred and were read as signal disorders, performed a boundary demarcation function, signalling the territorial divisions between established communities. Under such conditions there were different readings of the same disorder signals. For some, they denoted risk or threat. But for others, the incidents expressed identity and belonging. These very different perceptions reflect how disorder at the borders of territorialized communities can be imbued with extra significance and ascribed additional layers of meaning. This is accentuated when there are extant inter-community tensions present as occurrences of social and physical disorder are read as communicating deeper messages about the distribution of risk and threat, identity and belonging.

Several of the urban neighbourhoods where data were collected for this research did not conform to this pattern of segmentation though. Instead they were organized around what might be termed 'laminated' social orders. The concept of lamination is intended to capture 'layers' that do not intermingle or interact, but lie across each other. The idea is that in a given area there can be distinct communities, maintaining very different social identities and ways of living, and that they effectively inhabit parallel lives and social worlds. These groups value different things and effectively establish distinctive and separate moral orders. This describes the arrangements in a few of the research sites in London, Manchester, and Blackpool.

The critical point is that under a segmented social order conflict and disorderly conduct are often found at the geographic boundaries between two or more communities, where their norms and expectations are most likely to 'rub up' against each other to generate friction. That is not to say that intra-community conflicts do not occur, particularly along inter-generational lines. But, the key conflicts

---

[3] In the literature on 'social capital' this kind of scenario is understood as representing a difference between 'bridging' and 'bonding' (see Putnam, 2000). The former references inter-community ties, the latter intra-community ones.

and thus sources of disorder, are those taking place with the inhabitants of other territorially distinct, and often adjacent areas.

In a laminated social order, diverse social groups with varying moral orders, co-habit the same territory, and intra-community conflict is more significant. Under such conditions, signal disorders play an important role in the complex ways that people infer fractures and fissures between those with whom they are co-present, as was evident on a large housing estate in Lancashire:

> First, the good thing about living here is, by and large, it's a very friendly estate... Unfortunately the bad thing about living here is over the last few years it has become increasingly lawless. Certain people have moved on to the estate who have attracted the wrong type of people themselves, as visitors and friends and these are people who have sullied the environment and living conditions for the majority. (Ing130)

This individual provided a detailed account of how the increasing presence of social and physical disorder could be attributed to these undesirable groups. Indeed, the disorders observed on the estate provided a more tangible and visible index of these deeper social problems, than any other indicator.

Thus a laminated social order involves a co-residing population with different and diverse notions of identity, and must accommodate different understandings of what is and is not orderly behaviour. As a consequence, conflicts are often threaded through relations between people who may not have shared understandings about standards of appropriate behaviour and yet must live side by side. Under such conditions, signal disorders act as visible signifiers of the differences between these people.

The precariousness and anxiety induced under such conditions was articulated in some of the interviews conducted in Blackpool. Unlike in many areas, where anti-social behaviour problems could be blamed on 'outsiders' coming into an area and causing trouble, in this case, residents were very aware that much of the misbehaviour involved young people living on the estate. The following was fairly representative:

> It's a nervous place to be honest. For example, this Saturday afternoon, there's about 5 or 6 boys ranging from 10 up to about 13 or 14 and they were on the car park out here, just running across people's cars, just running and jumping on them! This went on for an hour and we went out saying 'get down' and you get a load of abuse, and then it starts getting more than abuse and you tend to pull back and go in then. So you do feel intimidated. (Brun092)

There is a clear recognition in this account of how the inability to control the activities of the young men from the estate pervaded the atmosphere rendering it a 'nervous place' overall. There is also reference to behavioural effects and intimidation. In this case, and in other similarly situated neighbourhoods, the recurrence of disorder was read as signals about ongoing risks and threats posed to residents by other residents. In urban environments where people are navigating through a flood of potential information, the appearance of things is important. The ability to develop deep knowledge is limited, and thus conduct and judgements about security depend to a significant degree upon a reading of surfaces and what can be seen.

In an earlier era, both Georg Simmel (1976) and Robert Park (1916) recognized that as the urban experience induced new ways of doing and being, the visual and visualizable elements of sociality became of increasing significance in terms of how people made sense of and respond to their environments, and co-present others. Maintaining a sense of social order where social organization is highly kinetic is dependent upon the manipulation and management of impression, surface, and the hermeneutic. The capacity for a 'deep' knowledge and understanding about people, places, and events is always limited by the onslaught of information that is a defining characteristic of the modern city. It is not that inhabitants of modern cities do not or cannot establish deep, long-lasting relationships with family, friends, and neighbours, but rather that these are in the minority compared with the far larger quantities of fleeting and surface relationships in which they become engaged in the conduct of their everyday life. To manage such fleeting relationships, the urban dweller must be far more adept at using and reliant upon what Lofland (1985) terms 'categorical knowledge'. Where individuals and communities are mobile and changing, many people with whom one interacts cannot be known on a personal basis, but only on the basis of the impression that they present or the role they are performing.

The almost paradoxical quality of urban environments then is that as more and more data are available in such spaces, in terms of the signals given off by unfamiliar co-present others, by the design of the physical buildings, and by social media communication channels embedded within these situations, so the reliance upon appearance and surfaces is accentuated. Rather than trying to process increasing amounts of data, urban life is oriented by ritualistically scanning 'the noise' that is present and quickly moving past it, in order to focus attention on the meaningful signals that have some bearing upon the design of conduct. Under such conditions we can start to see both how and why it might be that disorder matters so much for people. It is a visible, material, and indexical expression of the state of a community, where other information about the distribution of risks and threats is hard to get a fix on.

For members of a community or inhabitants of a particular neighbourhood who have more developed knowledge about the area, there is always the possibility that the presence of disorder may be less threatening. As Taylor (2001) identifies, individuals co-residing in a neighbourhood may differ greatly in terms of perceiving high or low levels of local disorder in their area. Having local contextual knowledge about the lived realities of local people and their problems provides the possibility of mitigating perceptions of any risks or threats posed. For example, knowing some of the protagonists of social disorder in an area, or their families, may mean that there is understanding that these people are not really 'bad' but are just having a difficult time in their personal life, which is manifested in their disruptive behaviours.

This process of 'defining the deviancy down' on the basis of situated local knowledge was observed to take place in some areas and for some problems. However, established social relations did not always have these beneficial effects. It was equally the case that prior knowledge of peoples' families could lead to anti-social acts being informally 'defined up' in terms of their perceived seriousness. Where families had reputations for trouble, when any of the members of that group were involved in disorderly conduct, that incident would be construed as connected to a wider pattern of behaviour. Especially in the case of young people, family reputation played an important role in shaping the signal that was seen as being sent by any anti-social conduct.

More generally though, conjoined with the fact that many people nowadays appear to feel less connection to their neighbours, the presence of repeated disorder on an ongoing basis within a neighbourhood can serve as a constant reminder to residents of the wider and deeper structural problems that they are negotiating. Introducing the concept of signal disorder into discussions of urban life provides a mechanism for unpacking how contemporary concerns about disorder are not driven solely by actual changes in the amount of this activity. Indeed, there has always been social and physical disorder present in communities, but what is happening currently is that it is assuming increased symbolic importance in a social context where people have less knowledge and understanding about these individuals and groups with whom they are co-present. As such, absolute levels of disorder in an area may be less consequential in shaping residents' overall perceptions of quality of life, than are the presence of disorderly incidents that serve to send signals about the area to those living in it, and beyond.

In more stable times, the capacity of less serious issues to trouble people and 'drive' patterns of insecurity is likely to be more limited. But in an era which is, in part, as a result of threats to national security in the form of terrorist attacks and neighbourhood security in the forms of crime and anti-social behaviour, increasingly defined by a pervasive and permeating sense of 'ambient insecurity' (Innes, 2003b), people are cognitively and emotionally on a heightened state of alert. They are particularly sensitive to and attuned to those events that might indicate a risk of potential harm. As such, disorder at a local level becomes a connotative signifier encoding the risks and threats posed by a whole world of trouble.

Conclusion: The Order in Disorder

The power of a signal disorder to shape or alter how people think, feel, or act in relation to their safety and security depends upon aspects of the situation in which they are located. A signal disorder is an act, or the material traces of one, that whilst not illegal, nevertheless influences collective safety and security. Conceptually, an analysis of signal disorders illuminates how public reactions to

infractions of norms and conventions of behaviour in urban envir
not random, or atomized, but possess a form of social organization. ҏ.
standings of crime and disorder risks and threats are situationally sensitive,
as indicators about what such problems might portend about current or possible
future threats to safety. Some disorder incidents that are dismissed as relatively
trivial by juridical institutions, assume a significant role in terms of how ordinary
people symbolically construct their understandings of different public spaces.
The empirical data presented herein have evidenced how there are patterns to
the ways in which people read and react to social and physical signal disorders.
In this sense, there is an order to disorder.

Different forms of disorder matter in different ways. Some disorders impact on
a comparatively small number of people, but intensively. Other incidents affect
more people, but more obliquely. Physical disorders tend to have less inherent
power to act as signals to people, but when they co-occur with other crimes and
disorders, a process of signal amplification arises and their cumulative influence
increases. Through patterns of both 'parallel' and 'serial' co-occurrence they
shape levels of 'incidental vulnerability'. This is one of three configurations of
vulnerability identified through the analysis; the other two being 'personal' and
'situational'. The point is to articulate how interpretations of disorder are both
shaping of and shaped by aspects of the wider social situation.

This accent upon the influence of the neighbourhood situation in terms of
understanding how specific disorder events are read, interpreted, and ascribed
particular meanings starts to move our thinking beyond that of prior accounts of
the role of disorder in social life. These have tended to cast disorder either as a
cause of other problems, such as crime, or as a consequence of wider and deeper
social forces, such as levels of socio-economic deprivation and inequality, or
prior crime rates. Grounded in the precepts and principles of the signal crimes
perspective, the approach outlined herein has started from an alternative
premise, that is, to question how and why particular forms and instances of
disorder are so influential upon individual and collective perceptions of safety
and security.

In urban environments people cannot and do not seek to process and interpret
all available information. To do so would be exhausting. Rather, they attend to
those units of information that can be anticipated to connotatively or denota-
tively indicate the presence of particular risks, opportunities, and threats—what
have been termed signals. Physical and social disorder is routinely encoded as a
signal because it provides a visible marker of where potential risks and threats
may be located across social space.

How Fear Travels

The Private, Parochial, and Public Harm Footprints of Criminal Homicides

Fear of crime is one of a limited number of criminological concepts that has travelled beyond the confines of the academy, gaining wider traction to become firmly established in the lexicon of public crime talk. There are, however, significant limitations with how it has been conceptualized and operationalized in academic studies, policy contexts, and public debates. These limitations pivot around a marked tendency to treat fear of crime as an abstract, ambient, and aggregate phenomenon. That is, it is not traceable or attributable to specific incidents, but held to be a generic product of overall crime rates. Related to this, crime induced fear is depicted as an attribute of population sub-groups, rather than a defined reaction to specific events occurring within particular neighbourhoods, networks, and communities (Ditton and Innes, 2005). These are problems compounded by the willingness to use 'fear of crime' as a generic label summarizing what are in actual fact, a diverse range of cognitive, affective, and behavioural reactions (Farrall et al., 2009). This includes anger and avoidance, which have been identified as amongst the most common reactions to crime threats and risks (Ferraro, 1995; Ditton et al., 1999). Indeed, much of what is labelled as fear of crime, if described with greater precision and clarity does not actually involve 'fear', nor is it just 'of crime'.

Such problems and limitations are as much methodological as they are conceptual. The study of fear of crime, or what might more accurately be termed social reactions to crime and disorder, has come to be dominated by the application of quantitative analytic methods to large-scale public opinion surveys (Ditton and Innes, 2005; Farrall et al., 2009; Kury, 1994; Sparks et al., 1977). Whilst there are notable exceptions to this tendency (see for example Girling, Loader and Sparks, 2000), there is a clear orthodoxy about how crime fear is studied. It is an approach providing useful measures of the prevalence and distribution of negative reactions, but it simultaneously inhibits thinking about the different ways in which public insecurity might be leveraged by the occurrence of a small number of high impact crimes.

In this regard, fear of crime is illustrative of a process described by Ian Hacking (1983) in his book 'Representing and Intervening'. Hacking cautions about how established concepts and ideas frame our perceptions of the world and the orders of reality we collectively manufacture. In particular, he traces the ways that such concepts can become ossified and solidified through the application of particular methodologies, and in the process structure individual and collective decisions about how we intervene in situations to tackle social problems. These are processes that are frequently seen but unnoticed.

Of course, there are incidents where 'fear of crime' is an entirely accurate descriptor of the reaction elicited. Certain serious crimes, when they occur, display a capacity to generate fear and anxiety amongst the public. However, current academic approaches to studying fear of crime are ill-equipped to capture the precise dynamics and mechanics of the social processes involved. There is a significant lacunae in our understandings of how collective reactions such as fear, emerge and evolve in the wake of high profile major crimes such as criminal homicides, and the factors that shape how reactions to these comparatively rare but impactive individual incidents 'travel' across social space. This is an important consideration for a signal crimes perspective.

This essay represents an attempt to rethink how we think about public reactions to major crime. Coherent with the notion that such incidents are functioning as signal crimes, the analysis describes specific reactions emerging, changing, and decaying across social space and time in the aftermath of incidents involving fatal violence. Informed by empirical data collected across a series of linked field studies designed to measure the community impacts of criminal homicides, the focus is upon understanding how fear and other reactions 'travel' in the aftermath of a major crime. The notion of 'travel' is developed to trace how social reactions to such incidents are diffused and disseminated across individuals, groups, and communities. A second conceptual innovation is to introduce the concept of 'the harm footprint'. Akin to the notion of an 'ecological footprint', the harm footprint idea seeks to capture the detectable patterns to the negative social reactions induced by criminal homicides. Three main 'harm footprints' are identified: private harms; parochial harms; and public harms.

The next section outlines some key resources that are drawn upon to frame analysis of the empirical data and construct a conceptual scaffolding for thinking about such issues. This is followed by several sections organized around case study-based accounts of how the impacts of particular major crimes travelled within and across different communities. The conclusion draws together the implications of the findings for how we think about social reactions to crime in general, and for the task of assessing community impacts of major crimes in particular. It is suggested that the distinction between forms of private, parochial, and public harm may have wider theoretical and practical utility.

On Homicide and its Impacts

A relatively small number of criminal homicides possess a particularly resonant quality. They exhibit a unique influence upon the public understanding of crime, with information about who did what to whom and why travelling widely across different communities and sometimes countries. In many ways they become freighted as vehicles for public deliberation about issues to do with crime, policing, and security more generally—the specific details of the cases affording ways in which, what would otherwise be abstract ideas and values, can be collectively articulated and debated. Some key facets of such processes are illuminated if we consider the state of homicide in England and Wales. There are now somewhere in the region of 600 criminal homicides recorded by police in England and Wales each year, and yet mere mention of 'The Yorkshire Ripper', Damilola Taylor and James Bulger would cue large numbers of people to recall horrific crimes, that at the time they occurred, were the focus of saturation mass media coverage, and still retain an ability to stir feelings of dread and fear many years later. A small number of crimes like these have a disproportionate impact upon how we collectively think about crime and security.

A growing body of social scientific literature has mapped and investigated different aspects of social reactions to homicide, including: how it is constructed in fictional and factual media representations (Jenkins, 1994); the police investigative response (Innes, 2003a); the repercussions for victims families (Rock, 1998); and the stigmatization of offenders' friends and families (Condry, 2007). In addition, studies trace the aetiology (Polk, 1994), victimology (Brookman, 2005) and geographic distribution of fatal violence (Shaw, Tunstall and Dorling, 2005). However, there is little systematic research that has considered how such crimes shape and alter the social settings in which they occur.

There is an assumption that crimes such as homicide have a significant impact upon local social orders. However, emerging evidence suggests that processes of social reaction to such events can be quite subtle and complex. For example, Carr's (2005) ethnographic study of a Chicago neighbourhood, recounts how, following two separate shootings in the area, neighbourhood residents sought to collectively mobilize to respond to the perceived threats signalled by these crimes. As he documents, the initial attempt to respond to the first incident stalled and failed. It was only following a second local killing that police and community became sufficiently motivated to do something in the face of a now incontrovertible threat, that they co-produced a more effective response.

That high profile major crimes can elicit significant reactions is well documented. In his study of the personal and political responses of homicide victims' families to the death of their friends and family, Rock (1998) charts the profound existential consequences and long-lasting sense of harm that can occur. But there can be wider consequences too. For example, Chancer (2005) analysed several high profile American crimes as case studies to show how they were generative of important legislative changes. Similarly, Simon (2007) has unpacked how a number of pivotal incidents have profoundly shifted the framing of crime more generally in political discourse and action.

In the UK, signal crimes such as the murders of Stephen Lawrence, Sarah Payne, and Holly Wells and Jessica Chapman, have been harnessed as the catalysts for large-scale, politically driven, institutional reform efforts (Rowe, 2007; Rock, 2004). The production of such institutional effects are frequently politically shaped as attested to in Tony Blair's autobiography. Recalling the murder of James Bulger in 1993, he describes how he purposively sought to use the sense of public shock and horror to leverage political advantage:

> Very effectively, I made it into a symbol of a Tory Britain in which...the bonds of social and community well-being had been loosed, dangerously so. (Blair, 2010: 57)

This kind of moral entrepreneurship by what Becker (1963) labels 'rule creators' is well documented. But whilst there are studies of the effects of particular cases upon the institutional architecture, and the politics and culture of criminal justice, the question about what impact such crimes have upon the neighbourhoods and communities where they occur, and further afield, has been neglected. This neglect is all the more notable given the number of studies that have sought to assess the influence of disorder and volume crime upon levels of fear of crime (see for example Hale, 1996; Taylor, 2000).

The significance of this gap in our knowledge is reinforced if we turn to consider how police have sought to develop practical tools to measure the community impacts of homicides as part of their efforts to manage the consequences of major crimes (Innes, 2010). There is, as yet, no national template or standard operating procedures in terms of how, when, or why Community Impact Assessments are conducted by police. Rather, there are local derivatives of some key principles. Typically these involve police contacting community 'leaders' or members of the public in an area where a significant event has happened, in order to gauge what the local reaction is and in particular whether there is any escalation in intra- or inter-community tensions. Their Community Impact Assessments may also make use of other 'open source' materials such as mass media articles or social media to try and get some sense of the impact that is being played out.

This innovation in police practice is inflected by a wider and deeper tendency of organizations to orient themselves towards risks of various kinds evident over the past three decades (Hutter and Power, 1997). Indeed, impact assessment methodologies have become established tools for public policy and practice. Across domains as diverse as health, gender equality, and environment, impact assessments are employed to predict and pre-empt the potential for different kinds of harm (Burdge and Vanclay, 1996). Coherent with these developments, police have developed similar approaches. However, whereas in other areas of public policy, impact assessments are routinely predictive and prospective, police applications tend to be more descriptive.

Research Design

The empirical data informing this study were collected through a series of field-work-based case studies conducted between 2003 and 2009. The first two cases (Dowler, and Shakespeare and Ellis) were studied as part of the wider project investigating community reactions to crime, disorder, and policing across several different localities. These incidents were not purposively sampled, but it just so happened that the research interviews were scheduled at a time after the incidents occurred and many respondents made reference to them. Preliminary analysis of these data suggested some interesting issues and a decision to undertake further similar case studies was taken. A further four case studies were conducted in subsequent years, with a more intensive focus upon tracing the incident impacts. These were purposively sampled in order to ensure that the incidents covered related to a variety of types of homicide.

Consequently, this essay is based upon detailed data drawn from a total of six cases. For each case, in-depth semi-structured interviews with a sample of members of the local communities were conducted. A total of 109 such interviews form the dataset analysed. The incidents involved cover a range of different types of homicide, from 'a domestic', to killings connected to gang activities. Included within the sample are cases that, at the time when interviews were conducted, were long-term unsolved police investigations, which may potentially identify a crucial variable in terms of interpreting the dynamics of community reactions. Indeed, taken together, the variations present in the circumstances of the cases affords the opportunity to start to unpack how the characteristics of the crime and its social setting interact in shaping the nature of community reactions.

A brief overview of the sample of cases and interviews is provided in Table 3.1. The interview instrument administered to generate data on public reactions to these crimes covered a range of topics so as to gauge respondents' reactions to the key incident, but also how these fitted with their more general perceptions and experiences of crime, disorder, and policing. The majority of interviews were tape-recorded, and where they were not, extensive and detailed notes were written. Thus the dataset collated across the series of case studies affords a number of detailed and thickly descriptive accounts of peoples' thoughts and feelings about the occurrence of particular crimes, and how they have made sense of these. A particular innovation of the methodology was the incorporation of a prototype 'qualitative GIS' tool. Qualitative GIS is an emerging method for generating thickly descriptive data to explore how social spaces are symbolically constructed (Elwood and Cope, 2009). In several of the cases this involved respondents being provided with maps of the local area, which were then used to investigate how they perceived that the occurrence of the homicide and other incidents had impacted upon the ways they thought and felt about their neighbourhood and other areas.

Table 3.1 Overview of cases and interviews

Case name	No of interviews	Case outline
Amanda Dowler, Walton-On-Thames, Surrey	10	The victim was abducted on her way home from school on 21 March 2002. Her body was not found until September that year. The case was covered extensively in national media. Interviews in the local community were conducted in 2003. At that time no-one had been prosecuted for the crime, although subsequently a man has been convicted for abduction and murder.
Laetitia Shakespeare & Charlene Ellis, Birmingham	28	On 2 January 2003 the two victims were killed in a 'drive-by' shooting whilst attending a New Year's party. The shootings were connected to a conflict between local gangs and the victims were not the intended targets. Interviews were conducted in 2003.
John Monckton, London	16	The victim, a wealthy banker, was attacked and killed in his home in Chelsea in November 2004. His wife was seriously injured in the same attack. The case garnered considerable media coverage and two men have been convicted. Interviews were conducted in January 2005 and 12 respondents were re-interviewed 14 months later following conviction of the suspects.
Jesse James, Moss-side, Manchester	21	A young black man who was shot in a park in a notorious area of Manchester in September 2006. The case received considerable media coverage, attributable in part to the potential similarities with the *Stephen Lawrence* case, including criticisms of the police investigation. The interviews were carried out in 2007.
Craig Ivey, South Wales	14	Ostensibly a 'domestic murder' in a fairly isolated Welsh town, the case is of interest because of the setting within which it occurred. The killing occurred in January 2008 and the field interviews took place within two weeks.
Rachel Baker (accused), Butleigh, Somerset	10	This was an unusual case involving the alleged murder of several care home residents by the home's manager between 2006–7. The setting was a small, affluent, and tightly-knit community. The interviews were conducted in January 2009 a few days prior to the suspect being charged.

Consistent with the strategy of analytic induction, respondents were sampled differently as the programme of work evolved, reflecting findings from the earlier studies (Znaniecki, 1934). So for example, interviewees for the *Monckton* case were identified on a geographic basis to investigate how distance from the crime scene shaped the tenor of social reactions. In subsequent data collection phases, different influences other than geographic distance were used to guide the selection of potential interviewees.

Analysis of the data from across the cases sampled identifies several distinctive patterns in terms of how and why individuals and groups react in different ways in the aftermath of a major crime. These are associated with relative 'geographic', 'temporal', and 'social distance' from the crime event. In developing these insights the analysis is focused principally upon 'theory-building'. Informed by rich qualitative data it seeks to establish a theoretical framework that can be used to explain and explore some key aspects of how criminal homicides, and by extension other types of serious crime, harm individuals and groups to shape the processes of social order. It should be acknowledged though, that the empirical data are limited by the practical difficulties associated with conducting fieldwork on a relatively infrequent type of crime such as homicide, and organizing in-depth exploratory interviews with members of the public about them. As such, the findings are necessarily tentative.

Social Reactions to Homicide

As a relatively rare but serious form of violence, criminal homicides often acquire the properties of a 'signal crime' influencing how people think, feel, and act in relation to their personal and collective security. The signal crimes perspective (SCP) posits that some crime and disorder incidents act as warning signals to people about the distribution of risk to their everyday security, with exposure to these signals structuring their beliefs and behaviour (Innes, 2004). A deviant act becomes a 'signal crime' or 'signal disorder' when it can be shown to have induced specific cognitive, affective, or behavioural changes to how people conceive of their security. A key contention of the SCP is that some incidents matter very much in terms of the social impacts they induce, but other ostensibly similar incidents are less consequential. As with many legal categories, 'criminal homicide' covers a wide variety of acts arising out of a range of different conflicts (Brookman, 2005). In terms of the potential to elicit intense reactions from a large number of people, some illegal killings (such as those involving a degree of deliberate predation) have a greater capacity to 'shock' and 'chill' the public at large, compared with a fatal assault arising between individuals intimately known to each other, occurring in emotionally charged circumstances (Innes, 2003a).

The fact that social reactions such as fear that are sometimes elicited in the wake of homicidal violence display different propensities to 'travel' between individuals and groups, in ways associated with the circumstances of the offence, raises an important question about how such diffusions are structured. In an important contribution to our understandings of the constitution of social order, Hunter (1985) has argued that the traditional distinction between 'community' and 'society' used to ground many analyses of the social impacts of social problems is both theoretically and empirically inadequate. Instead, he suggests distinguishing between what he terms 'private', 'parochial', and 'public social orders', differentiated along three key analytic axes: basic social bond; institutional locus; and spatial domain. On this basis, three principal kinds of social order can be defined as follows:

- Private: arises among family members and friends, and is founded upon shared values and mutually provided forms of social support. Spatially it centres upon the household and personal social networks grounded in 'strong ties'.
- Parochial: occurs between neighbours and depends upon interpersonal networks and interlocking local institutions, both formal and informal, that function to sustain the residential community and thus spatially centres upon shared conceptions of neighbourhood.
- Public: involves fellow citizens and is principally regulated through the auspices of the formal agencies of the state. Spatially this realm extends to the legal boundaries of a given state and beyond.

In analysing the communication of emotions and perceptions in the aftermath of collectively traumatic events, Hunter's framework has been appropriated because it offers insight into the patterns evident in the empirical data in terms of how fear and other forms of harm travel in the aftermath of homicides.

Private Impacts

Research on the aetiology of homicide repeatedly documents that most fatal violence occurs between family and friends (Wolfgang, 1958; Polk, 1994). This finding is important inasmuch as it serves as a counterpoint to journalists' concentration upon a select number of dramatic 'stranger homicides' (Reiner, 1997). Rather than 'cold blooded', the modal homicide tends to be a 'hot' crime, arising in an emotionally charged atmosphere between people who know each other (Collins, 2008; Polk, 1994). That is not to say that such events do not cause considerable suffering and harm (see Rock, 1998). But rather, that the affective consequences tend to be largely confined to immediate friends and family of the victim(s), and tend not to travel much further. In contrast to which, other homicides induce a far more wide-ranging impact upon public sentiments and sensibilities.

One of the cases studied exemplifies the key considerations associated with the largely private impacts of such incidents. The setting was a small, cohesive, and tight-knit village, typical of many similar communities in the South Wales Valleys. Indeed, many families had been residents for several generations in the village where the crime took place. Following the fatal violence there was a temporary sense of shock across the community, but this did not translate into any sense of harm for most people.

The killing resulted from an altercation between the current and former partners of a young woman living in the village. Her current partner (the victim) who was killed by her former lover (the assailant), and the woman were all well known within the community and it was also public knowledge that the assailant and woman's relationship had been a violent one. When interviewed, several respondents also recalled other violent incidents that the assailant had been involved in locally. The woman's new partner, who was killed, was not from the immediate area, but from a village a few miles further down the same valley. He was stabbed by a long-bladed instrument following a verbal altercation. Several interviewees repeated a local rumour that the source of the argument was that the woman was pregnant with the assailant's child, even though she was now in a relationship with the eventual victim.

The interviews conducted with 14 local residents confirmed that the incident had little measurable impact upon the community. Some interviewees expressed shock and sadness that the incident had been fatal, but the assailant was widely known to be a violent man and there was a relief he was 'off the streets'. This factor in particular shaped community reactions to the incident. Because it was a small, deeply inter-connected community, information and rumours were abundant, helping people to interpret and make sense of the incident. They had quickly moved to define this incident as 'a domestic' and so did not see it as involving any wider ramifications in terms of personal risk. There was some sympathy for the assailant's family expressed by respondents and perhaps that the woman was partly to blame. There was little evidence locally of much sympathy for the victim's family on the basis that he was not from the village, and indeed, little was known about his relatives. Fundamentally, the interviews revealed little evidence of community tension or wider impact. A number of those interviewed conveyed a sense of embarrassment that the assailant came from their community, and that they wanted to forget and move on, but nothing more profound than this.

The circumstances and social reaction dynamics of this particular case help to illustrate several key points in terms of understanding how and why particular crimes achieve impact. It is clear that the condition of the local community helped to mitigate any potential for wider resonance and thus the impacts of the crime did not travel much beyond those with a direct connection to the key protagonists. This is significant in that it tends to confirm that, at least in part, processes of social reaction are shaped as much by the community context as the crime itself.

Parochial Impacts

In his modelling of social order, Hunter (1985) uses the term 'parochial social order' to capture the sense of inter-connectedness and other associated benefits that can be derived by people co-present in a particular neighbourhood. It is a position resonating strongly with contemporary positions on social capital and collective efficacy (Sampson and Raudenbusch, 1999). The point is that extant local social networks can be mobilized for mutual benefit. Analysis of the empirical data collected following several of the homicides suggests though, that such networks can also act as channels to transmit and disseminate fear.

Making sense of the 'reaction patterns' present in the data however requires some updating of Hunter's original formulation. Looking across the data it is clear that there were two principal configurations in terms of how fear travels across established local social networks. There were cases where the pattern of travel remained relatively geographically confined to a particular neighbourhood—often where the crime occurred. This can be termed a 'parochial localized impact'.

In contrast to this however, there were also cases where the pattern of travel for the fear elicited was more 'parochial-distributed'. This was evident where processes of social reaction 'travelled' across social networks not based upon physical co-presence. So for example, if a member of a gay community is killed, then the crime may have little impact upon the immediate neighbourhood, but may prove to be a source of concern for other members affiliating with that community, even though they do not reside in the immediate vicinity (see Innes, 2003a). It is a 'travel pattern' reflecting the much commented upon fact that contemporary notions of community affiliation and belonging do not depend upon physical co-presence.

To discuss the contours of parochial impacts, reactions to the murder of John Monckton will be assessed. This was a complex case and it could be argued aspects of the social reaction were more in keeping with the conceptualization of 'public impact' to be detailed in due course. For current purposes though, it illuminates the kinds of patterns typical of parochial-localized impacts. This reflects how the unusual circumstances of the crime together with the socio-economic profile of the victims and their immediate neighbourhood, meant that the collective harm of the crime was geographically confined, but also travelled via established social networks to other wealthy Londoners.

The murder of John Monckton

In November 2004, John Monckton a wealthy senior executive, together with his wife and daughter, were attacked in their home in the Upper Cheyne Walk area of Cremorne Ward, Kensington and Chelsea. He was killed when two men tricked their way onto the property saying they were delivering post. In the process of trying to rob the family Damien Hanson and his accomplice Elliot White stabbed John Monckton and his wife, with the attack being witnessed by their daughter. John Monckton died from his injuries and his wife was severely injured. It was a crime that received extensive media publicity and profile. However, the pivotal insight afforded by the empirical fieldwork was that as the victims were targeted because of their wealth, the local travel patterns of the fear generated within local communities was strongly influenced by divisions based upon social class.

A series of in-depth interviews were conducted with residents in Cremorne, two months after the killing and then 14 months later, when 12 people were re-interviewed.[1] It is clear that for those living close to the scene of the crime it had been a significant event with profound implications for how they viewed their safety. The following was typical:

> The effect on me was that I locked the door. I have got a Yale lock but you could put your hand through the letter box and open it. I said to my wife because of the way that they had got into the Moncktons' house I said that 'we are going to lock the two dead locks on the door.' Because the only way into this house is through this street, you couldn't get in at the back. So the effect of it was we locked the door even when we're in. It's locked now actually. (004)

The majority of the respondents living in areas immediately surrounding the scene of the crime reported having introduced some form of behavioural modification in response to the murder and the fear it had provoked, including investments in situational crime prevention devices.

Harnessing principles associated with the qualitative GIS method, during these interviews respondents were asked to draw onto maps of the locality any areas that they considered to possess distinct neighbourhood identities. A computer algorithm was then used to process these data. The analysis identified three distinct areas plotted onto the maps by the majority of respondents. One neighbourhood was defined around Upper Cheyne Walk, where the Moncktons lived. The second was less specific and followed the boundaries of the local electoral ward. The third area identified by respondents was at the other end of the ward and related to a deprived council estate—'the World's End Estate'—distinct from the far more affluent Upper Cheyne Walk neighbourhood. The demarcation of the boundaries of these neighbourhoods were structured by their very different socio-economic profiles. Significantly, this in turn shaped the distribution of social reactions to the crime.

Interviewing people living near to the scene of the Monckton murder it was clear that it had had a significant impact upon their perceptions of neighbourhood security. However, for those living further away and who were of a different social class than the victims, the impact of the crime was far less immediate and pronounced. The following statements were representative of the views of those living on the World's End Estate:

> Because Mr. Monckton wasn't on my doorstep, you know, it was something that I didn't feel involved with. I just felt sorry for the whole family because of what had happened but it wasn't, although it was in the same borough, it wasn't on my doorstep. (009)

---

[1] The second wave of interviews were undertaken once the two suspects had been convicted. The purpose was to try and test whether a criminal justice resolution impacted in any detectable way upon the harm experienced.

I don't think it would happen here so much because...they knew he was a moneyed man, there was money there or there was things there they could probably sell, get money for...(003)

It can clearly be seen from these two quotations that social reactions to the crime were being structured by social class, partially reinforced by the influence of geographical distance. Class issues were framing a perception of 'social distance' between the victims and some other local residents, that over-rode considerations of geography. Indeed, more detailed analysis revealed that the concerns of residents on the World's End Estate were gravitating to a much greater extent around a homicide that had happened in that neighbourhood, near to a local pub:

I think the one closer to me had more of an impact, because it was on my doorstep. Um, and then, when this happened to this young lad it seemed as though it was not in my territory, d'you know...because, I told you, I finish at Beaufort Street. (011)

Unlike the Monckton murder that received full and sustained media attention across press and broadcast platforms, this second crime achieved little public awareness or profile. Yet, for some residents it was this latter event that did far more to signal the presence of risk and threat. What this points to is that, at least at a neighbourhood level of analysis, the community impact of the *Monckton* case was concentrated and intense, but did not travel that far either geographically or socially.

Factoring in some of the impacts induced by the second incident starts to unpick some of the complexities involved in the formation of collective reactions to crime in urban contexts. For it would be tempting and alluring to suppose that a clear homogonous reaction could be detected, in line with the kinds of discourse often featuring in mass media reportage of these kinds of event. Contrastingly though, the empirical data suggest something rather more subtle and nuanced occurring in terms of how reactions take shape and unfold. Groups and communities may react quite differently from one another depending upon how they are positioned in relation to the crime in terms of physical proximity and social distance. Relatedly, the presence of other prior crime incidents can play an important role in framing how any subsequent event is interpreted.

In an effort to understand how the impacts of the homicide were or were not interacting with the effects associated with more routine crime and disorder concerns, interviewees were asked about their key security concerns locally. Across the ward as a whole 'murder' emerged as the key priority. This might be expected given the circumstances. It is however extremely unusual. Abundant research evidence documents that in most neighbourhoods, most of the time, the public's focus is upon anti-social behaviour and social disorder (Bottoms, 2012). But what a closer analysis of the qualitative data reveals is that actually across the two affluent and deprived neighbourhoods residents' concerns were in fact being driven by the two separate homicide incidents.

Following on from the initial interviews, 14 months later, after the conviction of two men for the murder of John Monckton, 12 of the original respondents were re-interviewed. In this second wave of interviews, murder was still clearly the strongest signal crime. This evidences how the kinds of impact that arise in the wake of a major crime, in terms of how people think, feel, and act about their safety and security can be both intense and long-lasting. As such, this particular case helps to tease out two key dimensions that can be used to understand how homicides impact upon communities: the 'intensity' of any impact; and its 'duration'.

The duration of the impact of a signal crime and how its effects travel across time keys us into a number of interesting issues and considerations. Heinous crimes can fundamentally re-shape how people think about particular places and communities, with collective memories becoming configured around these incidents. The fieldwork examining the Monckton murder is important in this regard as it helps us to better understand some key influences upon the longevity of a signal and the decay patterns of their effects as well. For instance, in the process of tracking the local communities' reactions to the murders it became apparent that the fear and concern elicited by the main incident, was being supported and reinforced by connections that were being drawn with other problems and issues. When interviewed, one respondent told how, in the aftermath of the crime and the police's detailed enquiries:

> There were lots of things that later came out of that, which I think the police were told about. Like the children speaking up about things we didn't know about which kids were frightened to talk about, about this guy with the guns and...I worry more now because I think that there's a lot of guns around. (005)

What we can detect here is something akin to an 'aftershock' effect. There was the initial shock and fear that arose following the primary incident (the murder). But then, as the police enquiries unveiled the presence of other problems in the area, there were a series of secondary aftershocks as people found out more about previously 'subterranean' aspects of the 'underlife' of their neighbourhood. Other respondents similarly drew connections between the major crime and a series of other more 'minor' incidents. The cumulative impact of these was to prolong the capacity of the murder to serve as a focal point for a sense of underlying community concern and anxiety. The influence of the signal crime did not decay as fast as it might otherwise have done. How fear travels, in terms of its precise contours and dynamics of social reactions, following high profile major crime depends then, at least in part, upon how the incident relates to other occurrences—at least in terms of how they are perceived by local communities.

One further important dynamic of fear travel patterns revealed by the *Monckton* case concerns the role of well-connected and networked individuals in diffusing and channelling the emotions of local communities. There is a now voluminous academic and policy literature on the subject of social capital, much of which highlights the value of particular individuals as 'community mobilizers' and change agents.[2] Such individuals are often depicted as central nodes embedded within dense social networks of contacts and relations, because of which, they are able to get things done. There has, however, been far less attention given to the negative consequences that can flow through people positioned in such ways when the community of which they are a part is under stress. By way of example, in the area of Upper Cheyne Walk, the Vicar of the local church located opposite where the Moncktons lived, and attended by them, became an important figure in shaping the dynamics of the community reaction.

He recalled how, in the days after the crime when there was an enormous amount of local community concern and fear, a local police officer had told him that recorded crime figures suggested that Cremorne was actually a comparatively safe area of London:

> ...he said 'Well, did you realise that...' statistics, and I think he wanted me perhaps to calm the community. And to ask me whether they should leaflet the community, giving them the statistics. So I said statistics are not going to work, do some real work, I said 'Catch the buggers!', 'Catch the buggers!'

In an area like Cremorne, this man was an important conduit for information in the community and his evident lack of confidence in the police response was transmitted far more widely thanks to his network of connections, consequently amplifying the overall tenor of community concern. The key point for understanding how fear travels following major crime incidents is the important part that can be played by a relatively small number of individuals who function as 'messengers' for the wider community. These social actors can perform an important role in inhibiting the decay of the effects of a signal crime. But as will be discussed in more detail in due course, they can also provide the basis for community resilience.

Parochial-distributed impacts: The Jessie James murder

From the data collected, it is clear that not all homicides generate concentrated forms of impact channelled through neighbourhood based affiliations. On some occasions the reactions and reverberations travel across a social network. The unsolved murder on 9 September 2006 of 15-year-old Jessie James in Moss Side, Manchester, exemplifies the traits of the 'parochial-distributed impact' model. Jessie was apparently returning home from a party with friends at around 2am, when he entered a local recreation ground where he was shot dead at close range. His young age, assumed lack of links to local gang culture, and the national concern about gun crime and other violent offending assured that the incident attracted immediate and significant media attention. Locally, however, the reactions were more complex and convoluted.

---

[2] See for example Putnam (2000).

Building upon the findings derived from examining the *Monckton* case, in preparing to gauge the community impacts of Jessie James' killing, an effort to systematically investigate the effects of geographic proximity on the distribution and intensity of social reactions was devised. Accordingly, a sampling frame was constructed to ensure that people at varying distances from the crime scene were interviewed.

Analysis of the interview data collected suggests that the intensity of the reaction to the crime was not necessarily a reflection of how close one lived to the crime scene. Some individuals living close to the park where the victim was shot were manifestly negatively impacted by the crime, but others were not. Intriguingly, for some respondents living quite a distance away, the crime had obviously influenced them significantly. In seeking to make sense of the patterns in the data it emerged that these variations could largely be explained by ethnicity. That is, people from the black community, especially those with children, were more likely to attribute the James killing salience, than were white interviewees. There were a couple of individuals who did not conform to this pattern, but it seems that in these cases the presence of a perceived 'social proximity' to the victim, in terms of his identity and lifestyle, accounted for why these individuals felt they were affected by the harm that had been done.

These differences are illustrated by comparing and contrasting the following extracts from interviews with two separate individuals. The first respondent lived quite close to the scene of the crime, whilst the second was geographically more removed, but expressed far greater concern:

I: Are there any particular incidents you recall?
R: What, you mean the one that happened in the park, with Jessie, what was he called?
I: Jessie James?
R: That was just at the park over here
I: What was the effect of that on you—anything?
R: No...if a lot of people are quite truthful it didn't have an effect. It's happened before, it'll happen again. It doesn't affect me at all. It doesn't worry me...
(Respondent 008)
Yes...he was from the same school as my children go. He used to go Moss Side, Manchester Academy—there my daughter and my son is going...and that was very, very stressful for us...because we have children, our children. We can feel the pain...
(Respondent 010)

The frequency of violent crime incidents in this area, many involving firearms, had meant that, for lots of people, such occurrences had ceased to have a significant impact and a degree of tolerance was building up. It was almost as if previous incidents had partially inoculated them to the harmful effects. But the community networks present within the local black community meant that other groups of people did feel they had been affected by this shooting.

The two cases utilized to illustrate the 'localized' and networked dimensions of parochial community impacts have highlighted the extent to which the capacity of an incident to impact negatively upon public confidence and reassurance does not just inhere in the criminal act itself, but also reflects aspects of the circumstances and settings in which it occurs. Through prior victimizations some communities appear to be effectively sensitized, or more unusually de-sensitized, to the occurrence of subsequent crime problems. Other communities display vulnerabilities to specific crime types associated with particular socio-economic and socio-demographic characteristics. Attending to the parochial impacts of major crimes helps us to understand how fear and other negative sentiments can contort and reconfigure collective perceptions of safety and security.

Public Impacts

As rehearsed in the opening sections of this essay, some crimes acquire the status of public problems (Chancer, 2005). In such cases, the incident becomes an almost iconic focus for widespread popular concern and anxiety that transcends any one community. In order to investigate how fear travels within and across communities following particular crimes, the case of Amanda Dowler can be examined. The interviews were conducted in North Walton, Surrey approximately 24 months after the young female victim was abducted and killed. At this time no suspect for her brutal murder had been identified.

This was a crime that for an extended period of time was the focus of intense national and international media reportage. Some sense of the initial reaction more locally is provided in the following quotation from a man living in the area:

> ...the whole town was talking about it, the whole area was talking about it, about this girl had gone missing and we all wanted to do something, we all wanted to try and help as a community. (Nwal064)

What was especially interesting about the interview data collected was the sense in which intense and persisting impacts of the crime could be detected in relation to the behaviour of parents with teenage daughters even two years after the crime:

> Oh yeah. I think the whole of...I don't know about the community but lots of people we know took extra precautions to take care of their children...We still won't let our daughter walk alone...My wife makes sure um...she make every effort to go and pick her up or send somebody that we know to pick her up. (Nwal063)

The routine utilization of these precautionary measures was confirmed in a second account from a parent:

> She was pretty good anyway but if she's going to be 10 minutes late, I know it didn't help Millie, but she'll phone me. If she stops late at 6th form she'll phone me. If she goes out at night I'll pick her up, you know. (Nwal064)

From the point of view of assessing widespread public impacts, it is clear here how particular crimes have the capacity to induce profound concerns and significant changes to patterns of behaviour over an extended period of time.

In the previous cases examined earlier, it has been shown how, whether people identify themselves with the victim or crime in some way, induces nuances in patterns of social reaction. This is also present in reactions to the *Dowler* case. A particularly intense impact was detected within those groups for whom there was a sense of 'social proximity' to the victim. In North Walton the murder of Amanda Dowler continued to shape the concerns and anxieties of parents in the area for well over two years after the crime occurred. The crime had a considerable legacy in terms of its community impact, but the effects of the signal crime were decaying at different rates for different groups. It is also clear how the legacy effects of this crime were not just emotional, but involved the introduction of longer-term behavioural modifications by some local residents who continued to perceive the presence of an ongoing vulnerability.

Public impact with a parochial counter-reaction

Crimes that induce fear that travels across geographic and social boundaries to impact upon large swathes of people elicit a social reaction that is both 'deep' and 'broad'. One of the cases studied though, suggests that for some crimes that elicit public outrage and concern, there is an important and intriguing variation possible. It seems that where the overall public visibility of the crime increases, more locally, at the parochial level, a counter-reaction to how the incident is being publicly portrayed and defined can emerge. Typically, this parochial counter-reaction focuses upon a belief that the local area and its residents are being unfairly stigmatized by an incident that is atypical and not normal.

The key facets of this process are illustrated by data from interviews conducted in Aston following the shootings of Charlene Ellis and Laetitia Shakespeare in Birmingham in 2003. This incident received significant levels of coverage in the national media, playing into a more widespread sense of moral panic about gun crime. The case and developments in the police investigation were reported in detail for several weeks and it acquired the attributes of a public signal crime, shaping public discourse in relation to how people thought, felt, and acted in relation to crime and safety issues.

Interviews were conducted in the ward where the shooting took place with a sample of local residents shortly after the crime occurred and then 12 months later. One respondent in the second wave of interviews traced the pattern of social reaction within the local communities particularly succinctly:

> Well it gave us all a nasty shock when those two girls were murdered up here that was a very bad moment, everyone congregated in the local church, huge number of people about 700 came, on that memorial service, and they came again to honour the first anniversary of it, very impressive. But it didn't heighten my awareness, I just thought, 'ooh, you had to pass by very close to

where it happened', but it didn't stop me from going up there, it didn't suddenly become a Mecca for people who are anti social. It perturbed us for months, but that's gone now, yes, that was a bad thing. (Ast224)

This woman's account reflects upon how people interpreted the crime as being something that was troubling and perturbing, but ultimately a risk that could be managed by explicitly avoiding key dangerous locations. In contrast to a number of descriptions in mass media accounts though, she refutes the idea that this incident represented a 'tipping point' for the local area. Indeed, she implicitly conveys a sense of the community mobilizing and coming together, through the church service and other acts, to ensure that the area did not 'tip'. In so doing, she recounts how, in effect, the communities in the area successfully managed the risks attendant in the wake of this crime in order that a sense of normality could be restored.

A second Aston resident talked in even more detail about how people in the local area provided mutual support to each other reacting to the crime in a markedly different way to how it was portrayed in the media:

R: Yeah obviously I discussed it with family and the next door neighbour and people and they reassured me it wasn't quite as bad as it seemed,

I: What did they have to say about it that reassured you?

R: Erm, just mainly it doesn't happen all the time and it's only usually within gangs and they don't usually bother with people outside the gangs usually. (Ast235)

For this person, consulting with their local social network reassured them and diffused some of their concerns. The salience of what is described is that it foregrounds how, although mass media reports of high profile violent crimes can act as incubators for public fears, encouraging such reactions to travel, media effects can be over-ridden by more protean inter-personal communications. Similar sentiments and recollections were present in the accounts of other respondents living in Aston who were interviewed as part of this case study. There was an initial sense of fear and worry elicited following the crime, but this was quickly diffused by a collective process of interpretation and sense-making.

The tenor of this reaction points to the importance of community resilience and the potential to withstand negative consequences. For whilst fear did travel across local social networks in this instance, the local communities effectively limited the impacts experienced. As such, this case clearly demonstrates how community impact (and recovery) needs to be conceived as a social process.

In an effort to better understand the processual dynamics of the community impacts of crimes a deliberate attempt was made by the researchers to track how particular social reactions travelled across the different local communities in Birmingham. Analysing these data it was found that, in the wake of the double shootings and attendant publicity, people living in Aston held rather different views of the area than did those in electoral wards surrounding it.

Those living outside the area tended to view it as a dangerous locality and cited the killings as evidence of this. Indeed, many were now actively avoiding using services and facilities in the area, although they had previously done so, often for many years. Although not investigated by this research this does imply the potential for real material harm alongside more perceptual ones in the aftermath of deadly violence. In deprived areas, crime can act to alter perceptions of the area as a risky locale thus suppressing general public use and potentially inducing other negative consequences. In contrast, after an initial phase of perturbation, those living in areas surrounding the crime scene in Aston were content that nothing much had really changed and so they continued with their routine activities.

In this case then, we see a different fear travel pattern to the local social reactions observed in the *Monckton* case. In the latter, there was an intense and geographically focused sense of anxiety following the crime, but little concern evident in the neighbouring poorer areas. In Birmingham, it was locally that the fear dissipated and the surrounding areas sustained a perception of a dangerous place. As such, this case evidences how in the midst of widespread public concern regarding a particular crime, the members of local communities can effectively 'fight back' to establish a more balanced definition of the situation.

Community Impact as a Process

Collective impacts evolve and adapt over time. Usually this involves a process of diffusion and decay as the intensity of the harm wanes. On occasions though, particularly where a suspect for a serious violent crime is not identified by police, then the sense of negative impact can be amplified and spread. To develop understanding of how impacts can unfold and adapt over time, one further instance of homicidal violence can be examined. This particular case is interesting because of how the early public reaction was markedly different in the initial phases of the police response from the shape it came to assume later on.

Butleigh is a small village in a rural part of the Avon and Somerset police force area. So when police started exhuming the bodies of several former elderly residents of a local care home, considerable consternation was evident locally. When the police arrested and charged the owner of the care home with multiple counts of criminal homicide, this generated extensive national and regional media interest. However, based upon a series of interviews conducted in the village and further afield, the research data would tend to confirm that the impact of the crime conformed to the parochial-localized pattern, centering upon Butleigh village. Interviews conducted in Glastonbury for example, only about 10 miles away, suggested that even though the suspect came from there, and that there was an awareness of the case, it had not really acted as a source of concern for people. Indeed, a fair proportion of the local public did not accept the police allegations. For many, there was a sense that the alleged perpetrator of the killings was 'one of us' and could not possibly have committed the heinous acts police were describing and journalists reporting.

The defendant in this case was not convicted of all the charges of which she was originally accused.[3] Nevertheless, the incident appears to have acquired the properties of a parochial-distributed impact, because of the risks it signalled for older people and those with elderly relatives living in institutional settings. In effect, it may have served to 'sensitize' the public to a new set of risks. Overall then, what it demonstrates is how social reactions can evolve and adapt. In this particular case there was an initial reaction of shock because of the dramatic nature of the police intervention. In some (but not all parts of the community) this moved on to resistance to the police and a denial of the narrative they were developing. Subsequently, upon conviction of the suspect, there was a greater sense of acceptance and recognition of a new species of harm that had to be attended to. But the critical point for this analysis is that the nature of the reaction itself can only be fully captured by attending to its processual form.

Harm Footprints

Behavioural, affective, and cognitive reactions to major crimes are, to a significant extent, structured by degrees of 'temporal', 'geographical', and 'social distance'. The preceding discussion has sought to trace key aspects of the reaction patterns that can be detected in the aftermath of major crimes, and in particular, how the impacts of such incidents travel across space and time. In so doing, the empirical data have demonstrated some communities are able to display considerable resilience to offset potential negative consequences for neighbourhood reputation and security. Equally though, the analysis has clearly articulated how the occurrence of such incidents can have a long-term negative impact upon an area, contorting the reputations of places and communities, and also inducing fear amongst people not directly connected to the crime in any way. It is clear then that such events can cause real harm to both individual and collective security.

Harm is an idea that has, over recent years, acquired increasing prominence and traction. There are several competing formulations of harm within the academic literature, but what they have in common is an accent upon the importance of gauging negative effects and impacts. Scanning across the literature on harm deriving from a number of disciplines, two principal perspectives can be determined: 'the jurisprudential'; and 'the social'.

Jurisprudential philosophy maintains a clear demarcation between those infractions of the criminal law that induce harm and those causing offence. It is

---

[3] She was originally charged with two murders and was convicted of the manslaughter of one woman. In addition, during the trial the accused admitted 10 counts of possessing Class A and C drugs and perverting the course of justice.

a distinction traceable back to J.S. Mill's construction of liberal democratic state-craft and his assertion that the only justification for a state intervening in the lives of citizens and thereby curtailing liberty, is to prevent or ameliorate the effects of acts causing harm. Consistent with such tenets, Feinberg (1987) defines harm as a setback to one's own or others' interests that is also normatively defined as wrong. He stresses that this reaches beyond the purely physical and material to include emotional and subjective states. Excluded from this classification of harms are unpleasant momentary reactions and temporary states of unease that possess neither a profound or long-lasting impact.[4] Of course, the problem for empirical research is that the issue of when a nuisance or offensive act shifts register to become a harm is not clarified. A second issue is that it tends towards the individual as the key unit of analysis, thereby rather overlooking the potential for collective harms.

The tacit individualism underpinning jurisprudential renderings of harm is countered by a second perspective. Sutherland (1949) identified the quality of being 'socially harmful' as one of two necessary conditions for an act to be defined as a crime (the other being that it should be formally punishable in law). In so doing, the crucial distinction introduced when compared to more orthodox legal constructions of harm was his accent upon the 'social' component.

Sutherland's (1949) notion of social harm has been a formative influence upon the work of a group of critical criminological scholars who have deployed the notion of 'social harm' to outline an 'anti-criminology', critiquing both the conduct of criminal justice and of criminology as a discipline (Hillyard et al., 2004; Pemberton, 2007; Cain and Howe, 2008). Resonating with the arguments of an earlier generation of sociologists of deviance, the proponents of this position have declared that criminology has become infused with definitions of problematic and troublesome behaviour that simply reflect state power to authoritatively label some acts as 'criminal' and as such has lost its analytic purchase. They seek a focus instead upon the negative consequences of socio-structural forces upon less powerful communities.

Between these two poles are a number of avowedly more applied positions on harm. The most prominent being 'harm reduction' frameworks in relation to illegal drugs. These are the counter-point to more orthodox prohibitionist policies that seek to manage societal drug problems through criminalization (Inciardi and Harrison, 2000). However, in an incisive contribution based upon ethnographic research in Australia, Maher and Dixon (1999) suggest that the practical outcomes of harm minimization frameworks are frequently limited by the street-level enforcement practices of police, who typically tend to orient towards less long-term and abstract goals.

A further policy perspective on harm is provided by the UK's now defunct Serious Organised Crime Agency (SOCA). Rather than adopting the traditional law

---

[4] In legal scholarship, these tend to be categorized as 'offences' rather than harms (Harcourt, 1999).

enforcement paradigm associated with policing agencies, SOCA sought to define its mission as being concerned principally with reducing the harm caused by serious and organized crime groups (Harfield, 2006). It is a perspective rooted in several academic contributions setting out some of the problems associated with trying to measure the societal impacts of organized crime groups (Finckenaur, 1990). Several such accounts distinguish between 'economic', 'political', 'environmental', 'psychological', and 'social' forms of harm (see for example United Kingdom Drug Policy Commission, 2009). However, the problem with such framings concerns the boundaries between these categories when exposed to the empirical complexity of real life (for example, when does psychological harm, become social harm, or when does social harm become political?).[5] In sum, whilst variants of such frameworks have been employed and promoted enthusiastically by particular communities of practice, they tend to lack conceptual rigour and robustness.

A fourth influential contemporary definition of harm is a derivative of the literature on risk perception and management. Epitomizing this position, Sparrow (2009: 14) defines harm in a way that, 'covers the broadest set of bad things...it can be understood to include "potential harms" and "patterns of harm", as well as specific harms already done.' It is an approach founded upon a belief that the main purpose of governmental interventions should be preventing and minimizing the impacts of harmful events, rather than attempting to socially engineer perceived 'social goods'. Sparrow stresses that some harms are multi-dimensional, some are 'high level', whilst others are invisible or slow-acting. Across these various categories of harm, his interest is in encouraging policing and regulatory agencies to think in creative ways about how they intervene and define the aims of their interventions. A problem with Sparrow's (2009) approach though is that he tends to see harms and risks as more or less interchangeable.

Whilst recognizing that there are these inflections to how harm is understood and used, it does seem that much of what has been discussed in the preceding sections has concerned the perceptual harms of homicide. Rather than using fear of crime as a catch all label, it might be more appropriate to cast fear and some of the other negative emotions and perceptions that have been documented, as particular manifestations of harm. In this vein, it can be argued that what has been revealed through the analysis of the community impacts are five 'harm footprints' in terms of how collective reactions travel following both high profile and less publicly visible homicides:

- Private harm footprint—where the emotional, behavioural, and cognitive consequences are focused upon those individuals known to the victim and/or offender in some way, and do not spread beyond these persons.

---

[5] It is also worth noting a crucial difference here when compared to the previous position described. For whereas the anti-criminologists privilege the concept of 'social harm' as a master concept that is fed by forms of economic, psychological, and environmental harm, the practitioner perspectives tend to see them as separate but equivalent forms.

- Parochial-localized harm footprint—are cases where the occurrence of an incident has perceptual impacts upon a geographic community, but does not really travel beyond the members of this group.
- Parochial-distributed harm footptint—captures the ways that sometimes fear travels across social networks that are based upon non-geographic affiliations.
- Public harm footprint—occurs where a crime impacts upon the public at large, with fear travelling across community boundaries transcending any primary group affiliations.
- Public with a parochial counter-reaction harm footprint—involves a local group 'pushing back' in a situation where they or their neighbourhood are being stigmatized in the aftermath of a crime. They mobilize a resilient counter-narrative that seeks to define a more proportionate appraisal of the risks involved.

Conceived of in this way, the introduction of these five harm footprints can be seen to provide a significant extension and elaboration of the base components of the signal crimes perspective (SCP). The SCP maintains that certain criminal or disorderly events alter how people think, feel, or act in relation to their security. Empirical studies harnessing this approach have suggested it affords new insights into the role that anti-social behaviour and 'low-level' crime has upon levels of neighbourhood security (Bottoms, 2012). The empirical data reported herein start to demonstrate the SCP's potential for understanding how and why other types of crime impact upon communities, and importantly, that these forms of harm might be patterned and measurable. This development hints at the possibility of being able to identify a generic social and social-psychological process in terms of how individuals and groups interpret and make sense of crime and disorder, and the ways that these are imbricated in peoples' symbolic constructions of space.

Conclusion

Criminal homicides and their investigation are primary figurative tropes in how our culture seeks to impose moral order on the world. We are replete with analyses that deconstruct the rituals and frames employed by journalistic and more fictionalized representations of such crimes, and of the meanings encoded and social functions embedded within these narratives. In addition to this, there has been a growth in more structured research into the distribution and prevalence of such crimes, the impacts upon those directly connected to them, and the nature of police and criminal justice responses. But what has been lacking is a grounded understanding of the consequences of such events for the social situations and settings in which they occur.

Criminal homicides are, in many ways, the prototypical signal crime—displaying a manifest capacity to influence behaviour, and the ways people think and feel about their safety. Through a series of case studies this essay has sought to trace how such reactions 'travel' across space and time following fatal violence. In so doing, it has been shown that local reactions are frequently complex, shaped by social context, and intriguing in terms of what they suggest about how publics collectively make sense of crime. In many regards, the tenor and tone of local reactions was much more refined and nuanced than that provided in mass media coverage of the cases. There are though, distinct reaction patterns or 'harm footprints' that have been detected and described.

Taken together these findings have traced the outline for an alternative conceptualization of social reactions to major crimes. Work in this area has come to be dominated by the concept of fear of crime, which has struggled to accommodate and explain why it should be that a relatively small number of crimes have a marked influence upon public conceptions and perceptions of security. Instead, this essay has sought to delineate the presence of a number of distinctive 'harm footprints' that possess particular 'shapes' and dynamics.

The shift from focusing upon fear of crime, to understanding fear as a particular species of the harm associated with the occurrence of major crimes is important in terms of being able to manufacture a comprehensive account of the social impacts of these types of crimes. Absent of such a holistic approach, the kinds of wider collective reactions and sense-making processes that have been the focus of this discussion, will continue to be seen as entirely separate from the primary harms caused to those more directly connected to the homicidal event. In contrast to this, what has been distilled herein is how harm radiates out from the incident to impact upon victims, their families, friends and neighbours, communities, and the wider public. In so doing the analysis has picked out some important differences between initial 'shock' following a murder, and the subsequent 'aftershocks' that can arise as previously hidden issues and problems are rendered more visible.

In the age of information, with the rapid spread and development of social media and Web 2.0 and 3.0 technologies, and the informatics capabilities to process and analyse these 'big data' sources, social researchers are on the verge of being able to study social processes and structures in profoundly new and different ways than has hitherto been possible. The ability to 'scrape' and 'mine' social media sources affords new possibilities and opportunities to gauge and track public opinions and attitudes.

If we take the example of major homicides, police and other agencies are on the verge of being able to track, in fine-grained detail, public opinions and sentiments as expressed on social media in the wake of an incident, to see how public concern and anxiety is or is not 'travelling' and also how local communities are responding to the interventions made. The significance of this shift is that, in so doing, they will not be reliant upon opinion survey data, but can connect particular reactions to specific occurrences. So where currently survey methods resort to analysing fear of crime as an aggregate state or trait, sentiment-mining technologies applied to social media data make it feasible to dynamically track particular reactions to specific events. However, in order to engage in this type of work we need new conceptual framings that allow us to interpret and make sense of any patterns that are present in the available data.

Extending this line of thought, we might predict that 'reacting' in the kinds of ways that have been the focus of this essay, is only one way in which people might use social media in the aftermath of a major crime event. They might also use it to: report—adding new factual details to the public knowledge about what has happened (for example from witnesses); relay—passing on news to others they think might be interested, without adding to the content; and, rumour—improvising news, without necessarily being sure of its accuracy. Given the limitations associated with the data needed to pursue and develop this agenda, and the practical methodological difficulties involved in securing them, the insights reported herein are necessarily tentative and will require further studies to develop and test them more robustly. Nevertheless, they do suggest the possibility for developing an innovative and new way of researching and thinking about collective reactions to major crime events.

The notion of how fear travels captures the variety of influences that alter how negative social reactions are disseminated and dispersed, and the ways these social reactions can be amplified or mitigated. But to engage with such matters requires a second more subtle, but fundamental, conceptual reframing. This involves moving from population-based measures of fear to 'event-based' ones. It is predicted that in an age of 'big data' this will be 'where the intellectual action is'.

The Crimes That Were Not There

'Soft facts' and the Causes and Consequences of Crime Rumours

Sometimes people do not believe what they see. Belying the popular adage 'I'll believe it when I see it' that is often used to voice an intermingling of doubt and incredulity, it seems that the obverse is actually true and people will only 'see it when they believe it.' This is because in order to apprehend some phenomenon in the world around them, people require a classificatory framework enabling them to assign an object, actor, or occurrence, to a particular category and thus render it 'sense-able'.[1] In the absence of such a frame and the definitional and sense-making resources it affords, the capacity to recognize what something is and to explain its causes and consequences is manifestly limited. That this occurs reflects some basic operating requirements of human perceptual equipment. But, in addition to the neurological mechanics of perception, such matters also involve distinctly social processes. Namely, does the situation encountered cohere with our conventions and socialized expectations for this type of circumstance? And, how much trust can be imputed to the source of information that is being attended to? Such matters are of particular consequence given our contemporary modes of social organization where people are acquiring information 'polyphonically', on an ongoing basis from multiple channels of mass and inter-personal communication. The information relayed via these channels is sometimes coherent, but at other times conflicts with each other.

This essay focuses upon how people react to and negotiate conditions of imperfect information, where the validity and reliability of their 'knowledge' is

---

[1] That is, something that is able to be sensed, in terms of being perceived via human sensory capacities.

uncertain. That is, how do people orient themselves towards and conduct themselves in ambiguous situations? In particular, I am interested in a particular type of social situation where uncertainty and ambiguity abound—the aftermath of major and serious crimes. For in the wake of such events rumours tend to be profligate, impacting upon the organization of the social reactions of individuals, communities, and social control agents. Under the right conditions and in particular settings rumours can exert a profound and long-lasting influence upon peoples' beliefs, perceptions, and attitudes, and consequently behaviours. Thus they are imbricated in how people, both institutionally and interactionally, produce and reproduce orders of reality.

That crime rumours perform this role as shapers of perceived realities is a function of how they are frequently attributed the status of 'soft facts'. In negotiating many social situations, a premium is placed upon 'hard facts' and having valid and reliable knowledge. In contrast to which, soft facts are the forms of information and knowledge that are used to 'fill the gaps' when anything 'harder' is not available. Soft facts possess only contingent authority. Their 'softness' reflects the recognition by users that they are malleable, and liable to be revised and updated when more valid and reliable information becomes available. But in the meantime, they will do, even if they are improvised and of doubtful provenance, on the grounds that they provide a plausible explanation of what has happened. As will be detailed in what follows, these are precisely the qualities that account for how, when, and why crime rumours come to influence the establishment of definitions of the situation in the aftermath of major incidents.

Exploring such matters necessitates considering under what conditions crime rumours arise and acquire the sorts of tractability that exerts influence over peoples' perceptions and conceptions of security. Then relatedly, what consequences flow from such occurrences? The essence of the argument to be developed is that whether or not a crime really occurred is largely irrelevant in terms of a story's capacity to generate a profound social reaction. To mount this claim, several instances where crimes were not 'there', but rumours nevertheless channelled public attention and concern are examined. That this process can be observed reflects how patterns of social organization and social ordering pertaining to contemporary society, moulded as they are by a pervasive concern about crime, mean that it is frequently sufficient for people to believe that a troublesome event transpired, for it to act as a signal of risk and threat to them. In order to start to map out the conceptual terrain for such a claim, it is perhaps best to start with a story.

Crime Rumours as a Cause of Public Problems

On the evening of 22 October 2005 a small riot involving groups of Asian and Afro-Caribbean youths erupted in the Lozells and East Handsworth area of the city of Birmingham. During the violence: a 23-year-old Afro-Caribbean man was stabbed to death in Carlyle Road; three other people received stabbing injuries; a policeman was shot in the leg with a ball-bearing gun; and a further 31 people were treated in hospital. Cars were set alight and shops attacked (Muir and Butt, 2005). The violence itself erupted at 5.45 on the Saturday evening outside the New Testament church where a community meeting was being held to deal with concerns in the Afro-Caribbean community about emergent tensions with the Asian community in the area. At that meeting, attended by local political representatives including Khalid Mahmood MP, a Superintendent from West Midlands police announced that five men had been arrested in relation to an allegation that a black girl had been gang raped in an Asian-owned hair and beauty salon called 'Beauty Queen'. Whatever the police intention, the announcement of the arrests was interpreted as giving substance to a rumour about the rape that had been circulating within the local community for some time.

According to some reports (see Vulliamy, 2005) the rumour of a black woman being sexually assaulted by Asian men in a hair and beauty salon was being discussed in the local area since the summer. The rumour fizzled out only to resurface in early October and in so doing, the age of the victim decreased and the number of alleged assailants increased. But the rumour really took off when on the Tuesday before the violence flared, a DJ on a local pirate radio station started talking about the incident and calling on people to attend a community protest at the alleged scene. When later interviewed by *Guardian* reporters the DJ, Warren G, stated:

> I demonstrated because I believe that something happened... I have no proof and no facts, but I believe there are witnesses out there. (Muir and Butt, 2005)

The lack of facts did not, though, inhibit the spread of this unwarranted claim. The rumour was quickly picked up and further disseminated by other communication networks including several local radio stations and websites, as well as other informal community-based channels. This was crucial in sustaining the rumour and amplifying its intensity as people in the area were encountering similar information through multiple channels of communication—something that suggests there is a degree of validity and reliability to information that cannot be personally substantiated. In the aftermath of the riot, the police announced that their investigations had not established any forensic evidence or witnesses who could substantiate the allegation that was the subject of the rumour.

The incident outlined in the preceding paragraphs can be read as a particularly extreme illustration of W.I. Thomas' (1928: 571–72) famous sociological dictum that 'If men define situations as real, they are real in their consequences.' In Birmingham, serious and real material consequences flowed from the ways in which people acted on the basis of the definition of a situation that itself was founded upon unwarranted claims. Moreover, this particular case illuminates a number of the dimensions, both in terms of informational content and the conditions into which it is introduced, that are required for a rumour to be propagated and gain traction.

It is notable that there was a history of tension between the two communities that formed a backdrop for the rumour. These were infused by perceptions amongst some members of the black community that they were losing ground both physically and metaphorically to the Asian communities in the area. Concerns had been vocally expressed prior to the incident that Asian owned businesses were taking over in the area, and whilst the socio-economic position of the Afro-Caribbean community appeared to be stagnating, contrastingly the Asians were prospering. The incident of gang rape was also simply the latest in a series of allegations and counter-allegations about the criminal activities of groups of young people victimizing individuals from the other ethnic group. As such, the specific claims about the gang rape refracted a set of established concerns and collective memories already circulating in the area, collapsing them into a compact form of harm.

The way in which the public disorder unfolded is also suggestive of some of the unintended consequences that can flow from interventions by the authorities. In publicly announcing the instigation of an investigation into the rape allegation, the police Superintendent unintentionally gave a form of official imprimatur to the version of reality being sustained in the black community. The police initiative was no doubt intended to diffuse mounting tension and pressure arising from within the black community for something to be done about the 'heinous crime' that had been committed. Unwittingly though, the police intervention substantiated the community's belief in the validity of the allegation. For if the police were investigating, then surely there must be some substance to it? What the police had failed to appreciate here was that theirs was only one voice amongst many, and from the point of view of the community, there was a polyphony of information channels (mass-mediated and inter-personal) all repeating the rumour's content. This polyphonic effect was of vital significance in establishing a form of cross-validation, because although one source may be doubted, multiple sources all repeating the same information are harder to ignore.

In many ways the police were placed in an impossible situation. To not have investigated an allegation of a very serious crime and to attempt to resist the increasing political pressure for some form of enquiry into it, would probably have resulted in public violence anyway. But this is not the point. Rather the issue is about the tendency of authorities to rely upon 'facts' to disprove what, from a community's perspective, is believed to be a credible report of victimization. In this part of Birmingham, along with most parts of the UK, trust and confidence in the police on the part of young people from minority ethnic communities is markedly lower than for other groups in the population. Consequently, the willingness of minority ethnic youngsters to believe any 'facts' that are presented to them by the police is significantly constrained and thus the capacity of police 'facts' to offset and undermine rumours is limited. What we are moving towards, therefore, is an understanding that although rumours contain information lacking in warrants for their validity and reliability, they are persuasive and influential forms of communication.

To suggest that rumours are marked by information lacking in warrants for the claim that is being made, is not to say that they inevitably contain false information. As Shibutani (1966) correctly identified, the defining quality of rumours is not the 'rightness' or 'wrongness' of their content, but rather how they arise in ambiguous situations and under conditions of uncertainty, where knowledge is demanded but not forthcoming from authoritative sources. Just as 'nature abhors a vacuum', in uncertain and potentially troubling settings 'an information vacuum' will tend to be 'filled' as people in the vicinity of the gap strain for explanations and justifications for what has actually happened. Effectively, rumours involve information whose provenance is provisional and unsettled, in terms of whether it should be treated as 'truth' or 'untruth'. Rumours are claims where the empirical warrants for that which is being claimed cannot be assessed. In this sense they occupy a similar conceptual space in the processes of social life to other related phenomenon such as gossip, conspiracy theories, and urban myths, all of which exhibit a profound influence in terms of their capacity to shape social order (Dunbar, 1996; Best and Honuichi, 1985; Aaronovitch, 2010). For each of these modes of communication is predicated upon the transmission of information rather than knowledge, albeit some recipients may mistakenly treat the content as the latter.

Contrasted with conspiracy theories and urban myths, which tend to be 'macro-level' forms of communication, the status of rumours is more provisional and uncertain. It is in this sense that rumours work as 'soft facts', as opposed to 'hard' ones. They are temporary and unstable forms of 'knowledge' where issues of validity and reliability are pending, or suspended. They are used to infill the gap between a demand for knowledge and the ability to supply it. In conspiracy theories and urban myths there is a more established division of belief between a majority consensus that dismisses the veracity of the claims, and a minority group who hold that they represent a 'subterranean truth' that is frequently being actively suppressed by 'shadowy' powerful actors.[2]

If urban myths and conspiracy theories constitute 'macro' forms of unsecured information, then gossip can be said to assume the 'micro' version of this pattern, anchored in the routines of co-present social interaction (Elias and Scotson, 1994). Moreover, although gossip can be founded upon rumours, it is more routinely involved in relaying accurate information that is otherwise not widely known. So although gossip, myths, and conspiracies are frequently associated with rumours and act as a fecund source of them, rumours are in fact conceptually distinct and need to be treated as such. That conspiracies, myths, and gossip frequently function as generators of rumour is partly a result of the presence of what Damian Thompson (2008) has dubbed a powerful 'counter-knowledge

---

[2] There are, for instance, a number of variants circulating on the internet of the narrative that the United States government was aware of the 9/11 plot to attack the World Trade Centre and either elected to allow it to take place, or, in the even more stronger versions, actively collaborated in the destruction of the twin towers (Thompson, 2008).

industry.' According to this analysis there are now a plethora of entrepreneurial actors and organizations who deliberately seek to circulate theories and arguments in the public sphere that run counter to empirical evidence. Ideologically driven, often mimicking the established social conventions for claiming validity and reliability, they are able to present their alternative case in ways that are persuasive leading some people to form the opinion that it is at least plausible. To clarify, rumours, although related to these other forms, are more 'open' in that people have not concluded about their veracity or otherwise, and they tend to contain 'newer' information than either urban myths or conspiracy theories. Indeed, this temporal dimension is critical in clearly defining the conceptual boundaries between rumours, and conspiracy theories and urban myths. Rumours are enmeshed in more immediate processes of social reaction to troubling or difficult eventualities, although over time if they are sustained and gain traction, then they may sediment down to become part of a coherent mythology. Shibutani's emphasis on the role of ambiguous situations in the gestation of rumour clarifies the extent to which social groups will, when under stress, produce rumours as mechanisms that can inform how to act.

Rumour as a Consequence of Public Problems

One of the core ingredients required for a rumour to take hold and to be shared is a semblance of plausibility. A 'successful' rumour is likely to be one that coheres with established understandings of the characteristics of that which the rumour is attached to. It is, for instance, easier to generate rumours about the criminal and deviant conduct of individuals and groups if they are already assigned the status of 'outsiders' in some sense, rather than if the popular conception is of 'pillars of the community.' Likewise, locales that are renowned as trouble spots are superior candidates for rumours about other problems. The cognitive maps we collectively have of our social environments help to pre-figure our receptiveness to information about ambiguous situations and our attentiveness to this. Of course, this does not mean that rumours of other kinds do not occur, but rather that there is a general pattern.

Conditions of panic and high anxiety are especially vulnerable to being influenced by rumours that frequently serve to reproduce and sustain sensations of ongoing risk and threat. In August 2007 in the Croxteth area of Liverpool, a young boy aged 11 was on his way home from football practice when he was shot and killed in the car park of a local pub.[3] The death of Rhys Jones elicited shock and outrage across the national mass media, acting as a signal crime feeding established public concerns about young people and gun violence in the UK. The

---

[3] Carter, H. (2008) 'Teenager shot Rhys Jones while aiming at gang members court hears', *The Guardian* (9 October 2008).

media reportage quickly picked up on rumours circulating within the local community that this shocking incident must be tied to the activities of local youth gangs in the area. Initially, the police tried to reassure the public by refuting any such claims, but their counter-claims were confounded when journalists for several national outlets found and published extracts of videos posted on the internet by members of the 'Croxteth Crew' and the 'Nogga Dogz'.

The massive amount of media attention in respect of this case placed the police under enormous pressure to progress their investigation. Over the course of the next several months there were a series of appeals by police for members of the public to come forward with information to assist them with their enquiries, but seemingly these met with little success. There were a series of arrests (20 plus) but all of those involved were released or bailed. Eventually, the police did secure several suspects who were prosecuted, but this took a number of months.

In the intervening period though, they were confronted with a situation where rumours were circulating within certain sections of the local community about who was responsible for the shooting. These claims were not being made directly to the police, allegedly because people were too scared of the retribution that might be exacted by the local gangs. It is claimed that at one point the name of one individual was daubed in graffiti in the area. More definitely, in October 2007 an alleged member of the Strand Gang named a member of the Croxteth Crew on YouTube as being responsible. This represented both a peculiar and intriguing situation. Information was publicly available and widely known locally, but it was not sufficient for police to enact their formal social control functions against individuals suspected of involvement in a heinous crime. Perhaps even more significantly though, it points to the growing interconnections between the 'real' and 'online' worlds in shaping the causes and consequences of rumours.

It is well documented that the massive free-flows of peer-to-peer communication facilitated by the internet, in tandem with the diffusion of social media platforms and technologies, have made it particularly conducive to spreading rumours. It is a social environment that is especially suited to disseminating soft facts with limited provenances. But in the aftermath of the killing of Rhys Jones we can detect how rumours propagated in a virtual environment shape the 'offline' reactions of communities to real events. A second feature of the rumours in the Jones murder worthy of comment concerns how they were deliberate. In several of the cases outlined so far in this essay, there has been a certain sense in which the influence attained by specific rumours was an unintended consequence. But this is a situation where the rumour was purposive and intended. In this case the spreading of the rumour was undertaken to direct the attention of the police towards the opposing gang. In effect then, rumour was used to try to effect social control.

Deliberately starting rumours as a way of exploiting and manipulating uncertain circumstances occurs across a range of social settings. For instance, in the Spring of 2008 following the near collapse of the Northern Rock bank as part of a rapid contraction of the global financial markets, rumours abounded about the liquidity of a number of institutions. Most notably, in the UK, rumours were rife about the health of the very large HBOS banking and financial services group. These rumours provoked a significant downturn in the company's share price. The Financial Services Authority urgently launched an investigation into the incident, suspecting a 'trash and cash' operation, wherein persons unknown were maliciously spreading rumours to enhance their position in a practice known as 'short-selling'. 'Shorting' usually occurs when an investor borrows shares anticipating that they will fall in value. A profit can be realized in such a situation by selling the shares and then buying them back more cheaply. Rumours are also an engine for the related but inverse practice of 'pump and dump' in the financial markets. In this case, rather than deflating the worth of the shares, the aim of those spreading the rumours is to increase the perceived value of the shares above their 'real' worth in order to realize a significant gain. It would not be an over-statement to say that rumour making is endemic to the operations of financial markets and that effective operators are those who can access market intelligence in a way that enables them to puncture the rumours that are circulating and shaping the assignment of monetary value. Spreading rumours, particularly under prevalent conditions of uncertainty, is an effective way of attacking the value of a company, increasing the likelihood that a profit can be made. But identifying why individuals located in certain situations might want to deliberately start a rumour, does not answer the related question of why people attend to and believe them.

To understand why people may find rumoured information believable, even where there are insubstantial warrants for the claims being made, necessitates us turning to the ways in which the dynamics of inter-personal interaction, whether this be co-present or mediated, profit from the communication of rumours and other similar forms of information. This is a dimension insightfully articulated in Elias and Scotson's (1994) observations on the social functions of gossip. Set against a backdrop of ongoing community tensions between an established network of closely integrated residents and a more recent group of 'outsiders', the relaying of gossip produced and reproduced sensations of collective identity and belonging by demarcating differences between 'us' and 'them'. According to their analysis, the communication of gossip and rumours across each of the two groups, reflected their structures. The content of what was conveyed tended to conform to fairly well defined sensibilities of what the principal faults and failings of the other group were, and by extension, the contrasting valued attributes of the members' in-group.

Although they do not develop these implications, what Elias and Scotson's analysis recognizes is that there is an allure to being party to a rumour that is partly subterranean and not something that everyone knows. Moreover, there is 'soft power' to be realized by an actor positioned as a transmitter or conduit of a rumour, inasmuch as it displays a capacity to access information that is unknown to others. But in order to profit in terms of accruing any such soft power and taking it forward into the future, the source of the rumour has to possess a degree of credibility.

If plausibility is a quality of the content of the rumour, credibility is an attribute of its source (Fine and Ellis, 2010). One way people informally and tacitly assess the potential 'truthfulness' of a rumour in the flows and eddies of social life is through an assessment of the source and whether they occupy a position that makes it likely that they could come to know this information, as well as whether they have been a reliable source of accurate material in the past. As signalled in the preceding discussion, if the same rumour reaches someone through multiple channels and platforms then they are more likely to assign it credence.

In many ways then the tacit cognitive apparatus that people use to establish whether they should buy in to a rumour, gravitating as it does around evaluations of the interlinked notions of credibility and plausibility, is manifestly similar to the more formal apparatus employed by intelligence professionals. A central preoccupation for spies and others whose work involves secret intelligence is how to determine the truthfulness or otherwise of much of the material they come into contact with. To cope with such uncertainties intelligence assessments are fundamentally based upon evaluating whether the substantive content of the new intelligence is coherent with other things that are already known, and the extent to which the source has proven to be reliable in the past. One of the obvious and well appreciated problems with such a framework in the intelligence community is that it mitigates against information from a new source that is passing genuinely new information being accorded appropriate salience (Innes, Fielding and Cope, 2005).

Similar biases are evident in how people treat rumours in everyday life. If it is a rumour about people, places, or events that is in keeping with extant conceptions of these, it is more probable that it will believed and treated as a soft fact. It is also why, possibly despite expectations to the contrary, social institutions such as the mass media and the police function as key sources for rumours.

To identify the police as an important source of crime rumours in contemporary society is not to suggest that this is the principal focus of what they do, nor does it constitute the bulk of their increasingly sophisticated public relations strategies. Nevertheless, in the course of communicating information about their work through the mass media, they do with some regularity, engage in spreading information that amounts to little more than rumour and speculation. What is particularly intriguing is the way in which the symbolic authority of the police as an institution imbues their communications a credibility that leads any information they impart becoming suffused with an official imprimatur of reality. This extends to those occasions when they have deliberately sought to exploit this to expound some fairly speculative claims.

Reaction Patterns and 'Disinformation' and 'Misinformation' Rumours

The deliberate manufacture of rumours by police can be repeatedly observed as part of a wider 'reaction pattern' that arises as part of attempts to deny wrongdoing or mistakes following high profile institutional failures. A reaction pattern is a sequenced, ordered, and thus organized way that individuals, organizations, or institutions respond to a significant event. The elements of the police reaction pattern when confronted by institutional failure were most egregiously displayed by the revelations set out in the report of the Hillsborough Independent Panel in 2012. The panel presented compelling evidence that, in an effort to deflect and undermine public criticism of police failures, a 'Black Ops' campaign was mounted that deliberately sought to disseminate rumours about the behaviours of fans in contributing to the multiple deaths that occurred at the football match. These included rumours that the fans were drunk, and that they had assaulted police and medical staff who were trying to administer first aid to the dying. A similar pattern of behaviour was also evident in respect of a number of other cases involving police and/or corruption, including: the Stephen Lawrence murder; the shooting of Jean Charles de Menezes; the fatal assault on Ian Tomlinson; the notorious miscarriages of justice from the 1980s and 1990s, as well as Hillsborough.

The pattern unfolds like this. First, there is the moment where things go wrong. The initial emergency situation is misinterpreted, causing police intervention to amplify the harm. There follows the imposition of an official definition of reality seeking to submerge and suppress acknowledgement of any problems or failings. When this is challenged by a subaltern narrative 'from below', police and their allies engage in a collective denial of the credibility and plausibility of this account and its proponents, often labeling them as conspiracy theorists. A long period of campaigning ensues featuring repeated attempts to overturn the official account. At some point, political will cedes ground and a public inquiry is established, affording the power to retroactively revise the official history and rewrite the past. The process concludes with contrition and the promise that lessons have been or will be learned.

The *Hillsborough* case illustrates a further dimension of the ways in which rumour intersects with the construction of orders of reality in contemporary society. This is the contest between rumour and counter-rumour as different groups seek to assert and project their definition of the situation. Rumours of police manipulation of official reports and documents had long been circulating amongst the families of the victims and their supporters. These rumours were repeatedly and consistently denied by police, until the panel's enquiries demonstrated that collective and collusive manipulations had taken place. This returns us to Shibutani's (1966) prescient recognition that rumours are not inherently false, but merely lacking empirical warrants.

Compared with 1989 when the deaths at Hillsborough occurred, we are simultaneously both more and less at risk of similar problems recurring. In an information saturated landscape, permeated by social media and 24/7 broadcasting, the ability of police to suppress and deny stories of incompetence and to unjustly accuse others of wrongdoing is reduced—at least in terms of sustaining such allegations over an extended period. But these same communication channels and the speed they operate at mean that, when disasters do occur, rumours and conspiracies frequently start to circulate before the authorities have a chance to clarify and make sense of what actually has transpired.

The reaction pattern following the Hillsborough disaster provides a rather different account of the connections between 'crimes that were not there' and the proliferation of rumours, than the preceding cases. This difference pivots around questions of intentionality. The earlier cases discussed involved rumours as sense-making devices located in situations of doubt and uncertainty. Contrastingly, Hillsborough and the cases that conform to the identified reaction pattern involve the deliberate propagation of rumours to facilitate what Cohen (2005) holds to be 'literal denial'.

A distinction might therefore be drawn between 'disinformation rumours' and 'misinformation rumours'. The former are deliberate and malignant. The latter are more benign, occurring under conditions of uncertainty as people struggle for comprehension faced with incomplete information. Both can challenge and undermine institutional reputations. But the key learning point for institutions is that, in the contemporary information environment, they absolutely must resist the temptation to hide discreditable facts and spread disinformation rumours to deflect attention from their own problems. In the chaos and panic of an emergency, misinformation rumours are regrettable but understandable. Disinformation rumours possess an almost unquenchable corrosive legacy.

Rumour and the Symbolic Construction of Place

Rumours of involvement in crime, whether deliberately or unintentionally propagated, can lead to someone acquiring a disreputable social identity and reputation that attaches itself to the individuals concerned, and is incredibly difficult to shake off (Fine, 2001). But rumours can also play a role in tainting how people think about particular places (Fine and Ellis, 2010). Crime rumours are frequently influential in the symbolic construction of social spaces contributing to how some locales become labelled as troublesome places.

In the process of conducting fieldwork in a town in Surrey, the ways in which rumour plays into how people symbolically construct public spaces was illuminated. During interviews with local residents about their quality of life and local security concerns, a number of people mentioned a rape that was purported to have happened some time previously. Few of those spoken to in the local area seemed to be in a position to provide precise details about what had actually occurred, but a large number of them traced aspects of their concern back to 'the rape' on the canal towpath. For example, not untypically, one of those interviewed told how she:

> ...would never consider running along the towpath of the canal cause of rape or sexual assault. (Ash213)

The area around the canal was repeatedly identified as a location that local residents actively avoided. Some individuals were able to articulate a reason for this avoidance behaviour, but for others their concerns about this place remained less well defined. These effects persisted despite the fact that the allegation was now known to be false:

> There was supposed to have been somebody attacked on the canal about a year or eighteen months ago. Then that turned out that it didn't actually happen, but it caused fear in the village for a little while. (Ash212)

The fact that the allegation of rape was false was confirmed by a second local interviewee:

> This lady said she was assaulted, or raped actually, along the towpath. It was in all the media, papers and that but transpires she wasn't... But yeah it transpires she 'cried wolf' so, but you don't know that at the time. (Ash214)

As outlined in the first of these two accounts, when it became local knowledge that a violent sexual attack may have occurred in the vicinity it triggered marked concern. But as hinted at in the last sentence of the second extract, the fact that it was a false allegation was not initially known, and the alleged crime became a focal point for a flurry of rumours and suppositions about the possible victim and suspects, as elaborated in the following:

> First of all we heard about it word of mouth because one of the canals was blocked off and of course why is there police tape up? Why is there so much police? What is going on? And we got to hear about it. Also because initially the rumour was that the girl that was attacked perfectly fitted the description of one of our friend's daughters. So the fear issue was there. (Ash212)

In a small, fairly well-networked community, the sudden and unexplained appearance of a large police presence was a stimulus for speculation about what might have transpired. As conveyed earlier, there was an urgent issue that required an explanation. Then, when some details 'leaked' into the community about the fact that the police were investigating a rape, the substance of the rumours evolved to incorporate who might have been involved. As it turned out, the collective fear that the victim was a local girl was ill-founded. Nevertheless, the rumours pertaining to the crime spread rapidly through the community, because it seemed plausible from the point of view of local knowledge, for a rapist to have struck on the towpath. It was an area where there were established concerns about personal safety:

> See I've heard of rape, that was just in Ash Vale... I think that was down by Ash Wharf down near the canal. It's just the canal, everything happens on the canal, you get attacks on the canal. (Ash218)

As this respondent conveys, in many ways that 'the rape' was based upon a false allegation and associated rumours was largely irrelevant in terms of determining the influence it exerted. It persisted because of how it was cast as just one, albeit an especially serious incident, amongst a series of attacks that have taken place in this location.

Most notably, and as hinted at in the earlier extract, some 20 years prior to the new rumours about the occurrence of a rape, this same canal path, albeit a few miles away, was the scene of the abduction and murder of Marion Crofts. As a 14-year-old schoolgirl in 1981, she had been killed on her way to band practice, and the case remained unsolved until 2001 when Tony Jasinskyj was identified on the basis of a DNA sample he had given police because of his involvement in domestic violence. Although many local people were no longer consciously thinking about the Crofts murder, it undoubtedly continued to frame the collective consensus that this was a dangerous location. The conceptual relevance of this case for the current discussion is that it shows how crimes that are not 'there' in the here and now, can nevertheless directly influence current anxieties.

Returning to the more recent incident, in the absence of any detailed information from the police, who were in the early stages of their investigation, confronted by a flurry of highly visible police activities those residing in the area needed to assess what was happening. On the bases of snatches of incomplete information, soft facts started to be generated to the effect that a rape had happened and the victim was local. These rumours eventually turned out to be wrong on both counts, but that really didn't matter, as their impact was intense, and widespread fear and concern about safety had already become instantiated.

> What happened was a young lady from one of the barracks, I'm not quite sure but I think it is Purbright, had been in Aldershot on a night out. She got a little bit amorous with somebody and then she basically cried rape and said it had happened in the village. Why she picked our village is beyond me, but there were police around for quite a while... At that point it was fear. I have no other way of putting it... I never felt intimidated, then that happened, and it was like it can happen and can happen in the village... Even being so close to the Ranges, where of course it is wooded land, I never felt intimidated, then that happened. You start thinking well it can happen. It was never announced that it didn't, it was just through the pipeline that we heard this wasn't really what she said it was. (Ash212)

This more detailed account of the circumstances giving rise to the rumour and the social reactions that resulted from it confirms many of the points previously identified. In addition though, it adds one significant detail about the importance of a 'counter-rumour' once it became apparent that the alleged crime did not occur. According to this individual, no official statement was made confirming that what had been the focus for so much collective anxiety and concern was in fact a false allegation. As such, the assuagement of the community's concerns was left to take place through similar organic social processes to those involved in triggering the fear in the first place.

Even though this was shown to be a crime that did not happen, the rumours that grew up as part of the immediate community reaction to a perturbing event were sufficiently powerful that they continued to shape perceptions of safety and danger sometime after. In this particular instance, the content of the rumours exercised a potent influence upon how people in the area judged the safety afforded to them by their environment. As a location, lacking in opportunities for natural surveillance and being somewhat isolated in its geography, the canal area possessed characteristics that would make it emblematic of a risky place for citizens. Consequently, it seemed entirely plausible that a rape could have happened there.

One way of interpreting this is that the rumours of rape served a potentially useful social function, as a precautionary tale reminding people of the need to take care and actively manage their security. But what is of more direct interest here is the ways in which the rumour was generative of a 'sticky reputation' for a particular place. Even following the construction of a counter-rumour that should have neutralized, or at least mitigated the effects of the original one, the collective understanding that the towpath was a locale where trouble happened persisted.

That such symbolic constructions should prove so intractable and difficult to erase points to how people assemble judgements about their situated environments and the presence of risks and threats therein. It also confirms that rumours tend to arise and coagulate in social spaces that have reputations for being troublesome or problematic. This is because the notion that bad things happen here has immediate plausibility. To a significant degree then, rumour begats rumour. According to Wacquant (2007) in his discussion of the intensification of processes of 'advanced marginality' experienced by poor and dispossessed communities living both in the US and Europe, this is a reflection not just of the structural material disadvantages that assail them, but the comparative moral disadvantages that are overlain on their material circumstances. As he describes it, certain locales and those residing within them are increasingly subject to a form of 'territorial stigmatization' where a myriad of claims and counter-claims can be plausibly made. In this sense, we are starting to move from discussing the potential for crime rumours to provoke wider troubles, to thinking about how and why particular settings and certain conditions are generative of crime rumours.

This was apparent during qualitative fieldwork on a housing estate in the town of Blackpool in the North-West of England. The estate concerned was blighted by high levels of entrenched, inter-generational, socio-economic deprivation. It included a number of large high-rise tower blocks that the council used to house individuals with drug dependencies who were eligible for social housing. As one might expect, given such conditions, rates for crime and anti-social behaviour were high, and the area had, not altogether undeservedly, a well established reputation for 'trouble'. According to coverage in the local newspaper, there had been a series of murders on the estate. Upon further investigation though, it transpired that what had actually occurred was a number of suicides, often with people jumping out of windows from the upper storeys of the tower blocks. As is standard procedure for any unexplained and sudden death, the police would set up a murder investigation in order to enquire into the circumstances of the incident and explore the potential for foul play having been a causal factor. During the initial stages of their enquiries, when things tend to be fairly uncertain and they are trying to clarify what might have transpired, the police are often reluctant to say too much to the media in case they get it wrong. However, especially with the imperatives of 24/7 mass media reporting it is often in the initial hours and days immediately after an event, precisely when the police are inclined to communicate little about their progress, that journalistic interest tends to be at its most intense. In Blackpool, although they didn't have evidence to support such a claim, the local journalists in reporting the deaths had adopted fairly sensationalist headlines to the effect that there had been 'another murder on the estate'. Subsequently, when the police investigations concluded that the deaths were suicides rather than criminal homicides, a correction was never printed. It is perhaps unsurprising then that when interviewing people from other parts of town, many of them made reference to the high levels of murder in the area and the concerns it prompted. This constitutes a clear example of how crimes that never happened and were never 'there', nevertheless affected how people perceived levels of security in that area.

The Social Control of Rumour: 'Counter-rumour' Work

The institutional and interactional orders of contemporary social life mean that rumours arise with regularity and can prove profoundly influential in terms of how situations, events, and people are defined. Consequently, within many social control agencies there is a perceived need to try and limit and manipulate how the spread of rumours occurs across a range of social settings. For institutions and organizations, rumours of their bad or poor service provision can corrode levels of public legitimacy and reputation. For individuals, being the subject of a rumour can significantly influence the presentations of self that one must adopt when interacting with others. Given the 'stickiness' of rumours, and the ways they can taint how people and places are perceived over an extended period of time, considerable effort is often exerted towards diffusing or defraying rumours when they arise. However, it would seem that the capacity of most attempts to control or manage the spread and diffusion of rumours are, for the most part, limited in their effectiveness.

In circumstances where their discreditable actions and interventions are the topic of rumours, it has been well documented that in the past police have manufactured disinformation rumours to deny allegations of institutional failure. On other occasions though, they are required to engage in what might be termed 'counter-rumour' work. In relation to the public disorder case discussed at the start of this essay, it was intimated that a tendency to assume 'hard' facts are sufficient to subvert the power of soft-fact rumours is a common failure of how institutions seek to counter both misinformation and disinformation rumours.

It is now an appropriate juncture at which to consider some of the other ways that counter-rumour work is conducted, to develop a more rounded under-standing of what is involved.

As rationally ordered bureaucratic institutions, the capacity of formal social control agencies to effectively counter the spread of rumours and to manage their effects appears manifestly constrained. Their counter-rumour work typically involves issuing a denial of a rumours' veracity based simply upon setting out the factual information that is available. The limitations of such a response are mani-fold. First, the groups who are most likely to attend to rumours in the first place, are those whose trust and confidence in state institutions is lower. Therefore, they are unlikely to be persuaded or influenced simply by an alternate argument, even if the empirical grounds for it are more substantial. Consequently, their typ-ical response is that any new evidence has been fabricated by the authorities. A second problem is that, for state institutions such as the police, the preference has been to undertake their counter-rumour work through fairly traditional mass media platforms, whereas many of the rumours are spread by newer, faster, more informal modes of communication that are far less amenable to any semblance of central direction and control.

For example, in the aftermath of shootings and other such major crimes where their community impact assessments suggest there is potential for some form of 'existential harm' to be played out across the wider local community, police will often undertake a leaflet-based marketing campaign. Typically these leaflets will contain information that is intended to reassure residents about their safety and 'the actual levels of crime in the area'. Notwithstanding there is little to no thought given to testing the efficacy of any such measures, on sev-eral occasions during the fieldwork supporting this essay it has been observed that such an approach has antagonized local residents because they perceive the police to be belittling the harms induced by a very serious and often unpre-cedented community situation. Another favoured police tactic in the wake of major crimes is to step up levels of high visibility patrols in the area of the crime scene on the basis that these are anticipated to reassure locals. This may be the case for some, but an equally plausible outcome is that it heightens levels of fear and anxiety by functioning as a potent signifier of the trouble that has presented locally.

An additional form of counter-rumour work that can be deployed in con-junction with denial, or on its own, is to deliberately start a counter-rumour against the source of a previous rumour. The aim here is to attack the credibility of the other source in such a way as to render the audience so confused that they do not know what to think anymore. A setting in which this 'rumour as a response to a rumour' approach frequently occurs is when police prosecutions fail at court in major crimes. In order to justify the decisions that were taken, police will imply that there are other matters that perhaps were not considered by the court that continue to warrant their suspicions about the acquitted suspects.

It would seem then, that aware of the need to sustain legitimacy and public confidence, agencies of social control are increasingly mindful of the need to effect control over rumours that are spread about what they are doing and why. However, the capacity to respond effectively when a rumour starts to gain traction is frequently limited. In an information environment marked by speed of communication, and the ability to move vast quantities of information across social networks, the difficulties that state institutions have had in developing efficacious responses is perhaps understandable.

Nowhere were the implications of this information dynamic better illuminated than in the riots that occurred in London and several other English cities in the Summer of 2011. Several of the enquiries that were conducted once the convulsion of violence had abated pointed to the fact that the police's ability to respond effectively was inhibited, at least in part, by an inability to differentiate actual events on the ground, from those purported to be happening through a series of misinformation rumours. Attempting to monitor social media flows they were picking up rumours of lots of potentially bad things happening, but many of them turned out to be false. The material consequence was that police resources were so thinly dispersed that at no point could they muster sufficient force to 'grip' the situations where their presence and interventions were needed (Her Majesty's Inspectorate of Constabulary, 2011).

The scale and extent of the challenge posed by the contemporary information environment to agencies involved in social control work is further illustrated by examining what happened in Cardiff over the same period of the 2011 riots. Unlike many other English cities, Cardiff did not see any outbreaks of mass public disorder; only two incidents of looting which were rapidly contained. And yet over the period, South Wales Police logged hundreds of rumours from their officers on the street, staff from other public services, and members of the public, all of which had to be checked out in case they were true. All police leave was cancelled, and a significant surge in police presence on the streets of the Welsh Capital was manufactured. Only two incidents out of the hundreds rumoured to be occurring actually took place.

This serves to illuminate a number of important social dynamics related to the causes and consequences of crime rumours. First, it confirms that both individuals and institutions become particularly susceptible to the effects of misinformation and disinformation rumours in times of escalated tension and crisis. For all that institutions tend to be cast as rational, bureaucratic entities, they clearly display a potential to respond to rumoured information when under stress. It is evident that the contemporary information environment organized around a networked communication infrastructure, and the profligate nature of social media technologies, further embeds any such tendencies and increases the risk of acting upon soft facts (Castells, 1997). It perhaps also helps us to understand the extent to which rumour increasingly directs when, where, and in respect of whom social control is enacted.

Rumour as Social Control

At the same time as the practitioners of institutional impression management are working to limit the harm caused to the reputation and public image of their organizations, as intimated in a number of the cases highlighted earlier, rumours are increasingly integral to the conduct of social control. In an information rich environment, formal organizations are not immune to being swayed and directed by rumours. Particularly for those agencies involved in delivering emergency services to individuals and communities in trouble, rumours routinely attach to the work performed. A particularly notable recent example of this is to be found in Jonathan Simon's (2007) and Harvey Molotch's (2012) analyses of the aftermath of Hurricane Katrina. They both note how, in an emergency situation involving the mass evacuation of New Orleans' most economically deprived communities, the Chief of Police and Mayor of the city acted as sources for a series of rumours about serious acts of criminality taking place in the Astrodome where large numbers of the evacuees were being sequestered. It is not clear what the original source for the claims made was, but both Molotch and Simon are unequivocal in recording that all of the accusations of major crimes having occurred were subsequently proven to be false.

Whilst it may be difficult to establish how and why senior political and police figures were willing to make major public announcements of doubtful provenance in the full view of the world's media, the effects of their disinformation rumours are more readily discerned. They legitimated the invocation of an authoritative law-enforcement oriented response. The suggestion of criminals in the midst of an emergency situation fed a definition of the situation enabling the police to continue to practice a law enforcement role. Thus rather than having to re-calibrate their mission, to provide more social aid, significant proportions of the organizational apparatus could be retained doing more or less what they normally did—policing the poor and destitute.

Subject to acute stress, communities and particular information entrepreneurs within them or in contact with them, will gestate rumours. Importantly though, it is often the case that it is not simply one rumour that arises in isolation, but rather there will be a swirl of unsubstantiated claims. Under such conditions not everyone attends to all of the rumours. In complex and rapidly changing social situations, distinct 'epistemic' or 'rumour communities' can arise.[4] Membership of these rumour communities appears to be delineated on the basis of a wider world view and the extent to which the substantive content of different rumours in circulation between members accords with, or are antagonized by, these wider beliefs and values.

Overall then, rumour seems to be playing an ever more influential role in shaping the contours of social control, precisely because it is a modality of information that is not especially amenable to social control. In a multi-platform

---

[4] On the idea of 'epistemic communities' see Knorr-Cetina (1999).

media environment, suffused with peer-to-peer communications, where public trust in authority and expertise of many kinds seems to be waning, rumours display an overt capacity to shape how, when, where, and in respect of whom social control is enacted.

One area where such issues intersect and combine in especially interesting ways concerns the treatment of historic crimes. Innes and Clarke (2009) have suggested that one of the most important moves in contemporary criminal justice policy and practice in recent years, concerns the establishment and implementation of methodologies allowing for 'retroactive social control'. This term they introduce to cover the variety of ways in which past 'crimes' that were previously hidden from view, suppressed, or denied to have taken place at all by governmental authorities, can be recovered and redefined to recognize the harm done. Key variants of retroactive social control include Truth and Reconciliation Commissions, War Crimes investigations and 'cold case reviews' of long-term unsolved homicides. Intriguingly, rumours appear to play an important role in triggering the onset of such processes of recovery and redefinition. Rumours about 'what really happen' tend to persist and circulate amongst particular communities of onlookers, even in the face of official denials of their substance and attempts to suppress them.

This was strikingly evident in several recent cases involving historic allegations of child abuse. In the autumn of 2012 a public scandal broke about allegations that Sir Jimmy Saville, a deceased former BBC television star, had over a period of four decades, engaged in predatory sexual abuse against a large number of young children. As the story attracted increased publicity it was revealed that although rumours and allegations about Saville's offending (and that of several other celebrities) had been in circulation for some time and known to police and others, none of his acts had ever been defined as crimes; a particularly troubling example of crimes that were not 'there'.

But what was especially intriguing about the ways in which the story developed was that it produced a 'wave' of new allegations about crimes that were not there—in terms of not having previously been reported to or recorded by the police. It appears that the *Saville* case, and the ways it was reported in the broadcast media, and press, acted as a signal crime for historic victims, encouraging them to come forward and report to police events that had actually occurred many years previously. As a consequence, there was a sharp increase in the number of officially defined incidents.

This capacity to trigger 'crime waves' may be a generic property of signal crimes. The visibility and profile of these events may trigger enhanced public awareness and willingness to report crimes to the police. In a strict sense then, crimes that were not previously there, because they had not been reported to and recorded by police, are now rendered visible. It is a reaction pattern that is not restricted to historic serious crimes. For example, when police attend a neighbourhood following a report of a property crime, it is quite common for them to be told about a number of other incidents that they were otherwise unaware of. In his discussion of the making of 'crime waves', Sacco (2005) discusses how the transmission of rumours can contribute to the appearance of a crime wave. Herein we are also attending to something slightly different—how the occurrence of a signal crime can produce an actual rise in crime because of how it triggers changes in the public's reporting behaviour.

Specifically, in the wake of the publicity surrounding *Saville*, a number of new allegations were surfaced about abuse that had taken place in care homes in Gwynedd and Clywd in North Wales. Of particular interest though, is the fact that these allegations and rumours of police failure to investigate them properly had already been inquired into by Sir Ronald Waterhouse who had reported on them in 2000. But following the public visibility of the *Saville* signal crimes, over 100 alleged victims of abuse in North Wales were reported to have been identified—the majority of whom had not previously been disclosed as victims.[5] There was though, a further twist to the story. Waterhouse's public inquiry itself was accused by a victim in Wrexham of suppressing information about the identity of one of the abusers—a very high profile politician—or so it was rumoured. In the frenzied and febrile atmosphere of several weeks of revelation and scandal, a number of broadcast and print journalism outlets reported that the names of several abusers were circulating freely on the internet. They then took the step of reporting this information in full. The problem was that it rapidly became apparent that it was a misinformation rumour and in the process they had falsely accused a very high profile political figure of being a paedophile.

Taken together, these kinds of case clearly display just how important rumours and rumour management has become in the discovery and definition of crimes, and in shaping the social control work of criminal justice institutions. Persistent rumours about previously suppressed or hidden forms of criminality break the surface now and again. In this sense they foreshadow the instigation of retro-active social control where the public definition and remembrance of crimes past is fundamentally reconfigured.

Rumour and Reassurance

Whilst the content of some rumours engender them as suitable candidates for being controlled in order to restrict their negative effects, others function to support social control. In some settings, rumours attached to crime incidents perform more beneficial functions. For instance, in 2005 in the leafy and affluent village of Little Bookham in Surrey, a young mother was out walking her baby son when she was seriously assaulted. In the course of the attack she sustained knife wounds to the neck so severe that she was left paralysed.

---

[5] <http://www.bbc.co.uk/news/uk-wales-20946138> accessed 8 January 2013.

The brutal nature of the violence performed, combined with the tranquil setting in which the attack occurred, meant that the incident rapidly acquired the properties of a signal crime. It received in-depth and sustained coverage from all the major national mass media outlets for a number of days. Both the media coverage and police community impact assessments pointed to the fact that the incident was exhibiting a profound influence upon how people in the village and surrounding localities were thinking, feeling, and acting in relation to their security. If the media coverage is to be believed, these impacts were spread over a fairly wide area. Indeed the media reportage, shifting as it did between updates on the police investigation and more speculative contributions from 'crime experts', acted as an accelerant for new rumours that circulated daily amongst those living in Little Bookham. In the village itself, a toxic cocktail of fear, anger, and shock was very much in evidence amongst the local residents. It was a community on a heightened state of alert, concerned either that one of their members had been targeted by a violent stranger, or perhaps even more disturbingly, by someone from within.

As the days passed the sense of fear fused with a mounting concern about the apparent lack of progress in the police's investigation and frustration with the failure to locate a prime suspect. Then, several days into the investigation, an important development occurred. Police announced the discovery of a male's body in the village, the circumstances of which they intimated suggested that the cause of death was suicide. At first, in line with their standard practice, the police revealed very little information about this new development, despite considerable media pressure for them to do so. Amongst the villagers though, the police's refusal to officially identify the body or to publicly link it with their current investigation was irrelevant. Almost immediately upon its discovery, rumours started about who the new dead person was and that he was indeed a good candidate for being a suspect. As aspects of the rumour were confirmed by people from within the rumour community the credibility assigned to it grew. The police may have been refusing to provide any authoritative indications either way, but within the rumour community, which in a small tightly-knit village encompassed most people, the perpetrator was considered to have been identified and to have committed suicide. The sense of ongoing threat, therefore, rapidly dissipated. The palpable fear and trepidation that had haunted the village for a number of days evaporated. It seems that the rumour, although at that stage little more than a set of soft facts, sufficed in terms of giving the villagers an explanation for what had happened and that the problem had now been resolved, even though the connection between the deceased and the crime had not been officially confirmed by the authorities. What this amounts to is an illustration of how rumour can be used to draw reassurance about safety when this has been rendered fragile.

In the absence of meaningful definitions of the situation from authoritative sources, accounts circulated within and across particular rumour communities can provide a reasonable explanation for what has transpired and thus act to reassure. Events that, at least potentially, possess a capacity to profoundly destabilize the collective security of local people are effectively framed in such a way that most people can continue with their mundane, everyday routines. When individuals and groups perceive they have an adequate account of what has transpired, and crucially why, an occurrence that could have signalled trouble and induced more seismic implications, can instead be categorized as a misfortune.

Conclusion: The Work of 'Soft Facts'

Certain 'crimes' exert a form of 'presence in absence'. Incidents that are not actually present in the here and now, and indeed may never have even occurred, can nonetheless directly influence the ways people think, feel, and act in relation to their security. In particular, when individuals and groups find themselves in ambiguous situations where insecurity interacts with uncertainty, there is a tendency to try and construct an explanation for what is occurring, even when the information to enable this to be done with confidence is lacking. The radical insight afforded by attending to the phenomenon of crime rumours then, is that whether or not a crime actually happened is largely irrelevant in terms of 'an incident's' capacity to generate a profound and consequential social reaction. Effectively, the political and social consequences of crime are often decoupled from the reality of any incident itself. Consequential social impacts and effects can arise purely on the basis of perceptions and beliefs that people hold about crime. Insecurity frequently gravitates around social problems that are not actually there.

Although levels of crime have been receding from their highpoint in the early 1990s, the topic of effective crime management has retained its salience in political and public debate because of the dramatic reductions in public funding of criminal justice institutions that have been implemented. These are conditions in which misinformation and disinformation rumours about crime and social control prosper and thrive. Significantly though, it has been documented that rumours can function to provide reassurance and security, and not just insecurity. This is a necessary and important corrective to the general literature on rumour because sometimes rumours work to reduce collective anxiety following a traumatic episode. They can serve as 'convenient illusions'.

This leads us on to consider how crime rumours and false allegations travel through space and time. It would seem that to a significant degree rumours are context dependent. They are liable to become particularly consequential in ambiguous situations and those where inter- or intra-community tensions are already in play. In such settings rumour communities may be especially important in providing a communications infrastructure to pattern how multiple overlapping and interacting rumours are disseminated. Rumours tend to move more easily where they conform with peoples' extant belief and value systems.

Coherent with this, it has been suggested that rumours are often deployed by social actors as soft facts. Albeit their authority is recognized as precarious and provisional, in the absence of any more solid information, the rumour makes do in providing a plausible explanation of what has transpired. The repercussion of this is that the kinds of early rumours that emerge following crime incidents can possess 'first mover advantage', having an important role in establishing a definition of the situation for a wider public audience that can prove very difficult to shift subsequently.

In public policy terms this is a confounding problem. Agents of the state who might be minded to try and counteract rumours or manage their consequences often expend considerable energy trying to demonstrate the factual inaccuracies of what is rumoured to have occurred. The efficacy of their assumptions about the ability of 'facts' to counteract 'rumour' do not though, appear well-founded. In particular, if people distrust the police or government anyway, they are unlikely to believe the veracity of any alternative account offered, no matter what warrants support it. That this is so is also a correlate of the information architecture that has arisen and threaded itself through our webs of social relations. The internet and World Wide Web in particular has demonstrated a particular proclivity to aid the movement of rumours, conspiracy theories, urban myths, and gossip. This is now occurring on such a scale that some commentators who have previously countenanced an eschewal of any imposition of forms of governance or authority onto the structures of the internet, have started to identify a need to provide some form of quality evaluation for the information being provided by different online sites.[6] But we should not absent the more conventional mass media of any blame as they also routinely actively participate and play a role in how rumours about crimes and other troubling events travel.

In a world where a premium is placed upon 'hard facts', and the defining task of many of our key social institutions, including science, law, and the criminal justice process, is to establish mechanisms for the production of valid and reliable knowledge, the frequency with which the information environment we have created generates rumours, conspiracies, and myths that people believe is increasingly viewed as a social problem in its own right. Rumours as soft facts tend to lead to instability, often evolving and developing in terms of the news that is relayed, as understandings are updated or refined. They can turn out to be correct or false in their assertions. But the point is they are frequently influential and persuasive initial guides for action when something needs to be done.

Ultimately then, whether a troublesome event 'really' happened is largely irrelevant in terms of the impact that it can have upon a community or neighbourhood. Perceptions have consequences. Rumours of crime incidents can have presence in terms of shaping behaviour and conduct in the here and now, even though they are absent. By charting the varied ways in which rumours arise, as

---

[6] For example, see David Aaronovitch's article in *The Times* (16 September 2008), 'Easily caught in a web of sinister untruths'.

both cause and consequence of problematic and troubling situations and events, but also as a source of reassurance, this essay has documented the complex ways that rumours are imbricated in the construction of orders of reality.

It is tempting to reduce rumours to little more than the 'noise' of urban life. It is a tendency that social control institutions appear especially susceptible to. But to do so is to misunderstand the potential significance and power of crime rumours in shaping the contours of public insecurity. Rumours can in and of themselves act to signal the distributions of risks and threats across social space. In many ways such rumours are akin to phantoms—not 'real' but very capable of eliciting fear and anxiety.

The Long Shadow of the Twin Towers and the 'New' Counter-terrorism

A Case Study of the Institutional Effects of Signal Crimes

More than any similar attack before or since, the events of 11 September 2001 conveyed the capacity of terrorist actions to inspire shock and awe. Images of two planes arcing across the New York skyline to explode into the Twin Towers of the World Trade Centre have been seared into the collective memories of a generation precisely because of the visual and visceral nature of the destruction. These were acts designed to send signals. They distilled in elemental form the logic of the signal crimes perspective, and how certain events alter collective perceptions, emotions, and conduct.

These social reactions have been reinforced and amplified by a series of subsequent terrorist attacks in a number of world cities, including amongst others: the Madrid train bombings in 2004; the explosions in London in 2005; the killings in Mumbai in 2007; the attack at Glasgow airport in the same year; and latterly, the attempted beheading of Lee Rigby in Woolwich in 2013. Added to these there have been a far larger number of plots intercepted and interdicted. Collectively these incidents have generated a widespread sense of uncertainty about the precise scope and scale of the threat from violent Islamist extremism that is being confronted, and uncertainty too about how to respond appropriately.

This uncertainty has been evident following each of the attacks not prevented where a fairly standard reaction pattern can be observed to have taken place. After the initial public outrage and anxiety has subsided, some form of enquiry reveals that the perpetrators were 'known' to the authorities, but not assessed as a priority. In effect, the individuals concerned had been categorized as a risk but not a 'threat'. This sense of an 'intelligence failure' to detect and prevent motivated individuals from committing mass violence was present in the findings of the Presidential Commission established following 9/11 (Kean and Hamilton, 2004), and has been part of the story of all subsequent successful terrorist attacks.

Cumulatively these incidents have been generative of a series of profound and consequential social reactions, not least amongst the social institutions charged with countering terrorism. The resulting adjustments and reforms to institutional processes and systems can be understood as the effects of signal crimes that have dramatically displayed vulnerabilities and weaknesses in the protective framework that these institutions provide. It is these institutional effects that are the focus of this essay.

By constructing a history of the present of recent developments in UK counter-terrorism, the intention is to trace out how signal crimes can impact upon institutions. The discussion is designed as a case study capable of illuminating broader patterns and trends. Early sections of the essay are presented as a case study of the development of a more preventative disposition to counter-terrorism policy and practice. This feeds into a discussion of a wider set of cultural shifts that have taken place over the past two decades as the social order has sought to accommodate new security risks. The conclusion translates the findings from studying counter-terrorism to thinking about the institutional effects of signal crimes more generally.

The analysis is informed by empirical data collected as part of two distinct but linked research studies. The first was based upon in-depth interview data collected between 2003–5 in South London, Greater Manchester, and Birmingham, focused upon developing a more evidence-based understanding of the community context of extremist radicalization and thinking about how policing could be reconfigured to respond. The second study involved periods of field observation and 42 interviews with counter-terrorism police and community representatives (n = 53) in four areas of England and Wales during 2009–10, focused upon assessing the ongoing development and effects of the Prevent strand of counter-terrorism policing.

Framing Terrorism

History is replete with nation states of very different persuasions having to respond to political and social movements willing to invoke violence to challenge the governing regime's legitimacy and integrity. In some settings and circumstances these states have responded using military resources, whereas in others, the preference has been to rely on the auspices of the criminal justice apparatus (Laqueur, 2001). In practice, whether the 'war' or 'criminal justice' 'frame' assumes primacy depends, in part, upon how the acts and actors involved can be defined.

There is now a voluminous literature debating what is and is not 'terrorism' and how it should be classified. This reflects the inherently contentious nature of terrorist acts. States and their governmental agencies that have been attacked frequently seek to wield their social authority and power to label their assailants as 'terrorists'. Those subject to this labelling process often contest this, seeking instead to project an identity of 'freedom fighters'. Such considerations are further complicated by the possibility that states themselves might commit terrorist actions against their own citizens.

Seeking to synthesize and summarize the main currents of thought cutting across these myriad contributions, Paul Wilkinson (2000: 12–13) maintains that terrorism comprises the following key ingredients:

> ...the systematic use of coercive intimidation, usually to service political ends. It is used to create and exploit a climate of fear among a wider target group than the immediate victims of the violence and to publicise a cause, as well as to coerce a target to acceding to the terrorists' aims.

Elaborating and developing this synthetic approach, the vast majority of studies conclude that there are three key differences that separate terrorism from other forms of violent crime. These are:

- Political violence—a necessary condition for defining an act as terrorist and thus distinguishing it from other forms of violence is that it is conducted in pursuit of some political objective.
- Communicative violence—accompanying the preceding point, almost all definitions acknowledge that terrorist acts are marked by a desire to communicate an intimidatory message beyond the immediate victims. The violence is expressive and designed to send a message to the authorities.
- Asymmetry of power—more contentiously perhaps, many contributions identify that terrorist violence tends to arise when a relatively powerless group identifies a need to mobilize a response to a more powerful adversary. For example, Black (2004) as part of his wider geometry of social relations, proposes that terrorism is frequently an attempt at social control and self-help by relatively weak minority positions.

That said, the categorical boundaries between violent crime and terrorist violence are frequently blurred. For example, Anders Breivik's shooting of 69 people on the island of Utoeya and the additional eight killed by the bomb he left in Oslo in 2011, albeit motivated by a far-right political discourse, is probably closer in form to a 'spree killing' than traditional forms of terrorism. Similarly, the fatal knife attack against Fusilier Lee Rigby in Woolwich, London in 2013, may have been inspired by extreme Islamist ideologies, but in terms of how it was carried out, the assault had clear affinities with other violent street crimes.

Given the particular focus of this essay, of especial interest is the notion of violence as communicative action. Terrorists purposively design their violence as forms of signal crime. They are provocations deliberately seeking to elicit fear, and oftentimes to trigger a significant reaction from state authorities. This reflects how they are engaged in signalling different messages to different audiences. For those designated as 'the enemy' the violence should instill fear and a sense of risk. But at the same time, a message should be conveyed to the supporters of the group or network concerned that effective action to address the grievance is being taken. Terrorist campaigns need social support, both material and existential if they are to be sustained.

This is a quality picked up by Richardson (2006) in her discussion of 'the conducive surround'. Drawing upon studies of a number of terrorist campaigns across the globe, she maintains that both actual and perceived wider support for their cause on the part of those engaging in terrorist actions is vital if they are to be able to sustain their motivations and active involvement (see also Cronin, 2011).

The complex interactional dynamics of these kinds of factors are captured in a grounded fashion by Slucka's (1989) ethnography of the Divis Flats in Belfast. He identified how acts of violence by the Provisional IRA (PIRA) were responsible for important shifts in local public opinion. An important innovation that he introduced into his analysis was to differentiate between 'hard' and 'soft' support for the terrorist groups. Hard supporters were committed to the aims of the PIRA providing active material and moral support for the violence committed by the activists. But he also delineates an important role for a group of soft supporters. People occupying this position may not engage in behaviours that actively facilitate violent actions in pursuit of particular political ends, but they nevertheless provide ideational support.

A key element of this conducive surround that emerges from Slucka's analysis is the work involved in sustaining it by a terrorist group. As he articulates, in a situation such as Belfast where 'normal' policing services had effectively been withdrawn and a highly paramilitarized presence established, one way the PIRA garnered social support was through the supply of social control in communities. Pivotal in shifting public opinion away from a neutral or oppositional register, in favour of the PIRA, were the activities of police, army, and security service. Slucka tracks how, whenever these institutions were seen to over-reach themselves and engage in unnecessarily coercive interventions, there was an upturn in support for the PIRA.

Commencing this discussion of the institutional effects of 9/11 and associated incidents with a comment on terrorism in Ireland reflects how it was this situation that framed UK counter-terrorism policy and practice. Considerable experience and expertise had been built up in relation to how to manage aspects of the Irish threat. But one of the immediate consequences of 9/11 was the demonstration that much of this was of only passing relevance in terms of dealing with what has latterly come to be termed 'Al-Qaeda inspired terrorism'. Much has been written about aspects of the response to 9/11, herein, given the interest in tracing the impacts upon key institutions, the focus is restricted to the development of the Prevent programme in the UK.

Counter-terrorism Policy Development: A Short History of the Present

The initial reaction to the events in 2001 in policing and security agencies across the Western world was one of profound uncertainty. There was uncertainty about what to do in terms of responding appropriately, and in terms of being able to know and scale the threat. For despite the experience gained in places like Northern Ireland, the violence enacted in September 2001 with its combination of suicide and mass homicide, together with the failure of the intelligence apparatus to detect it, was interpreted as signalling the arrival of a profoundly different set of risks to be managed.

With the benefit of hindsight, it is now clear that the response that was manufactured blended a series of 'offensive' military actions, together with significant investment in the more 'defensive' use of intelligence agencies and policing. These are all part of the institutional effects of 9/11. Due to limitations on space and reflecting that far more has been written about the militaristic aspects of the response, the focus here is how policing and criminal justice have been adapted in countering the acts of Al-Qaeda affiliated and inspired events.[1]

Institutional uncertainty about how to respond effectively has persisted over a number of years. It has been sustained and reinforced by the macabre innovation and imagination of those motivated by violent jihadist ideologies, who have demonstrated a repeated ability to circumvent preventative measures that have been put in place. Retrospectively, it is possible to trace a sequence of plots and attacks marked by shifts in methodology. For example, in a few short months in 2007, two unexploded car bombs were found near the Tiger Tiger nightclub in London. The day following their discovery, two men inspired by Al-Qaeda's propaganda tried to drive a jeep into Glasgow Airport. These incidents followed the discovery, earlier that year, by West Midlands Police of a plot by a number of Muslim males residing in Birmingham to kidnap and execute a British Muslim soldier. Over a longer time frame, there have been: a succession of successful and unsuccessful plots involving passenger and cargo air transport; inter-personal crimes against politicians by committed violent jihadists in Holland and the UK; and disrupted attempts to attack sports stadia and shopping complexes, with successful versions of this in Mumbai. The variability in terms of who has been involved in such efforts and how they have sought to undertake these acts have posed ongoing prevention and detection challenges to the authorities.

---

[1] Two good summary overviews of what has taken place in the aftermath of the original attack are Burke (2011) and Wright (2007).

Smelser's (2007) evocative description that terrorists and counter-terrorism agencies are 'locked into a rhetorical battle of symbols' appositely captures the principal dynamics. The terrorist assailants are seeking to cause a symbolic harm to the state, something evident in their choice of targets which are often iconic, or freighted with deeper meanings. Concomitantly, police and security agencies seek to signal their capacity and capability to effectively control the terrorist threat they are confronted with.

It is precisely this dance of action and reaction that marks the emergence and evolution of the CONTEST counter-terrorism strategy in the United Kingdom. The initial reaction of institutional uncertainty following events in 2001 was significantly amplified when Mohamed Siddique Khan and his colleagues detonated bombs on the London Underground in 2005.

Developing the UK's CONTEST policy

There were two key influences on the initial formulation of the cross-departmental CONTEST strategy. The first was the experience gleaned in Northern Ireland, moderated by a recognition that the Al-Qaeda problem was different. The second influence was the increasingly multi-agency approach being used to tackle crime more generally. Reflecting this combination of influences, CONTEST was constructed around four key pillars: Prepare; Protect; Prevent; and Pursue.

The Prepare strand focuses upon establishing processes and systems in anticipation of a range of different types of potential attack. Protect involves a range of situational crime prevention activities, seeking to reduce risks and threats to elements of the critical national infrastructure. The aim is to minimize the opportunities for an attack and limit consequences should one occur. Pursue is more in the traditions of police and security service involvement in counter-terrorism work, and the identification and securing of motivated suspects. Subsequent sections examine Prevent in more detail.

The original version of the CONTEST strategy was established in 2004. In practice, whilst it promised more preventative work, the centre of gravity remained very much with the 'Pursue' strand and established counter-terrorism intelligence and covert policing work. This changed in 2007 when the new Labour government launched what became known as CONTEST II. A key driver for the 'refresh' of the policy framework was a growing frustration that very little preventative activity was actually taking place.

The 'radical' thinking that went on at this time and how it was impacted by what had occurred in London in 2005 were described by a senior counter-terrorism police officer who was interviewed as part of this study:

> There was a three month window of opportunity before Sadiq Khan and his comrades committed the attack...The reason why the service said they weren't pursuing them was because they weren't high enough on the intel radar. However, why didn't we just send a couple of uniformed officers to knock on the

door and say 'Hi Mohammed, I'm from the counter-terrorism unit, we really need to have a chat.' ... They've no idea what level of detail we know, very, very powerful that. (Police, 2659–24)

This quotation engages with two themes threaded through this essay. The first is how policy and practice developments arise in response to aspects of signal crimes. In this case, the officer describes how one of the effects of the 7/7 bombings in London and similar events was to trigger a re-thinking across the policing and security agencies about how they might practically deal with the kinds of problems they were confronting. In so doing, he further articulates one of the principal challenges for these organizations. Tracking and monitoring 'risky' individuals in any serious way is an extremely resource intensive activity, and as such, choices and assessments have to be made about which individuals and groups should be the primary focus of attention.

Locally such decisions were increasingly informed by the development of Counter-Terrorism Local Profiles. The concept underpinning these documents was that they should provide an 'all-source' local intelligence assessment about the prevalence and distribution of local risks and vulnerabilities so that choices about where to allocate resources and effort could be taken. The kinds of informational inputs included in these profiles was described thus:

It will be based on the number of intelligence logs that have come in, number of Rich Picture locations ... number of CT operations in certain areas. It will be based on other factors, sort of vulnerability indicators deprivation indicators and all that was put into a formula by our analysts and they came up with a threat map, and then we allocated resources as we were able to that threat map. (Police, 2611–11)

That was the theory at least. Several other operational 'users' of these profiles were less persuaded about the insights they actually provided. It is certainly the case that there are now a number of cases where these risk-based judgements about who to track and who not to have been shown to have been wrong. This is a product of the unavoidable probability of identifying false positives and false negatives; that is, focusing upon actors who were never really likely to progress on to engage in violence, but equally missing those who do.

Despite such challenges and problems, a fundamental commitment to Prevent and the principles of the wider CONTEST strategy has been sustained. This reflects how, despite the considerable level of effort and activity, there has been a steady stream of viable plots. Some sense of the scale of the problem, at least as perceived by the authorities, was provided in speeches by the Director General of the security service in late 2007, indicating there were around 2000 individuals being monitored on the grounds that they posed a direct threat to national security because of their support for terrorism. This figure was deemed to have increased by around 400 from the previous year. It was also noted that during

2007, 37 individuals had been convicted by the courts in 15 significant terrorism cases.[2]

These metrics are significant in capturing how the strategic threat being confronted was understood by senior policy-makers and practitioners as not being limited to a few isolated individuals living overseas. Rather, it gravitated around small groups of young Muslim males who were experiencing deeply felt 'anomic' dislocation, and who were being indoctrinated into using violence in pursuit of a broader ideological agenda. Importantly, this was framed by an increasingly sophisticated understanding of the processes of 'radicalization'. When the original version of CONTEST was formulated, there was very little understanding or insight into the social and social-psychological involvement sequences via which people were recruited into terrorist violence. Indeed, in many quarters there was a tendency to view this as a problem relating to a few pathological individuals.

By 2007 however, there were a growing number of accounts of radicalization recognizing different routes via which particular individuals had come to affiliate with other violent jihadists and acquire violent motivations (eg, Richardson, 2006; Horgan, 2005). Alongside which, there was increasing acknowledgement of a combination of 'push' and 'pull' factors at work, where the former detached people from their mainstream social contacts and the latter attracted them to the ideas of particular Islamist groups (Innes et al., 2007). Sageman (2004) provided one such influential treatise by focusing upon how social contacts and networks shaped patterns of recruitment into violent Islamist groups.

Consequently, CONTEST II saw significant investment in the Prevent strand, through the Preventing Violent Extremism programme. Critical to its operationalization was the identification of 'communities' as a key site for intervention. The accent placed upon Prevent and its attempts to 'get upstream' of the problem to inhibit processes by which people were being radicalized, rather than just waiting to interdict plots once they were underway, proved controversial. In particular, the allegation was that the Prevent programme was constructing Muslims as a 'suspect community' (Pantazis and Pemberton, 2009) and that its 'real' purpose was to 'spy' upon Muslim communities, rather than building community resilience and promoting cohesion (Kundani, 2009).

CONTEST II defined five main and two supporting objectives for the Prevent programme.[3] These were to:

- Challenge the ideology behind violent extremism and support mainstream voices;
- Disrupt those who promote violent extremism and support the places where they operate;

---

[2] These figures are summarized on p.15 of the HM Government (undated) report 'Prevent Strategy: A Guide for Local Partners in England' that was made available in 2008.

[3] Home Office (2009).

- Support individuals who are vulnerable to recruitment, or have already been recruited by violent extremists;
- Increase the resilience of communities to violent extremism;
- Address the grievances which ideologues are exploiting;
- Develop supporting intelligence, analysis, and information;
- Improve strategic communications.

Alongside these objectives, the Home Office published more detailed guidance for practitioners about how Prevent work should be conducted. In terms of practical application, three main types of activity were identified: 'counter-radicalization' focused upon inhibiting the spread and influence of extremist ideas both generally and in specific cases; 'de-radicalization' involved acts to reduce the influence of extremist ideas where they have gained traction; and, 'community cohesion building' pivoted around increasing the resilience of communities so that they are less likely to be influenced by extremist views. For example, the 'Channel' programme targeted individuals risk assessed as being vulnerable to extremist influences and provided intensive mentoring and/or theological support to counteract any such malign forms of persuasion. The balance between these three streams of work reflected concern both with those who had become motivated to engage in violence or actively support this, as well as those individuals who might be vulnerable to such influences.

To justify this approach, the head of the Security Service at the time stated on the basis of polling evidence, that some 100,000 UK citizens thought the attacks in 2005 were in some way justified (Manningham-Buller, 2007). Another survey conducted in October 2006 found that 82 per cent of British Muslim respondents believed British Muslims had become more politically radicalized and a similar proportion believed the 'war on terror' was really a 'war on Islam' (The 1990 Trust, 2006). The Pew Global Attitudes Survey (2005) reported that 24 per cent of Muslim respondents thought there were times when suicide bombing was justifiable and 22 per cent felt the 7/7 London bombings were in some way justified. Importantly, a second survey conducted for the Channel 4 'Dispatches' programme found marked differences in the attitudes of different age groups, with 31 per cent of those aged 18–24 years compared with only 14 per cent of those aged 45 or over reporting support for the London bombings (NOP, 2006). Not dissimilar patterns were evident in a YouGov survey in July 2005, where 24 per cent of respondents had some sympathy for the feelings/ motivations of the 7/7 bombers and 56 per cent said they could understand why the 7/7 bombers behaved in that way. [4] In the same survey, 14 per cent said they were aware of groups of young British Muslims who are preaching hatred of the West and 41 per cent said they believed Muslims would be reluctant to report suspicious behaviour to police for fear of getting other Muslims into trouble.

---

[4] YouGov/*Daily Telegraph* Survey (27 July 2005).

In qualitative interviews conducted with police involved in Prevent work, many of them recounted how they had encountered views consistent with these kinds of opinion survey data:

> This became the opportunity to take all of your frustrations and your anger and the vitriol and the things that have been pent up for a long, long-time. That was undoubtedly challenging for the officers who had to deal with that at the beginning of almost every relationship they were trying to forge. (Police, 2659–24)

Such views were difficult and challenging for the authorities at the time. But as is now well documented, there is a malleability to 'public opinion' in terms of how it is constructed through polling instruments according to how questions are asked, when, and of whom. Accordingly, it is potentially insightful to compare such data with other sources. For example, the British Crime Survey (BCS) was a robust annual survey that questioned randomly sampled members of the public about their experiences, perceptions, and attitudes about a wide variety of crime, disorder, and policing issues. Although it did not ask about terrorism and counter-terrorism issues directly, it contained a battery of questions on various aspects of policing. Two particular advantages of analysing the BCS are that it has a sufficiently large sample to allow for comparison of attitudes and perceptions amongst Muslim respondents with those of the general population in England and Wales. Moreover, as an annual survey, it is possible to explore trends in these views, rather than simply a 'snapshot' at one point in time.

If the more assertive critiques of Prevent were correct that it had been profoundly alienating and had constructed Muslims as a suspect community, then it seems reasonable to assume that this would be reflected in attitudes towards and perceptions of policing. But the reality of the situation appears to have been rather more complicated. For instance, Table 5.1 examines four indicators focused upon perceptions of policing comparing Muslim views with those of non-Muslims.

As can be seen, Muslims were slightly less likely to believe police would treat them with respect than people from other backgrounds, albeit a large proportion endorsed this statement. But for the other three indicators, Muslim respondents had more positive views of the police. Extending this analysis to look at similar data over four years of the British Crime Survey between 2004–5 and 2008–9, a key period in the implementation of the Prevent strategy, demonstrates that this pattern remains fairly consistent.

These views are important when set against other data from the same source showing Muslim respondents were more likely to say crime and disorder had a negative impact upon life in their local communities. For example, compared with the general population sample Muslim respondents were far more likely to say that they were worried about becoming a victim of crime. Relatedly, a greater proportion of Muslims expressed concern about 'drug dealing' and 'public drinking' being key local problems. Around 25 per cent of the general population

Table 5.1 Comparing attitudes to the police

Police in this area ... (Strongly agree or agree)	Muslim N = 963	gen. population N = 44601
would treat you with respect if you had contact.	81	84
understand the issues that affect this community.	70	65
are dealing with things that matter to this community.	63	53
I have confidence in the police in this area.	63	53

Source: British Crime Survey 2008–9

surveyed saw drug dealing as a key local issue, a figure that rose to 45 per cent amongst Muslim respondents.

However, disaggregating the analysis further refines the emergent picture. For instance, the 'confidence in the police' indicator in the survey captures some of the subtleties that lie beneath the headline figures. In Figure 5.1 comparative BCS data for males expressing confidence in the police is provided.

Young Muslim males have less confidence in the police than do their older compatriots. But there is an important 'cross over effect' in the graph as older Muslim males were significantly more likely to report being confident in the police than older men in the general population. A second gender effect on this indicator was also identified for women, but in reverse. That is, Muslim women aged 45 or over, reported less confidence in the police than did women of the same age in the general population. It is possible that these two patterns are linked, in that young Muslim men were experiencing some negative contacts with police on the street under the auspices of Prevent and reporting these to their mothers.

One further area where analysis of the BCS provides important data relates to perceived levels of community cohesion. The sense of living in an area that is cohesive is increasingly recognized as a useful measure of community resilience and well-being. Between 2004–5 and 2007–8 the BCS asked respondents whether or not they agreed that they lived in a place 'where people from different backgrounds get on well together?' The results for Muslims compared with the general population are set out in Figure 5.2.

In the first two years Muslims were more likely to say that they lived in a cohesive area. However, this dipped in 2006–7. This covers the period immediately following the bombings in London. Importantly however, it quickly recovers to a level comparable to that of most people. Although, it is difficult to be absolutely sure about the cause of this dip, it would be consistent with the general thesis of this essay that significant signal crimes (such as the London bombings) can be felt in terms of the effects they have upon public cognitions, affect, and behaviour.

Contrary to some cruder critiques of Prevent, the present analysis suggests that its effects have been situated and complex. Rather than wholly negative and

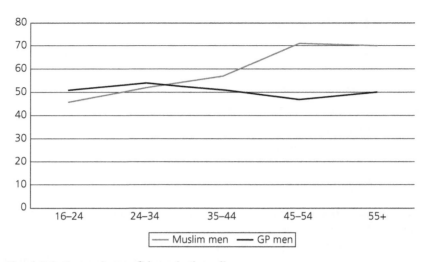

Figure 5.1 Comparing confidence in the police
Source: BCS 2008–9

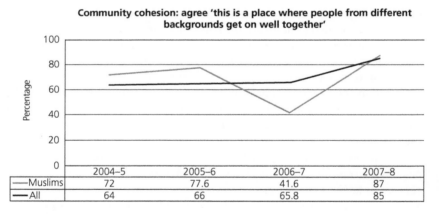

Figure 5.2 Trends in community cohesion
Source: BCS 2005/5–07/08

profoundly alienating for the UK's Muslim faith communities, there has developed a grudging and reluctant acceptance of Prevent type activities. For most Muslims, although some of their experiences of policing and Prevent have not been positive, and there was a dislike of aspects of how the policy has been implemented, this was balanced by an acknowledgement of violent extremist radicalization as a social problem needing to be addressed.

Given the combination of implementation problems and political contentiousness, it is unsurprising that a change of national political leadership resulted in a distinct policy shift. After being elected, the Coalition government quickly moved to introduce significant revisions to the focus and delivery of Prevent. In part, these reflected the onset of public sector austerity and the perception that the high levels of funding for Prevent could not be sustained. But there were also political and ideological motives at work.

Many of the problems that the Coalition government highlighted in justifying their review of Prevent were also identified by those involved in implementing the CONTEST II strategy at local levels. The following quotation for example, reflected the concerns voiced by a number of interviewees:

> What's happened is Prevent money has been used by groups who we'd call 'poverty pimps' like they go to areas where there's funding, take the funding, don't really deliver anything meaningful and we're none the wiser at the end of it. (Community, 2654–01)

But there was an important political edge to how the policy framework was reformed. A sense of this is provided in the foreword to the revised Prevent strategy penned by the Home Secretary Theresa May (2011: 1):

> The Prevent programme we inherited was flawed. It confused the delivery of Government policy to promote integration with Government policy to prevent terrorism. It failed to confront the extremist ideology at the heart of the threat we face... funding sometimes even reached the very extremist organisations that Prevent should have been confronting.

This is a coruscating critique, casting the inherited policy as 'flawed', 'confused', and 'failing'. Especially loaded was the last sentence. As Robert Lambert (2011), former head of the Muslim Contact Unit in the Metropolitan Police Service describes in some detail, within the Counter-Terrorism Command the approach developed over several years had been to encourage Salafist groups to lead on the local delivery of many Prevent activities. This was inflected by a deeper orthodoxy to be found in the work of Special Branch officers, and the belief that those closest to a problem are often best placed to address it. In this particular case, adherents of Salafist versions of Islam were held to be theologically close to many of those inspired by Al-Qaeda's ideology, with the important difference that Salafists reject the use of violence. As such, it was argued that they provided credible role models to young men who believed in an extreme version of Islam.

From the Coalition government's point of view however, the involvement of Salafist groups was problematic because some of their beliefs were antithetical to core tenets of Western political liberalism. As such, it was argued they should not be recipients of state funding, even for the purposes of reducing the risks of terrorism. Ensuring that this no longer happened was a core objective of the Prevent review.

To a degree, the key point of difference was between short-term and long-term objectives. For the police and Security Service officers tasked with inhibiting the potential for serious politically motivated violence, encouraging theologically and politically radical groups to help address the problem in the here and now, appeared an effective solution. For the Coalition policy-makers however, there was a concern that encouraging such approaches might unintentionally promote more militant versions of Islam over the longer term.

The revised Prevent strategy formally separated community cohesion and integration work from those functions focused upon countering terrorism. There was also a deliberate move away from the more communitarian ethos pursued under the Labour governments, with far greater emphasis upon involving educational establishments and healthcare providers in identifying vulnerable individuals who might be susceptible to radicalizing influences. At a practical level, this placed significantly more accent upon using the Channel programme to counteract any such malign influences. In sum, the overall focus of Prevent has become much more concerned with individuals deemed to be at risk and posing a risk, than the community contexts that serve to position them in these ways.

Accompanying these policy shifts, have been significant alterations to the social organization of counter-terrorism. In the United Kingdom for example, as part of the change processes described earlier, a network of regional counter-terrorism units were established around the country. Hosting teams of specialist counter-terrorism police officers, alongside individuals from the Security Service, these units were a manifest response to the changed threat environment that the key agencies now perceived. It was no longer deemed effective to have all counter-terrorism assets based in London, given that plots were emerging in towns and cities across the country.

Similar processes of reaction and reorganization can be observed in the US. Thacher (2005) has documented the introduction of the Joint Terrorism Task Force concept as an attempt to overcome some of the intelligence pathologies induced by the highly fragmented and fractured nature of American policing. Likewise, Fosher's (2009) ethnography of the Homeland Security Department in Boston, further captures some of the deeper organizational effects that have radiated out from the signal crime that occurred in September 2001. Indeed, the fact that the American government perceived a need to establish a whole new Department of Homeland Security to overcome some of the limitations of its prior approach is striking evidence of just how profoundly governmental institutions were effected by 9/11.

Aggregated together, these policy manoeuvres and organizational reconfigurations can be interpreted as one of the primary institutional effects of 9/11 and subsequent events. As Simon (2007) has noted in relation to the politics of criminal justice reform more generally, high profile crimes where there is a perceived failure, routinely induce a political imperative to be seen to be doing something to redress the vulnerability.

Interpreting and accounting for reform

From even this cursory overview of key counter-terrorism policy developments over the past decade, significant shifts and adaptations in the overarching approach are apparent. However, the extensive policy analysis literature across a number of substantive domains teaches that one should not assume tight coupling between policy prescriptions and how these are translated into action on the ground. Indeed, what emerges from examining the relations between counter-terrorism policy, strategy, and practice is the sense of a layered or 'laminated' response wherein different strata of the state's reactions to terrorist risks and threats are operating with very different guiding logics. These can be conceived as constituting forms of revolution, evolution, and involution.

Recalling the accusation made by the Home Secretary in 2011 that the previous iteration of Prevent had 'failed' and was 'flawed', the political diktats of countering terrorism mean that there is a tendency to present key policy developments as 'revolutionary'. That is, they are constructed as representing significant changes from what was done in the past. Often this reflects the fact that such policy reforms are stimulated by perceived failures in managing the problem, but also the practical realities of how politicians have to try and get attention (and hopefully some electoral credit) for their initiatives.

But for the layer below, the senior leaders in the security agencies and police who must translate the rather abstract policy frames into specific operational strategies, all this talk of change and revolution is not especially helpful. They prefer a sense of 'evolution', identifying continuities between what has been done previously and any new requirements. Of course, from time to time, there are genuine innovations and wholesale shifts to strategic thinking, but where possible, the tendency is to establish a longer term trajectory of development.

However, a rather different guiding logic seems to be in play when we turn to examine practical delivery on the ground, some elements of which were identified during interviews with key practitioners who were less than certain about how they were meant to follow new policy edicts:

> We were then tasked to deal with people who fell out of that operation and that has been problematic in that we have had no specific training for carrying out that intervention. How do you go to somebody who's believed to be involved in a group...and say to them 'what grievance have you got, what are your worries, talk to us' when they already possibly, are well down the path of radicalisation? So how do we get trained into that? How do we manage that process and how do we deal with that? (Police, 2611–12)

As this officer, who was involved in delivering Prevent within communities identifies, there was a lack of clarity about precisely how to translate policy prescriptions into specific actions.

Exposed to the complexities of real life situations, the messy and intricate details of peoples' biographies, and the difficulties of identifying risks of radicalization *in situ*, there is a far greater sense of what might be labelled 'involution'. Involution refers to a process of increasing complication and complexity. Applied to the realm of counter-terrorism work, it helps to capture how, in terms of actually trying to make any strategic and policy frames work, actors on the ground

113

must improvise and use discretionary decision-making as they attempt to work out practically viable ways of preventing and pursuing individuals and groups who might represent a danger to public safety.

Co-producing Counter-terrorism

Based upon the fieldwork conducted in four police force areas, combined with in-depth interviews with practitioners engaged in the delivery of Prevent and community-based recipients of such interventions, it is possible to identify four ideal-type modes through which Prevent-based counter-terrorism work is delivered. These modes can be delineated on the basis of who does the defin-itional work of identifying a problem or issue that needs addressing, and then, who assumes lead responsibility for tackling it (Table 5.2).

Differentiating between whether it is the police and their partner agencies who lead the processes of problem definition, and service delivery, or whether com-munity networks perform these roles, four principal modes of Prevent activity can be distinguished. The 'protective' mode is where police and other formal agencies clearly 'own' the intervention. The tactics they engage in can vary from disruption to legal sanctions, but crucially the problem is determined and responded to by the police and/or security agencies. This equates to the more orthodox and established approaches they have historically taken to counter-terrorism activities, and certainly what happens under the 'Pursue' strand of CONTEST.

Community mobilization involves the problem definition and response being undertaken through informal social control resources. These responses can range from violence through to awareness-raising. Critically, police and their local authority Prevent partners may be wholly or partly unaware of the activity.

The focus of much of this discussion though will be upon 'Type One' and 'Type Two' modes of co-production, because it is these components that are 'new' to the conduct of counter-terrorism. The former relates to how, in some situations, police act to deal with issues brought to their attention by communities. This has been previously documented in other situations in the research literature.[5] Under Prevent, this mode is engaged either because a problem is sufficiently troubling that it is beyond the scope of purely community-led interventions to impact

Table 5.2 Four intervention modes

	Police defined	Community defined
Police delivered	Protective	Type One co-production
Community delivered	Type Two co-production	Mobilization

[5] See for example, Carr (2005).

upon it, or because police can fashion a response to build community trust and confidence.

Type Two co-production is where police identify a problematic issue, but enable or encourage community-based actors to deal with it. This can either be through material and practical support, or more tacit forms of backing. Engaging this style of collaboration in Prevent work tends to reflect the fact that some problems are complex and cannot be effectively treated through application of the criminal law.

Protective and community mobilization modes

Protective counter-terrorism involves police and their partners identifying risks and threats and implementing actions to address these. As Brodeur (2010) catalogues in his discussion of 'high policing', much of this work involves the development of covert intelligence and relatively clandestine forms of operation. But not all counter-terrorism depends upon formal social control.

Fieldwork conducted across four areas of the country identified considerable amounts of informal social control being performed by community and third sector groups to tackle aspects of violent extremism, outwith any involvement of the governmental agencies formally tasked with this role. Indeed, the significance of this community involvement was frequently neglected and underappreciated by formal agents of social control.

One man interviewed told a story of how, when a well-known extremist figure started proselytizing locally, the community decided to 'push-back' themselves:

> What we done as a community we thought if we send the police in it looks heavy handed, he gets the publicity he wants and he will get more followers. We got community people to actually confront them on their stalls and after a couple of weeks of coming here and then facing the confrontation, he ran away from this road. (Community, 2654–01)

Across the interviews and periods of field observation, repeated instances of communities acting to tackle potential problems were identified. Confirming the sentiments in the previous quotation, in a second area, a Muslim interviewee with considerable experience of working with the police was asked what would happen if 'unwanted groups' started trying to radicalize young people. He replied:

> People that are quite active within the community, would probably sit down, would have this discussion and then effectively try to rally the community around them ... and people start to think well this isn't right, we don't want this in our community and then the barriers go up and they will then prevent people from being able to do what they were trying to do internally.

He was then asked by the interviewer 'Would they tell the police?'

> I don't reckon they would no ... I think it would be a, not a last resort, but quite close to being the last resort. I think the involvement with the police is

something that is way, way down the line. First of all see if we can do it in-house. (Nctt7312)

Involving police as a last resort was a common theme across the interviews. This seemed to reflect two main influences. The first was a distrust of the police and their motivations; the second though, was a general confidence in the efficacy of informal social control available in Muslim communities. There is good evidence, from a range of studies, that many British Muslim communities possess higher levels of social capital and community cohesion, than is found in other areas. As a result, there was a generalized feeling that where possible, community mechanisms should be used to craft solutions to problems.

The following account details the kinds of response leveraged from within a community when concerns started to be raised about a young man in the area. Of particular interest, are the intertwined mechanisms of power and influence engaged:

> I said 'why should we, just for one individual's sake sort of make an effect on the Mosque, where the Mosque will get blamed when everything comes out in the open?' So then we spoke to the parent and we said 'you need to go to the police, otherwise we will then go.' And at first he said 'no, no'. I said 'no, why should we, we are lying for your son, and today he's done something minor, tomorrow he'll do something big. Are we still going to hide him?' And then at that point he saw sense and he went himself. (Community, 2659–31)

Whilst there was undoubtedly a preference for solving these issues internally, it was also recognized that this was not always possible. Some of the more interesting responses involved interactions between police and communities.

Type One co-production

Co-production involves a particularly engaged form of partnership or collaborative working between distinctive groups or organizations. Where other forms of partnering accommodate dominant or 'lead' partners, the unique quality of co-production is the accent upon participant equality and shared endeavour. For an initiative to be genuinely co-produced requires three phases of activity to be present: co-defining the problem; co-designing the solution; and co-delivery of any response. The first of these requires participants coming together to confirm what the issue is that needs addressing. Following on from this there has to be mutual agreement about what is to be done. Finally, there needs to be the active participation of all in responding.

These three phases are present in the two main forms of co-production. 'Vertical co-production' involves two or more actors where there is a power differential between them, for example, where a state agency works with community groups to address an issue. Contrastingly, 'horizontal co-production' occurs where two or more similarly situated acting units engage with each other. This might include where one community organization undertakes to work with another one, or similarly, where two separate state agencies collaborate. Horizontal co-production is more commonplace than the vertical form. That said, both Type One and Two co-production are instances of vertical co-production, and featured in the more progressive counter-terrorism approaches present in two of the four research sites.

The emergence of this co-productive counter-terrorism had been presaged by some innovative thinking in respect of the police role. This involved importing approaches from neighbourhood policing into the work of units focused upon the Prevent agenda. In one area in particular, the Prevent teams started wearing police uniforms and being very open about the nature of their work. As the head of the unit described it, his officers were:

> ... based locally in uniform and overtly counter-terrorist, so they will state who they are. (Police, 2611–11)

This represented a marked break from the orthodox approach of counter-terrorist and Special Branch methodologies where the assumption had long been that this kind of work had to be performed by plain-clothes officers. The backgrounds of the individuals recruited to work in this way was also different. Where many Special Branch officers have traditionally been recruited fairly early on in their careers, the majority of those brought in to deliver Prevent in this area had learned their craft in neighbourhood policing settings, or as police trainers. They brought a different way of doing things with them. One of the first things the unit did was to build a structured and systematic network of contacts across all the local communities. The purpose of this was described by a female officer who had been pivotal in its development:

> We never ask any of our contacts to give us intelligence, we'd never task them ... however if you have something ... (Police, 2659–15)

As the quotation intimates, the importance of building this network of community contacts was to provide channels for communication should people have any suspicions or concerns they wanted to relay to the police. It was not assumed that this communication channel would always be 'on', but rather it could be used when needed.

Because the local police were not actively asking for information and intelligence, it was seen more positively by representatives of the local communities. Several cases illustrate how it was being operationalized:

> Another Mosque in [Place Name] rang up one of my sergeants and said 'we've got three guys coming here, and they were doing the proper radicalization thing.' They were trying to draw kids in, they were trying to have little meetings, they were being quite radical. 'We'd appreciate your support if you could come and help us, and speak to these three individuals because we don't want them here but we're a little bit concerned.'

This exemplifies the principles of Type One co-production. The police and community had agreed what constituted problematic activity in the area, in respect of the activities of a known extremist group. They had identified instances of this occurring and confirmed police intervention was needed. As the police Inspector further described, the agreed course of action was fairly 'low-key':

> So [Officer Name]'s gone down, confronted the three individuals. 'The Mosque don't want you here, what are you about? Do you want to talk to me about it?' They didn't. They went. We know where they went. (Police, 2611–11)

The Inspector went on to recount how information about the group was circulated more widely amongst other community groups, in order to create a 'hostile environment'. Consequently, the extremists were subject to an ongoing sequence of locally generated disruptions and were not able to settle in any new premises—thus fulfilling the third criteria for genuine co-production—co-delivering the solution. As a framework this starts to build up a more nuanced understanding of how counter-terrorism work in the post 9/11 setting has been adapted. In particular, the use of disruptions and forms of intervention that are not predicated upon the invocation of criminal law is a feature of both Type One and Type Two co-produced counter-terrorism.

Type Two co-production

The more unusual and innovative form of counter-terrorist intervention observed during the fieldwork was based upon Type Two co-production, where police identified a problem, but encouraged the community to lead the delivery of any solution. The details of this way of working were illustrated by a similar scenario to that described earlier, in that there was a radical group booking local meeting rooms to try and engage with vulnerable local people and begin the process of converting them to their cause. In this case, the community and police agreed that a police-led intervention would be unhelpful. This was because the group concerned were not officially proscribed and had not done anything that could be construed as illegal. As such, the concern was that any police involvement would be exploited by the group for propaganda purposes. So instead, police agreed that informal social control exerted by representatives of the local community might be more effective. One of the local Prevent officers described the sequence of events:

> The community was telling the venues he was booking under different names. We disrupted the first one on the night dynamically, but then they phoned round all the others and without any pressure from us they cancelled. So not only was he being approached on the street, he was turning up at venues and being told, 'look here's your money back.' We haven't seen him for months. (Police, 451)

In this case, the local community representatives contacted the venue owners to inform them about who had booked their rooms, and that they would withdraw their future custom if these meetings were allowed to take place. All of the bookings were cancelled. Alongside which, the leader of the group was being actively challenged whenever he tried to hold less formal street meetings. This is a compelling illustration of the power of Type Two co-production and how such innovations have developed under the auspices of the Prevent programme.

Although infrequent, other examples of interactions between formal and informal social control providers were evident. For example, in another city several community groups were empowered through some subtle assistance from the police, to help disrupt a proposed visit by a leading radical preacher. Police received intelligence that the English Defence League were proposing to hold a counter-demonstration at the time of the visit. Both police and Muslim community elders wanted to ensure that no confrontations took place that could be exploited by extremists on either side. Accordingly, the local Muslim groups set up public meetings and organized barbecues in order to:

> ...keep the young people away. Mainly, just for you know worrying about our young people getting involved and getting arrested...In the local park we had a football tournament, we had a BBQ...and family fun day. So it's basically trying to get the whole community out...we had over 100 people turn up that day. (Community, K)

These diversionary activities proved highly effective, successfully diffusing the evident potential for tension and confrontation.

Such initiatives were founded upon the work of a number of key individuals who played pivotal brokering roles between sources of formal and informal social control. Several of these individuals were professional community workers:

> Youth workers or community workers so this is the core people that it actually comes out from...the majority of the people don't know what's going on outside...We've got a lot of volunteers active in the community who are not actually paid workers or anything like that, but they just want to do things for their own family. (Community, K)

As this account makes clear, Prevent-based activities were not restricted to the professionals, many others were involved too. But what these professional community organizers provided was a core repository of 'soft' skills that are needed to network, coordinate and mobilize other interested actors in an effective manner. Bridging the activities of formal social control providers such as the police to the quantity and quality of community-based informal social control, reflects mounting evidence that the former plays an important role in propagating the latter. Notably, Sampson (2011) in an important revision to his prior studies on the role of collective efficacy in preventing crime, has recently identified that a supportive institutional framework in an area appears to provide an important scaffold around which effective citizen involvement and participation in solving local problems can grow.

There are affinities here with Sennett's (2012) notion of 'dialogic' engagement, drawn from his wider research into the necessary and sufficient conditions required for social groups from different backgrounds to cooperate and collaborate effectively with each other. Dialogic engagement involves the recognition of fundamental differences between potential collaborators, and the effort involved in negotiating ways to work together whilst acknowledging these differences. This approach Sennett contrasts with 'dialectic engagements' that seek a synthesis in the divergent views prior to any effective cooperation. As far as Sennett is concerned, dialogic engagement is the more difficult to achieve, but ultimately the more productive, viable, and sustainable in an era of multi-cultural and pluralistic politics. The relevance to the current essay is that those areas where Prevent was observed to be more effective, had adopted dialogic ways of working. That is, there was an acknowledgement on all sides that different parties may want and need different things to happen, but ultimately there was a shared mutual interest in trying to inhibit extremist violence.

It is important not to overstate the prevalence of this co-productive approach to countering terrorism. It remains a minority position. The more established covert approaches associated with 'high policing' units continue to predominate and consume the majority of funding. That said, the significance of the sorts of innovation described earlier should not be neglected as they denote how the challenge of Al-Qaeda affiliated terrorism has caused revisions to aspects of how police conceive and enact aspects of their role. This instigation of a more overt and preventatively oriented approach to managing terrorist risks and threats is just one way in which the institutional effects of 9/11 have been made manifest.

Surveillance, Culture, and the 'See Through Self'

To this point, the discussion has focused upon the direct effects of 9/11 and associated events upon the conduct of counter-terrorism. There are, however, a wider set of additional linked institutional effects that can be charted over the past decade. These include, within academia, a significant invigoration of terrorism studies as an interdisciplinary subject area attracting contributions from a wide variety of backgrounds (Weston and Innes, 2010). There have also been a growing number of cultural artefacts produced, including films, novels, and plays, that have crafted representations of social life, identity, and order in the post-9/11 environment. These have frequently projected a dystopic vision, suggesting that in the quest to attain a semblance of security from terrorist risks and threats, we have sacrificed the other important public goods of liberty and privacy.

A particular focus for such debates has been the permutation of surveillance technologies and their embedding into the routines of everyday life. Indeed, challenged by the intelligence failure to identify the plot to bomb the airliners in 2001, the decision by the US government to significantly increase the capacity of their agencies to monitor and analyse all forms of electronic communication was one key strategic reaction. Initially packaged under the 'Orwellian' moniker of 'Total Information Awareness', this was quickly revised to become the 'Terrorism Information Awareness' programme, the point being that, confronted by a profound uncertainty about the contours of the risks and threats posed by Al-Qaeda affiliated terrorism, a more comprehensive monitoring and tracking of electronic data trails promised much. Consequently, under the auspices of these programmes, a significant increase in the capacity of state agencies to collect and analyse vast quantities of electronic data was established.

The extent of this investment has latterly been revealed by the leaks about PRISM and the US National Security Agency (NSA) to *The Guardian* by Edward Snowden. PRISM is a clandestine mass electronic surveillance programme that has been in operation since 2007. It collects stored data on internet communications by making demands to Internet Service Providers. In this it is augmented by ECHELON which is a signals intelligence collection and analysis network spanning intelligence agencies in Australia, Canada, New Zealand, the UK, and the US. This software system focuses upon the interception of telephone calls, faxes, and emails. The point about the investment in these monitoring and surveillance technologies is that it has been both material and moral. Materially, to make these systems work has required vast additional resources. But accompanying this and allied to it, there has also been a moral investment in such systems and processes. Implementation has required a belief that such an approach is both an effective and justified way of seeking to counter terrorist threats, given the wider implications they have for citizens' privacy.

Generally, surveillance can be conducted in three principal modes. 'Targeted surveillance' focuses explicitly upon individuals or groups where other intelligence gives rise to suspicions that they might be involved in illegal or harmful acts. In the post-9/11 environment however, a lot of public debate has focused upon 'profiling surveillance'. This subjects individuals to monitoring and tracking on the grounds that some aspects of their personal background, or behaviour, fits with a set of 'risky characteristics' that have been identified from analysis or a precursor dataset. This has proven contentious because of its discriminatory consequences for people who might be erroneously put under surveillance, and doubts about the validity and accuracy of the predictions and 'sorting' decisions made. Finally, there is 'mass surveillance' founded upon harvesting massive volumes of communications data, and using computerized data mining algorithms to process and interpret them. Compared with the 'targeted' and 'profiling'-based logics, mass surveillance approaches expose far greater numbers of people to monitoring and tracking. Much of the concern expressed about the activities of the National Security Agency in the US, GCHQ in the UK, and other intelligence agencies following the Snowden leaks, was how they had surreptitiously implemented forms of mass surveillance through establishing a major international data-mining infrastructure. Critically, this appears to have included some form of tacit partnership with the multinational corporations whose activities underpin much of the internet and World Wide Web.

But in terms of understanding the patterns of institutional reaction to major signal events, the key analytic point here concerns how government investments in data monitoring and analytics were coherent with broader and deeper trends in society. Attempts to develop and use an enhanced surveillance infrastructure to better manage terrorism risks are part and parcel of wider shifts in the governance of social life. As electronic communications and social media have become an increasingly important component of how social life is conducted and negotiated, so a range of powerful actors have sought to enhance their abilities to collect, analyse, and interpret such data for multiple purposes.

Predating 2001, there had already been major investments in CCTV systems in the UK for the purposes of trying to prevent and solve violent and property crime. More recently, many private corporations have significantly increased their ability to manipulate 'big data' for the purposes of increasing their sales and maximizing their profitability. It is not just state intelligence and security agencies that have increased their surveillance capacities; they have been at least matched in terms of scope and scale by private sector data-matching and aggregation.

Some sense of this effort is provided by Marwick (2013) who cites marketing information from one of the leading US firms involved in this field, claiming they hold around 1500 separate 'data points' on every US consumer. The essential craft of this work is to use data-mining algorithms to match data from a range of disparate sources, to create consumer profiles about who people are, how they think, and most importantly how they are likely to behave. Incisively, Marwick (2013) points out that although the prevalent discourse is of 'big data' analytics, these big data are actually composites of lots of 'little data', some of which can be highly personal.

Although corporate and state surveillance activities involve very different motivations, these private and public sector developments should not be construed as entirely separate. In addition to the kinds of cooperation that appear to have been given to the NSA and GCHQ, policing and security agencies are rapidly becoming a key client base for corporate data-mining tools. By way of example, in the UK, most police forces have subscribed to the MOSAIC platform which combines consumer records with recorded crime and social deprivation data to construct neighbourhood profiles that can be used to tailor the style of policing delivered in particular areas. The value of having access to the kinds of data collected by the private sector and the powerful algorithms they have developed to extract interpretations from them, is increasingly recognized by those involved in all kinds of crime prevention work.

Investments in the state surveillance apparatus for the purposes of terrorism risk management should therefore be understood as an accelerant of wider and deeper trends, rather than an entirely novel trajectory of development. Developing this line of argument, Harvey Molotch (2012) suggests that one of the key points of intersection is the ways former military equipment manufacturers have identified new markets for their technologies as we attempt to manage the sense of insecurity that pervades late-modern social life. He documents how the threat of terrorism has been used to justify and account for the introduction of new surveillance technologies into an array of sites, particularly airports and subways, that are marked by 'ambiguous danger'. In such sites, previously mundane objects have been translated into signifiers of threat (Neyland, 2009). For instance, following the interdicted plot to bring down a passenger aircraft using liquid explosives disguised in a soft drinks bottle, taking quantities of any liquid onto planes was banned by the aviation authorities. A previously accepted practice was redefined as a security threat. A consequence of this is that 'rebooted' and newly reconfigured threat detection technologies are required to identify these newly risky objects and their owners.

Molotch's (2012) argument is that confronted with the challenges of an ever expanding litany of ambiguous dangers, we have been persuaded to become increasingly dependent upon 'technological fixes' to manage our anxieties and uncertainties. Purveyed, more often than not by firms previously focused upon selling kit to the military, they actually corrode those facets of social life that might actually make us safer and feel safer. For one of the fundamental problems of surveillance technologies is that they institutionalize perceptions of risk and a lack of trust. In effect, by virtue of their presence and operation they inherently signal some form of problem pertaining to a situation.

These subtleties were illustrated in one of the areas where fieldwork was conducted. Some months prior to the data collection starting, a terrorist plot to kidnap and murder an individual was uncovered by the authorities involving a number of men from the area. This was the latest manifestation of concerns that the authorities had about the activities of a number of individuals living there. Reflecting this, a decision was taken to introduce a public CCTV network into the area to support counter-terrorism operations. It generated an extremely negative public reaction when it was revealed in 2010 that, what had been presented publicly as a general community safety initiative of the Safer Birmingham Partnership, was in fact being underwritten by funding from the West Midlands Counter-Terrorism Unit.

The extent to which this attempt to introduce a sophisticated surveillance system equipped with automatic number plate recognition technology undermined other good work by Prevent officers in the area, is described in the following extract from an interview with a resident in the area:

> We felt totally betrayed. Well we couldn't walk away because we'd worked quite hard and the only way to deal with it was to stand and fight it, and deal with the situation…The relationship between the police and the community was severed, you know there was a void left there, it was like total mistrust. (Community, 2654–04)

As is clearly described, from the point of view of the local community, the uncovering of the 'real' purpose of the camera system confirmed suspicions that really police were trying to spy on them. But at the same time, this episode provides some support for Molotch's contention about some of the unintended consequences of the proliferation of surveillance technologies and how they can undermine other security generating efforts.

Undoubtedly the enhancement of the infrastructure for monitoring and intercepting electronic communications of different kinds was partly triggered by the events of 9/11, 7/7, and other similar occurrences. However, to attribute these developments in the prevalence and distribution of surveillance wholly to problems of crime and terrorism is misleading. That the adoption of such monitoring technologies was deemed acceptable and politically permissible was because they 'went with the grain' of a broader pattern of social development. Whilst there have been legitimate concerns expressed about the decline of social trust, privacy, and liberty induced by the diffusion of powerful mechanisms of surveillance, these are all symptoms of the emergence of an essentially new information environment.

That our collective constructions of what constitutes 'public' and 'private' are correlates of the wider media ecology in which we are situated was noted by Joshua Meyrowitz (1985) some years ago now. His thesis was that via its ability to engage in affect-laden forms of communication, broadcast mass media was altering our very conceptions about the location of the boundaries between public and private information. These are patterns of development that have been accelerated by the ubiquity of mobile and social media enabled devices, and especially Web 2.0 technologies. The latter are especially significant in light of their support for user-generated content and the capacity to self-publish material online available to anyone who chooses to access it.

In the context of this essay, the key point is that in the post-9/11 environment the social dynamics and mechanics of surveillance and the new information environment are complex. Under the auspices of trying to manage risks of terrorism that are rather uncertain in their form and display a proclivity to shape-shift, state agencies have increased their ability to proactively harvest data from a variety of sources to inform their work. At the same time, they have been afforded the opportunity to more passively collect and 'mine' huge volumes of data that are generated by virtue of citizens engaging in a variety of other online social interactions; activities that leave potentially revealing electronic data trails. A lot of what might be considered private information is being voluntarily 'given away' by people participating in online social networks. Any cursory glance at a series of Facebook 'walls', or the electonic chatter taking place via tools like Twitter, immediately conveys how people have become accustomed to revealing their intimate thoughts, feelings, and behaviours to a social audience that also inhabits these digital spaces. These are increasingly accessible to, and used by, state agencies and private corporations.

In this sense, one of the more subtle but highly consequential institutional legacy effects of the attack on the Twin Towers has been its role in inducing a shift in the ethics of social identity formation. So where, for previous generations, Charles Horton Cooley (1902) could talk of 'the looking glass self' to describe how people recursively constructed their self and social identities from the imagined impressions they have of how others view them. Instead today, such relations are governed by a more 'see through self'.

In an era suffused with surveillance technologies that track and generate data on different aspects of our interactions and behaviours, people increasingly orientate themselves to others on the basis of a see through self. There is an expectation that they will be observed and monitored by others, and that it is hard to step out of such arrangements. Co-opting these arrangements, state agencies can use them to track movements by monitoring the geo-tagged devices that we carry with us and by accessing the accounts of users' thoughts, feelings, and actions that they voluntarily post on these social media sites. Corporations can 'mine' and combine different data traces to provide behavioural insights into these users' motivations and conduct that they may not have been consciously aware of. The result is that swathes of social life are effectively being rendered more 'transparent'. Consequently, social relations are worked out in a situation where potentially discreditable and stigmatizing information about our own and others' past behaviour or opinions is easily discoverable and knowable. An awareness of the ongoing possibility for others to be aware of these discreditable aspects of our social identities conditions social interaction, and the ways individuals and institutions act towards each other.

Whilst the recent emergence of such conditions is undoubtedly of general interest, introducing a discussion of developments in electronic surveillance, alongside changes in 'on the ground' counter-terrorism practices is intended to make a wider analytic point. This concerns how major signal crimes like 9/11 can induce a multiplicity of complex effects upon how institutions think, feel, and behave. The consequences of such events can reach across different domains of social life. The trajectory of development that can be observed in relation to electronic surveillance shows how such effects acquire traction when they 'go with the grain' of wider social forces. Enhancement of the ability to monitor and track electronic channels of communication would have happened anyway as a correlate of more and more of social life shifting online. But this has been accelerated by the desire of states to use this as part of their wider counter-terrorism effort. As such, whilst the emergence of an ethic of the see through self cannot be attributed directly to 9/11, it is part of a wider set of social consequences that have been induced by such events.

Conclusion: The Arc of Social Control

Every era has moments that come to define them. Every generation acts to establish those events that collectively clarify who they are and what they are not. In the early part of the twenty-first century a number of our key moments and collectively defining stories have pivoted around events of politically motivated violence. But they are not limited to these. More generally, high profile signal crimes have played a key role in provoking and inducing changes to the interactional and institutional orders of social life.

The influence of signal crimes upon institutional reform processes becomes particularly acute when some form of institutional failure is present. For example, in the field of social work, the failures identified in the cases of Maria Colwell in 1973, Victoria Climbie in 2000, and Peter Connelly, are all signal crimes that had profound impacts upon the institutional response to vulnerable looked-after children. Similarly, the multiple fatal shootings by Michael Ryan in the town of Hungerford in 1987 and Thomas Hamilton at a school in Dunblane in 1996, both of whom used licensed weapons, contributed to sharp changes to the regulation of firearms ownership in the United Kingdom.

There are many other incidents that could be cited as signal crimes that induced institutional effects. The list would be very long indeed. But the more intriguing point is that, drawing back from the situational detail pertaining to the specifics of individual incidents, these signal events seem to replicate similar patterns of reaction. Following initial discovery of the incident, there is widespread shock and alarm about the harm perpetrated. It then transpires, at some point, that key institutions missed opportunities to prevent the harm, requiring some form of formal inquisition. The sense of public disquiet that this causes is fed by wider cultural representations. This may then lead to wider and deeper changes to the social institutions involved.

This institutional reaction pattern can be conceptualized as forming an 'arc of social control'. The initial incident that surfaces and highlights problematic and troubling issues signals the need for innovation in the conduct of social control. As adaptation and reform is brought forward, so it is rendered highly visible and the focus for public debate and contention. As time passes, the contingencies and necessities of acting in complex real situations refine and partially reshapes what is actually done in practice. Consequently, with the passing of time, the level of public visibility and contention subsides and the former innovation settles down as part of the future institutionalized reactions that are provided to problems of this kind.

Attending to institutional effects in this manner starts to unpack the complex and intricate ways in which signal crimes can influence the interactional and institutional orderings of social life. These effects can be widespread, traversing cultural, social, and state institutions; as has been illustrated by the case study of developments in counter-terrorism policy and practice. But the fundamental point is that the effects experienced by institutions are similar in form to those upon individuals. Powerful signal crimes clearly possess the capacity to change how key social institutions think, feel, and act.

VI

Control Signals

At the side of the road leading north out of the city of Chichester on the south coast of England, there lies a sun bleached memorial, the inscription on which is now indecipherable. This is the Smugglers' Stone. It sits near an area known locally as 'Brandy Hole Woods'. Legend has it that groups of smugglers would use this area as a place to store their contraband in times past, hence the name. As such, it confirms how the legacy of some crimes can echo across time to subtly but indelibly shape our contemporary cognitive landscapes. The stone marks the location where, in 1749, several members of 'the Hawkhurst Gang' were led to the gallows and hung.

Belying the contemporary assumption that mobility and networked organization are somehow wholly new characteristics of serious criminality, throughout the 1740s the activities of the gang ranged along the South Coast of England from Deal in Kent across to Portsmouth. They were widely feared and it was rumoured at the time that the gang could raise 500 men to their cause within an hour. The execution memorialized in Chichester followed a particularly brutal double murder committed by members of the gang.

On 5 October 1747 the Hawkhurst Gang, together with a group of affiliates including about 30 other local smugglers, decided to mount a raid on Poole Customs House, where contraband that had been seized from them some weeks earlier by the authorities was being stored. The raiders encountered no resistance and made off with two tonnes of tea. To celebrate their success, on their return journey to West Sussex they stopped to breakfast in Fordingbridge, before dividing up and distributing their bounty across the Southern counties of England.[1]

It was not until the next year that one of the smugglers was caught. William Galley, a Customs Officer, and Daniel Chater, a resident of Fordingbridge, who

---

[1] A more detailed narrative of the crimes and their antecedents can be found in Platt (2011).

had witnessed the smugglers together during their return journey, were called to give evidence at the trial. However, fearing the consequences of their testimony and that they would identify other members of the gang, the two men were intercepted on their journey to court by the smugglers, and brutally tortured and killed. In due course, seven of the smugglers were apprehended and on 16 January 1749 were sentenced to hang the next day, at a special court established in the Guildhall, Chichester. One man named Jackson died in Chichester jail overnight. The other six were executed as instructed by the court. Reports from the time record that a crowd of thousands turned up to witness the hangings.

Once dead, the bodies of the condemned were taken down and put on public display at strategically selected sites where they would be highly visible. Bodies were hung in chains on the Portsmouth Road near Rake, at Horsemonden, at Rook's Hill near Chichester, and two at Selsey Bill on the coast. At the spot where they were hung, outside of Northgate, the Smugglers' Stone was also erected, inscribed with the following message:

> Near this place was buried the body of William Jackson a prescribed smuggler...As a memorial to posterity and a warning to this and succeeding generations, this stone is erected AD1749.

In an era predating a regular and organized criminal justice apparatus, where the 'touches' of the state on the lives of citizens were far less frequent and intense than they are today, with limited literacy levels across the general population, and constrained methods of mass communication, these rituals of punishment were a way of signalling the willingness and capacity of the state to protect social order. Such punishments were crafted as representations through which the state could project its authority and legitimacy. The state sanctioned deaths of the smugglers was being used to send a warning message. In this regard it exemplifies how, as Garland (2010: 132) describes:

> The state execution, with its elaborate cruelties and ceremonials, was designed to teach political lessons to enemies and to impress the state's power on the population.

But in many ways the uniquely fascinating aspect of this story is not the execution, nor its public nature or popularity. Rather, it was the deliberate act by the officials of taking the cadavers down from where the punishment was exacted and their strategic relocation to several places where they could be displayed in such a way that their public visibility would be maximized. The signal that the authorities were seeking to send was not haphazard, but reflected a deliberate intent. Specific actions were undertaken in relation to displaying the corpses of the condemned in an effort to boost the power of the signal. The effort was designed to showcase the state as a source of security and social control at a time when this was manifestly precarious.

At a moment in history where the internal capacity of the state to actively propagate and manage social order was circumscribed, the reach of mass media limited, governmental authorities faced problems of how to communicate with the mass of the population about the workings and functions of law. The drama of high profile punishments was one mechanism by which such limitations could be overcome. As such, this historical narrative conveys a deeper truth about social control; the extent to which it is predicated upon communication. Projecting the visibility of acts of social control in the way previously described was an elemental form of control signal.

These are qualities that have not been resigned to history. They remain part of the design and delivery of contemporary criminal justice interventions. For example, the notion that punishments should communicate beyond those being punished is intrinsic to theories of general and specific deterrence (Kennedy, 2008). It remains common for sentences being handed down from the bench, particularly in relation to heinous or innovative crimes, to be accompanied by comments from the judge to the effect that the punishment is intended to convey to onlookers the gravity of the harm or offence caused.

A control signal can be defined as an act of social control sending a message to an audience. This messaging can be intentional but also an unintended product of social control interventions. The significance of the control signal concept is that the communicative work and properties of social control have rather been overshadowed by a focus upon instrumental behaviour change in the literature. Where such considerations have been included within analyses of social control, rather than cast as intrinsic to how the control itself is accomplished, they have tended to be discussed in terms of symbolic meanings and thus reduced to secondary considerations compared with the material effects of the action. As a result, the extent to which effective and efficient social control depends upon and pivots around communication has been neglected. The defining idea of a control signals analysis is that the material effects of a social control action or intervention are irrevocably dependent upon processes of tacit and explicit communication. It is to this issue that the current essay attends.

Given these imperatives, selecting policing as the empirical and conceptual vehicle to investigate the intricacies associated with the communicative properties of social control is both deliberate and important. This is because many of the most influential studies of social control have derived from investigations of control in carceral settings, most notably prisons and mental asylums. These settings are in effect relatively closed and bounded social systems, features that have implications for what dimensions of control are illuminated and which are shaded from view. Policing is interesting in this respect, because it is about the conduct of social control in communities, in more 'open' non-bounded settings. Conducting social control in these 'wilder' less controlled situations induces different problems and challenges.

In what follows, the discussion attends both to social controls as reactions to crime and disorder, but also public reactions to these control events themselves. Adopting this approach leads to an important distinction between 'signals of control' and 'signals to control'. The latter are intended to protect the social order in some way. They are designed to effect control over problematic or troublesome conduct. Signals of control, in contrast, are the products of any such acts or interventions.

The focus in the opening sections of the essay is upon how policing, in the broad sense, communicates signals to communities that serve to shape sensations of safety and security. Data drawn from the 18 research sites where members of the public discussed their experiences, perceptions, and attitudes towards policing and community-based informal social control in some detail, is used to map the principal forms of control signal that can be identified. It is shown how these control signals can be: positive or negative in their effects; targeted or unfocused in terms of whom they are directed towards; deliberately manufactured or more organic in relation to how they occur. They can have diverse objectives, seeking to influence potential or actual perpetrators, victims or a wider public audience. Related to which, the effects of specific control signals may not last long and may fade rapidly, especially when they are over-ridden by signals emanating from other events. This is especially the case when signification contests arise between more and less positive aspects of social control. In turn, this raises the possibility that, in a historical moment marked by declining public trust in state institutions, the potential for control signals to have positive social effects, bolstering security, may be becoming more circumscribed.

Thinking in these ways opens up the means by which the power of control signals to influence levels of public security and reassurance are conditioned by wider cultural forces. How interventions conducted by police and other institutions of social control are seen and interpreted depends, in part, upon the ways individuals, communities, and citizens think, feel, and act in relation to these institutions more generally. Individual control signals do not occur in isolation from the problems they are enacted to solve, nor indeed are they separate from many other control interventions. Rather, individual control signals interact and intermingle with a range of other influences upon public experiences, perceptions, and judgements about safety and security. It is these more abstract and theoretical considerations that dominate the latter sections of the essay. It closes by turning to reflect upon how acknowledging the communicative properties and qualities of social control creates an impulse for a reformulation of the ways that it is understood to work in the fabrication of social order.

Control Signals and Their Effects

Spooling forward a few hundred years from the executions marked by the Smugglers' Stone and shifting substantive focus from one mode of social control (punishment) to another (policing) it is striking how similar communicative processes can be observed in terms of the interactional and institutional patterns of social control. Since the mid-eighteenth century the capacity of states to uphold and enforce law has expanded considerably through the institutionalization of the police and allied agencies of criminal justice and social regulation. Intriguingly though, much of what the police do, shares similar social functions to the attempts to increase the visibility of capital punishment described previously. That is, through their actions they are involved in projecting the symbolic authority and legitimacy of the state to manage contraventions of social order, using their legally endowed powers to do so (see also Manning, 1997). Police work is suffused with the transmission of control signals designed to deter people from engaging in acts that are defined as criminal or breach conventions of order, whilst other aspects of policing are intended to convey reassurance and protection from risks, threats, and harms deriving from the conduct of other people.

The point of a control signals analysis though, is to move beyond these generalities and connect particular practices and interventions with specific perceptual, attitudinal, emotional, and behavioural effects. That this is possible is confirmed from data collected during 2011 in London via a survey of approximately 600 residents from one borough. As part of a series of questions they were asked 'Is there anything that has happened in the past year to increase your confidence in the Metropolitan Police?' to which they were invited to offer a response. In effect this question starts with a distinct effect—'increased public confidence' and then seeks to identify the causes of this. Because the answers were provided in free text form rather than structured by pre-determined response categories, a degree of interpretation is required. But overall the majority of responses pivoted around three key themes. The first concerned aspects of the work of the local Safer Neighbourhoods Team, including the level of visible patrolling and engagement they were providing.[2] The second group of responses mentioned responding to crime and disorder, but with a crucial caveat stressing that it was how they were treated by officers that mattered to people as much as whether any perpetrator was apprehended.[3]

The third set of responses was more interesting. The research site was one of London's less crime-prone Boroughs, but unusually that year there had been a non-domestic murder that had attracted considerable mass media attention. In their replies to the question that they were posed, a sizeable proportion of respondents recorded that the professional way in which police managed this murder had a distinct positive influence upon their views of the police. The police response to the homicide had radiated out across the area to touch far more people than were directly connected to the crime itself. It had acted as a control signal.

Control signals are clearly present in the aftermath of many heinous crimes and are programmed into aspects of how police departments respond to such incidents. When stranger murders or the violent deaths of children occur, the scale and intensity of the police response is often intended to symbolize the

---

[2] Safer Neighbourhoods was the Metropolitan Police Service's brand of the national Neighbourhood Policing programme.

[3] That these aspects of police practice should generate increased confidence is consistent with much available research evidence, and as such is not so surprising (Tuffin et al., 2006).

moral opprobrium attached to such acts, at least as much as being practically necessary for identifying and detaining any suspects (Innes, 2003a). It is now also
standard practice following such crimes for the police to introduce high visibility
patrols in the area surrounding the crime scene to signal their response and
reassure the public when their insecurity might be heightened.

That major crimes afford vehicles for the police to send signals to the public
about their capacities and capabilities to exert control have been especially
sharply figured in some recent developments relating to 'cold case reviews'
(CCRs) of unsolved murders. CCRs emerged originally in the late 1980s/early
1990s, with many police forces establishing small squads or teams to specialize in
the task of looking back over past case files to try and identify new 'investigative
opportunities' (Allsop, 2013). Although there is not a prescribed methodology
for conducting CCRs, many forces now pursue a fairly standardized approach to
them. This typically involves each case being re-looked at every few years in order
to audit the original decision-making processes used in the first investigation,
and to establish whether anything different could be done in order to progress
the state of the knowledge held by the police. In many cases where new developments have been made through the auspices of a CCR, this has been driven by
new technological developments, and the potential for improved investigation
and detection afforded by socio-technological assemblages such as the National
DNA Database in the UK (Innes and Clarke, 2009). There is a relatively small yet
highly significant collection of cases where suspects have been identified and
convicted as a result of work conducted by a cold case review. This includes murders where individuals had been falsely accused and imprisoned, and cases with
the highest public profile imaginable, such as the Stephen Lawrence murder.

When developments take place in cases such as these, supplementary to the important consequences for justice and for the victims' families, there are equally significant implications for policing and social order. For what is signalled by the
solving of 'old and cold' cases is the ability of the police to mobilize 'awesome' scientific technologies, capable of connecting perpetrators of heinous acts to their
crimes through analysis of microscopic traces of dust, in order to secure justice despite many years having passed. They provide moments of 'shock and awe' policing
in terms of just what can be accomplished in terms of ensuring people are made to
account for their crimes. It would be misleading though, to only focus upon these
high profile control signals. Similar processes of symbolic communication are routinely instantiated within more mundane and routine forms of policing.

Patrol, Visibility, Reassurance

There are periodic debates about the significance and importance of police visibility and presence.[4] Over four decades of opinion polling now clearly evidences

---

[4] For a summary of these debates see Fielding's (1995) book on community policing.

that public value is attached to a uniformed policing presence at a local level. What thinking in terms of control signals provides is a way of articulating just how and why particular forms of police presence may be valued by communities.

The National Reassurance Policing Programme that ran between 2003–5 across 16 trial sites in England provided a concerted effort to explore what effects policing had upon levels of neighbourhood security. Overall, the research identified that the control signals emanating from the actions of police officers could incur both positive and negative effects. Indeed, one of the principal findings was just how sensitive public audiences were to fairly subtle shifts in the public presentation of policing in general, as well as the particularities of specific interventions.

For example, the following statement was fairly representative of the complaints that members of the public voiced:

> Oh I don't know, the police are now like this invisible thing that fly round in cars. (F&W068)

Sentiments such as these are important in implying that from a community viewpoint police can be visible, but effectively not present. Uniformed foot patrol, where officers were visible and accessible for interactions with members of the public, were the kind of police presence that registered most positively with communities. Indeed, under the auspices of the experimental policing programme, the public were quick to pick up on a shift towards more foot patrol:

> There's a progress that's happening at the moment where the police are moving around here and you do actually see them lately, cos you didn't used to. I mean, if that progresses steadily like it seems to have done in the last 12 months, that would be great. You feel as if something is being done on your behalf... (Ash216)

This quotation starts to illuminate how control signals work in a similar way to other kinds of signal event, with a connection between expression, content, and effect. In the interview, the signal 'expression' is the increased police visibility and presence, whilst the 'effect' of this is the sense of 'progress' and local improvement being made.[5]

The importance of signalling the visible presence of control has been embodied most self-consciously in the figure of the Police Community Support Officer (PCSO). Introduced around the turn of the millennium, as non-warranted providers of several key policing services, these figures were explicitly designed to focus upon performing a reassurance function through visible patrolling and engaging communities. Because they possess only limited powers (they cannot arrest people) the PCSO role has been controversial. For example, the *Daily Mail*

---

[5] This passage confirms that the principal analytic components associated with the signal crimes perspective, namely 'expression', 'content', and 'effect', can be diagnostically applied to acts of social control.

has continued to refer to them as 'plastic police', periodically running stories that apparently show how they are poor substitutes for 'proper' police constables. In many neighbourhoods however, the reception has been more positive, at least where the PCSO possesses the right kinds of soft skills and personality traits.

In the town of St Helen's on Merseyside, for example, when young people aged 14–18 were interviewed about their relations with the police, they were far more positive about their interactions with the PCSOs than they were with the local police constables. As they described it, many of the response policing officers were not much older than the young people themselves. As a consequence of which, it was felt that they needed to demonstrate their authority by being surly and rude in their interactions with the local youngsters. In contrast to this, the two local PCSOs were older middle-aged women with children of their own. In the accounts of the young people, interactions with the PCSOs were far more relaxed and they achieved much more through 'soft policing' methods than the 'hard policing' that typified the stance of the police constables.

The 'doseage effect' of police visibility

Police visibility is important in signalling to communities the potential for formal social control to be available to help protect a social order if and when it is breached. However, it is important not to over-simplify the relationship between visible social control and its effects. For example, when PCSOs were first introduced in Birmingham the public reaction was initially positive. However, this waned rapidly. When asked what accounted for their change of heart, several residents said that they were just walking up and down and not doing anything to solve local problems.

This points to two refinements required in understanding control signals. First, that visibility is as much cognitive as it is physical. The extent to which police and other agents register in public consciousness depends upon what they are seen to be doing (eg, interacting and engaging with local communities), rather than just being present and visible. Second, there are limits to visibility. Indeed, there is evidence from the fieldwork of a 'doseage' effect in relation to the visibility of policing. Too much police visibility can have deleterious consequences for community confidence and cohesion, just as too little police presence can. The fundamental contours of this were surfaced during a simple empirical test of public perceptions of police visibility.

The test involved two sets of large photographs of police officers on foot patrol. In one set the officers were dressed in fairly traditional blue tunics and helmets. In the second set of images the officers were in fluorescent high visibility jackets. Across the two sets of pictures the different images varied the number of officers involved, between one, two, and four officers. Researchers then took these images out onto the local high street and showed them in different orders to a random selection of members of the public. The results were striking. All of the pictures involving more than two officers elicited negative reactions. When asked why they responded negatively, people's responses were that having so many officers present signalled to them that there must be an emergency.

Precisely this reaction was replicated during some of the fieldwork when increases in officers were introduced. Where this occurred, people would say things like:

> Although a heavy police presence curtails any trouble, or the likelihood of trouble, it gives you the impression that there must be something going on here—look at all the police about. (StH118)

Perceptions of officers' uniform in the pictures added a further layer of nuance to public responses. Around half of those questioned expressed a preference for the image featuring one or two officers dressed in the fluorescent clothing on the grounds that it rendered them more visible. But a similar number of people suggested that the high visibility jackets connoted an emergency situation, preferring the images of police in their more traditional blue uniforms.

The general tenor of these results was confirmed during a natural experiment occurring whilst the fieldwork was being conducted. In two separate research sites homicides occurred during the period when the research teams were interviewing members of the public about their neighbourhood security concerns. Consistent with their standard operating procedures for homicide, in both areas the police significantly increased levels of uniform patrol. In one of the sites this produced positive reactions from the members of the public when they were questioned by researchers. But in the other site a very different negative reaction was elicited. The critical difference between the two sites being that in the first, the police explained to local residents what was happening and why they would see more police patrolling. In the second area, no such explanations or justifications were provided.

The logics of perceptual intervention

Consistent with such findings, Ditton and Innes (2005) identify a need to study far more carefully the logics of what they term 'perceptual interventions'. A perceptual intervention is a measure designed to alter both what is seen and how it is seen. That is, they are intended to change how individuals and groups see the world around them, rather than just being concerned with a material situation. The natural field experiment described previously is an example of a perceptual intervention by police inasmuch as the increased presence was not designed to help detect the crime, but convey an enhanced sense of protection to local communities at a moment of risk.

Similar logics pervade a number of the practices and processes associated with neighbourhood policing. The point is that by promoting neighbourhood security, perceptual interventions can leverage increases in peoples' willingness to enact informal social control to solve minor conflicts. It is here that the 'community support' function identified in the label of the 'Police Community

Support Officer' becomes important. Their role is not the same as a police officer; they are involved in the provision of services that can underpin and buttress levels of community activity. As such, much of what they do should be concerned with the supply of perceptual interventions.

Such interventions are not, of course, the only source of control signals. They interact and sometimes compete with other everyday policing interventions. How these convey messages to a wider populace are exemplified in the following story told by a resident from Colville ward in London:

> I saw on Portobello Road, I saw them in action in a very good way, where a very big, a very aggressive black guy was...he was basically screaming abuse at two police officers who were remarkably calm and remarkably sort of together in dealing with him...so I think the police officers were very good in calming the situation, which I think in the area can become explosive quite quickly. (Col201)

In many ways this is an ideal type of the police role, acting professionally to diffuse a situation threatening violence. It is resonant with many of the themes that classic accounts of the police function have taken to be the defining capacities and capabilities of democratic policing. But what this account particularly neatly encapsulates is the ways that such mundane policing actions communicate messages to a wider social audience. This man, telling the story after all, was not involved in the encounter, he was an observer, an onlooker. But the effect that it had upon him was to frame a positive perception of the police.

Woven into the preceding account is an important theme about the treatment of the suspect by the police that coincides with wider currents in the policing literature. This encounter, located in an area with a history of tense police–community relations and interactions, was important to the interviewee in respect of how the police treated the aggressor. There is increasing interest amongst many scholars in interrogating the ways that process and treatment variables profoundly impact upon aggregate levels of public trust and confidence (Jackson et al., 2012). Informed by theories of procedural justice these accounts are building a strong case about the extent to which the overarching public legitimacy of the institution of policing is tied to whether police treat members of the public fairly across the variety of ways in which they interact with them (Bottoms and Tankebe, 2012).

Consequently there is much interest in improving the quality of police–public interactions, and with good reason. Skogan's (2006) quantitative analysis suggests that it takes between 9 and 14 good encounters with the police to compensate and offset the damage to public attitudes resulting from one bad interaction. But caution is needed in terms of what can be achieved through establishing procedurally fair policing. It is perfectly plausible, for instance, that whilst at the micro-level each interaction between police and a community member involves fair treatment and good interactional skills in managing it by the police, cumulatively police are reproducing the disadvantage of that group by surveilling members of the community at a rate disproportionate to other communities. Equivocations of this sort notwithstanding, it is undoubtedly the case as Loader (2006) asserts, that procedurally just and fair treatment of citizens by the police conveys important signals to them about their sense of belonging to and membership of a democratic polity.

A similar instance of unexceptional policing having important effects upon a social audience is recalled in the following extract where the interviewee describes a pacification effect derived simply from the presence of the police. It is critical to this account that the police don't actively need to do anything:

> Me mum was with me one day and we got on the bus and one of them [a police officer] got on the bus and it was around the time of day when the kids come home from school. And they was all as quiet as anything. It was lovely going home knowing that you was safe on the bus. (F&W083)

This reassurance effect appears to be strongly connected to the general value ascribed by the public to police presence. In some of the areas studied this seemed to relate to dealing with problems as they arise, but in other neighbourhoods the reaction was more about having someone available and accessible should issues occur.

What is interesting about this and many other similar examples detailed in the interviews is how the reassurance effect is not a deliberate outcome of police activity, but more organically derived. This contrasts with those occasions where the police deliberately set out to design interventions intended to signal the presence of control. Many police forces periodically undertake special campaigns involving high profile raids on the premises of multiple suspects. These interventions are often explicitly choreographed for the mass media with the intention that they should showcase vigorous police activity to a wide audience. In this sense the control signal can be said to be deliberately manufactured.

Innes (2003b) distinguishes between organic and manufactured social control as part of an effort to circumvent some of the limitations of established conceptualizations of formal and informal social control. Manufactured social control is where the regulation or control of troublesome or problematic behaviours is the intended outcome of an intervention. In contrast to this, organic social control refers to where enhanced social control is a secondary benefit of an action originally performed for another purpose. Applied to the task of disaggregating the communicative properties of social control actions, this distinction becomes particularly helpful in capturing the different ways in which control signals can shape perceptions, attitudes, and values.

Reception and Interpretation: Negative Control Signals

The critical difference between manufactured and organic control signals is between a message being sent and it emanating relatively naturally from an event.

In both cases there may be only low levels of 'signal coherence', where audience interpretations differ as to the message that is being transmitted by the event. Recognition of the fact that there might be multiple interpretations of a control event, and more significantly, that control signals can trigger effects other than those they were intended to have, is vital to enriching our understanding of public reactions to policing, punishment, and social control. Even manufactured control signals are not always positive in terms of enhancing security.

Control signals can be said to have 'negative effects' when they defray public conceptions of security, or damage public trust and confidence in institutions of the state. Where police and other institutions fail to protect the public in some way, or where they engage in wrongdoing that leads to miscarriages of justice, then negative control signals with significant legacy effects can occur. There are many examples of such events to choose from. The series of miscarriages of justice brought to light in the 1980s and similar cases since then; the failed investigation into the murder of Stephen Lawrence; and the more recent revelations about the institutionalized cover-up following the Hillsborough disaster; and activities of undercover police officers serving with the Metropolitan Police, are all sources of negative control signals. Both individually and collectively they have had decaying effects upon public perceptions and attitudes towards the police, as well as other institutions of the state.

But coherent with the general approach to the study of signal crimes, such negative signal events do not pertain just to high profile catastrophic failures. They exist also in the micro-dramas of control that occur in more everyday settings. The salient issues are rather neatly encapsulated in the following account where the interviewee is describing public responses to a drugs raid mounted by the police. In terms of interpreting their reactions and understanding why they read the police behaviours in this way, it is important to know that this was an area of London with longstanding and serious concerns about the impacts of drug dealing. Consequently, when the police raid was launched a number of the local residents turned out to observe, initially pleased that their concerns had been recognized and action was being taken. But as this respondent recalled, the impression management of how police were seen to be interacting with the individuals they arrested as they were led out of the crack house, totally changed community perceptions of what was occurring:

> I: I tell you what, one thing that was extremely annoying was to see the police laughing with the drug addicts...All smiling and interacting with them. Extremely annoying.
>
> R: Why?
>
> I: Because it felt like they were on their side. Everybody mentioned it. Everybody got annoyed, 'Just look at them, they're smiling at them', got annoyed. But when you think about it that's, what happens between the police and their regular clientele...But the perception, the community perception, was one of absolute fury. It seemed as if they were colluding in some way. (Col206)

The police officers were probably using interactional strategies with their arrestees to try and manage and defuse a potentially volatile situation. But from the point of view of the wider audience, they sent a rather different message:

> It sends you a signal that somehow it's acceptable to the police for that drug substance abuse to be allowed in the neighbourhood and I don't think they understood that. (Col206)

That police interventions can be read in this way, starts to highlight some of the subtleties and delicacies that are involved in terms of how control signals work positively and negatively simultaneously.

Policing is contentious work. As such, how police interventions are viewed is often finely balanced, depending upon situated histories and past events, as much as the nature of any action in the present time. This was the case on a housing estate in North West England where there was a lot of consternation about the activities of drug users and drug dealers. Their presence was perceived by other residents as having a massively detrimental impact upon quality of life, causing a lot of disorder and local crime. Police had long been aware of the drugs problems on the estate and sought to address it through high visibility, 'spectacular' raids. They were, in effect exemplifying the use of 'control signals' trying to send messages through their actions: to the law abiding, that they were tackling the problem; and to those participating in the drugs markets that they were closing in on them. However, more often than not this was not the signal received. This was due, in large part, to a series of failed police raids on the flat of a well-known drug dealer. Periodically, when this individual was 'targeted' police would speed into the estate in several vans, officers dressed in public order protective gear would leap out, and proceed to execute the search warrant. However, these raids were mostly unsuccessful and the police would leave empty handed, despite good intelligence that drugs were being dealt from the premises.

The reasons for these failures to find any illegal substances were revealed by a member of the public who had observed the police raids on several occasions. When interviewed, he told how, because there was only one route in and out of the estate, those living in the estate's high rise tower blocks had a natural vantage point from which they could observe any police arrival. He added that whenever they had drugs to sell, the male would stay in the flat 'dealing', whilst his female partner would sit in a car at the bottom of the flats. Subsequently, whenever the police turned up she would phone her partner to warn him of the impending police action, so that as the officers started climbing the stairs, a package would be lowered out of the flat's window. The woman waiting below would unhook the parcel and drive off until the drama in the flat had been acted out. Watching the police being repeatedly out-smarted through this simple artifice, served to undermine community confidence in them. It acted as a negative control signal conveying a sense that for all their talk of being 'intelligence-led', the police were not really on top of the problem.

These examples of how control signals motivated by good intentions can induce negative effects articulate some of the complexities and sensitivities that shape the tenor and tone of public reactions. For a complex institution such as policing then, in terms of how overarching public views and sentiments are formed, it is true to say that there is an interplay of positive and negative control signals. Some interventions will be viewed positively; others result in more negative effects. The effect of a policing intervention will differ markedly according to the values and predilections of the audience.

Informal, Organic, and Anti-social Control Signals

Policing and the other institutions of the criminal justice process are not the only source of control signals in everyday life. That this is so, is implicitly articulated in one of the most competent definitions of the police role provided by Egon Bittner (1972) where he asserts the defining quality of policing, is 'the emergency maintenance of social order'; the key term here being 'emergency'. Police supply a legally endowed capacity to use coercive force to intervene where there has been an acute breach of social order or where one is threatened. But most of the time, social order is sustained by resources and capacities that are not dependent upon formal social control.

Organic control signals are frequently important in this regard, as they influence perceptions of control and order in fairly subtle ways. For example, neighbourhoods where the properties are well tended and looked after, implicitly convey a set of expectations about appropriate standards of behaviour. But similar perceptual interventions are increasingly embedded in the designs for public and private spaces as an intrinsic element in how our behaviours and subjectivities are moulded and shaped. These 'ambient control signals' designed into the aesthetics of the built environment operate on the basis of subtle signalling processes that steer conduct and behaviour almost imperceptibly.

An example of this is in the physical design of a subway leading towards the main Cardiff University campus. On the footpath leading towards the underpass and through it, is a small channel of slightly raised cobbled stones running along the middle of the pathway. At first glance this looks merely like aesthetic detailing, but when the number of pedestrians increase, its function becomes more apparent. Because it is uneven and less comfortable to walk on, it helps to channel walkers into a contraflow system. In effect it creates a gap between two sides of the narrow tunnel and helps to stop people moving in opposite directions from colliding into each other, interrupting the movement of people and reducing the risk of tension and conflict.

The process at work is one where the physical environment sends subtle signals to those moving through the space about how to use it. These embedded design features are becoming increasingly commonplace, providing subtle indicators about what are the expected ways of behaving in that particular situation. Such developments reflect an increasing utilization of knowledge about human perception, cognition, and how these can be moulded by the layout of physical space by urban planners. These forms of control signal may be relatively weak, but are nevertheless effective in guiding and steering aspects of our collective conduct in unobtrusive ways much of the time.

Anti-social control signals

Social control enervated by informal interventions is typically more limited in terms of its 'power', where this is understood as the ability to influence a wider audience of onlookers, when contrasted with formal social control acts. It can, however, be highly effective for those directly engaged. The ways in which informal social control interventions act to signal the presence of effective control mechanisms at a highly localized level are exemplified in the following account from London:

> We are a neighbourhood where we do tend to believe we can police ourselves. We're less likely to snitch, inform, because people believe they can sort it out. An example would be Fireworks Night. The children were throwing fireworks. A local mother grabbed one of the young gentlemen very strongly by his lapels, and told him in no uncertain terms she would be very unhappy about if he continued to do it. Now this wasn't someone that he knows that well, but he knows she knows who knows. My Aunt [name], they went to school together. They all know who you are, 'I know who you are and I know your mother' and that's actually something you hear a lot … that is done almost constantly round here. (Col206)

As recalled in the second half of this quotation, the intervention by the local mother was designed to signal to the youngsters concerned that their behaviour was out of order. The signal sent was also that because of the tightly bonded local social networks, repercussions would occur if their anti-social activity persisted. Importantly, the purported sanction did not have to be imposed; it was sufficient to let the boys know that it *could* be activated.

But overlaid on these themes, the first two sentences of this story have important implications for our understanding of when and why informal control signals might be preferred to formal ones. As was strongly implied, this was not a neighbourhood with a history of high levels of trust in the police, but this does not mean it was bereft of social capital or collective efficacy. In fact, quite the opposite was the case. According to interviews with a number of local people, this was a highly cohesive community where informal social control was routinely mobilized. What is interesting was how control signals were nonetheless important in sustaining and reproducing this sense of cohesiveness and belonging. For what they indicated was an ongoing preparedness by local residents to regulate each others' conduct without involving the police.

The previous interviewee elaborated their account of how the local social order was collectively manufactured to describe how and why informal social control performed by residents did not necessarily follow the contours of criminal law:

> I not only know my neighbours, I know what they're doing that's illegal ... They know my family history, they know me inside out ... In fact I was saying to someone the other day, I could honestly say I don't know anybody in this neighbourhood who is legal. (Col206)

This combination of everyone engaging in criminal behaviour in conjunction with mutual knowledge about these 'illegalities' supplied an important constraint upon willingness to interact and engage with formal agents of social control such as the police. For if one did inform police about the illegal activities of neighbours, the risk was that they would reciprocally disclose what you or members of your family were up to. This starts to reveal the extent to which local cultures and situations matter in shaping when informal control signals are invoked. Within this community in London for example, they most definitely were not present for all the acts that could be officially labelled as crimes. Instead they were activated on those occasions where local conventions and expectations about acceptable behaviour were breached, especially where violence, disrespect, and theft from within the local community were involved.

This segues into a final species of control signal that needs to be considered. Cinema films and literary accounts of organized crime have long revelled in depicting the uses of spectacular violence to impose a degree of order and control over its participants. There is more than a grain of truth in this. Varese (2011), for example, points to the 'paradox' of the use of violence by those involved in organized crime as being that the more violent someone is believed to be, the less violence they actually need to commit. A few instances of strategically conducted extreme violence can be highly effective in sending a signal to potential rivals and a wider community, that this is someone who should not be 'messed' with.

Having documented the main forms of control signal, the remaining sections of this essay turn to consider the wider implications of these for how social control is theorized at a more abstract level. This reflects how the meta-narrative threaded through these empirically grounded examples of social control as integrally communicative action, is something that has been largely neglected in many previous accounts.

Social Control and Symbolic Communication

Social control occurs when social order is at risk or threatened in some manner and acts or interventions designed to protect it are enacted, either prospectively or retrospectively (Innes, 2003b). The most conceptually rigorous definition of social control is provided by Cohen (1985), with aligned formulations featuring in several other studies (for example, Black, 1976). Cohen (1985) maintains that social control involves programmed responses to deviant, problematic or troublesome behaviour. He was motivated to define his position in this way because of concerns about the 'plasticity' of social control as a concept, and the ways it had been appropriated and applied to a range of different situations and contexts, not always consistently.

The definitional problem Cohen was seeking to counter arises, at least in part, from a failure by many accounts to be clear about whether they are focused upon control *of* the social, or control *by* the social. The former references where the focus of concern is with those processes where the behaviour of people are collectively regulated and conditioned. The latter addresses the ways in which shared conventions and expectations for conduct are formulated, expressed, and upheld. It is this sense of shared and collective orientations that distinguishes social control from self control, for example.

Cohen's account is justly celebrated for identifying how, in the context of a profound 'destructuring' impulse that started in the 1960s, processes of 'net-widening' and 'net-deepening' took hold of redistributing the prevalence and allocation of social control in society. This involved a move away from reliance upon specialist and closed institutions such as prisons and mental hospitals, to emphasize mechanisms that sought to induce control in other spaces. Embedded within these macro-level shifts, he introduced several distinctive conceptual variations, including differentiations between 'exogenous' and 'iatrogenic' social controls. The first of these concerns how the introduction of new classifications of problems acts as an engine for the expansion of the control net. Iatrogenic controls, on the other hand, involve the development of greater internal complexity within any such classificatory frameworks and their associated circuits of control. These result in people who come into contact with the institutions of control, finding it increasingly difficult to extricate themselves from these contacts, as the net is deepened. Elsewhere in the midst of this discussion he also elucidates a difference between those controls possessed of a 'hard-edge' and those formulated around a 'softer' one.

Cohen's principal focus was mapping the 'master-patterns' that he detected in terms of how the tasks and framings of social control were increasingly exerting a gravitational pull upon other spheres of social life. In this respect the influence of Foucault's (1977) writing on the role of panoptic disciplinary institutions of surveillance and the accompanying dividing practices of confinement, examination, comparison, and normalization, are evident. Foucault famously deployed Jeremy Bentham's eighteenth-century design of the panoptic prison as an analogue of far wider social developments. Through exposure to the continuous penetrative gaze of a central authority, the errant desires and expectations of inmates would be identified and revised through a 'micro physics' of control focused upon instilling conformity in their acts and behaviours as a mechanism for altering their deviant subjectivities. In so doing, Foucault provided a chilling, pessimistic, and dystopian epitome of a social order where more and more mechanisms of social control are threaded through the conduct of social life to regulate conduct ever more tightly.

The genetic traces of such accounts are evident in several other recently influential treatises. Garland (2001), for instance, discusses how the institutional order of contemporary society has become predicated upon a 'culture of control'. His 'responsibilization' thesis positing that active involvement in controlling crime has been increasingly required of citizens and many public and non-public agencies, has clear continuities with Cohen's earlier formulation. Relatedly, Simon (2007) documents an increasing tendency for almost the entire system of governance to be oriented towards a political obsession with 'governing through crime'. His analysis captures how policy development in criminal justice has increasingly been conceived of as a control signal in its own right. That is, at least from the points of view of their authors, key legislative measures and reforms introduced in the wake of high profile signal crimes are increasingly less important in terms of what they practically accomplish, than what they can be used to symbolically communicate. In the context of a divisive and morally fraught politics, such interventions enable politicians to send a signal to the electorate that they are 'in control', or at least 'doing something'. In this respect, perhaps we have not travelled so very far from the mid-eighteenth century and the kinds of social control politics memorialized by the Smugglers' Stone.

Following a decade or more now of reductions in aggregate official crime rates and more latterly, reductions in public spending on crime control measures, a pause to question the extent to which some of these more generalized claims still hold as accurate descriptors of the scene before us may well be warranted. But Garland (2001) does introduce an important caveat that moderates the dystopian vision when he asserts it is important that we do not mistake rhetoric and discourse for what is actually accomplished in reality. There is an important distinction between claiming that measures of surveillance and social control are becoming more virulent and prevalent, and concluding that they are able, in practice, to provide an ongoing, constant, stream of 'wrap around' social control across all settings and situations.

This is a theme developed in Alice Goffman's (2009) ethnography of the lives of men subject to penal sanctions in a Philadelphia ghetto. As she captures, gaps and crevices in the reach of state social control allow these men who are 'on the run' from the authorities to regularly avoid and circumvent attempts to bring them back within the ambit of the criminal justice system. She concludes that whilst Foucault's panopticon provides a compelling modelling of power, in reality its surveillant gaze is routinely and ritualistically circumscribed by a variety of situational contingencies. This leads her to conclude that the conduct of social control is more complex, temporary, and occasional than many contemporary accounts drawing inspiration from Foucault would allow.

There are clear echoes here with Erving Goffman's (1961) work on total institutions. On the surface there are manifest similarities between his and Michel Foucault's accounts, inasmuch as both seek to describe how closed institutional settings impose a social order designed to effect physical and psychic control over those subject to it. But Goffman is far more alert to the limits of the control that is practically achieved. He captures some of the ways in which the inmates in the mental hospital where he was working carved out little micro-rituals, niches, and crevices within the routines of the institution where they were

incarcerated. The power of the descriptions he provides is in displaying how social control often only partially succeeds, even in settings explicitly designed for
the purpose of regulating and ordering conduct.[6]

Many empirical studies of social control confirm this. In prisons, the staff do
not apply all of the rules assertively all of the time. If they did, it would lead to
rapid breakdown of the negotiated order between prison officers and inmates
triggering wider disorder (Sparks, Bottoms, and Hay, 1996). Likewise, on the
streets, agents of social control such as police officers, routinely utilize discretion
in making decisions about how, when, why, and in respect of whom to intervene
with, generally reserving use of their legal powers as interventions of last resort
(Hawkins, 2002).

What this points to is that the conduct of social control is not an all pervasive,
un-modulated stream of social ordering mechanisms, rather it is a bit more inter-
mittent and situational. There are some moments and spaces where attempts to
effect social control either prospectively or retrospectively are the clear focus, but
these are not constant and unrelenting. And it is because of this, that control signals are so important to understanding how the work of social control is performed. For what control signals do is fill in 'the gaps' between the chains of
specific control events to act as indicators for, and reminders of, expected conventions of conduct and what happens when these are not adhered to.

To accommodate this understanding requires us to reformulate how we con-
ceptualize social control at a base level. Donald Black (1976) identified four 'pure'
styles of social control. These he saw as possessing distinct ways of defining problems, favoured responses, discursive representations, and imputations of cause
and effect. 'Penal control' according to Black, is where formally proscribed pro-
hibitions are enforced on behalf of the wider group. This is different from 'com-
pensatory control' which is frequently initiated by the victim in search of
recompense. Black's final two 'pure' forms of 'therapeutic' and 'conciliatory' social control both stress a desired outcome of restoration and repair. In adopting
this approach to unpacking the notion of social control certain traces to a much
earlier topography can be detected. Writing as early as 1901, E.A. Ross was able to
list 23 mechanisms via which social groups seek to influence the conduct of
individuals.

The New Modes of Communicative Social Control

There are problems, however, with many of the formulations outlined in the
preceding paragraphs in that they do not adequately capture some of the complex and blended ways in which social control is now being conducted. Penal
institutions, for example, routinely make use of therapeutic interventions. As

---

[6] This interplay between Goffman's and Foucault's perspectives is elaborated more fully by
Hacking (2011).

such, whilst Black contends that the forms he identified are 'pure' modes of control, in practice they are increasingly frequently melded together. More than this though, there are several new modes of social control that do not appear to fit within Black's formulation, or to be captured by it. These include: retroactive social control; algorithmic social control; and, the operations of behavioural economics. Moreover, Black's account, along with most other seminal contributions, underplays the role and significance of communication in how social control is enacted.

Retroactive social control

Innes and Clarke (2009) argue that whilst extensive attention has focused upon the predictive, preemptive, and precautionary logics of contemporary social control, an equally important social movement has been its increased 'retroactivity'. This involves the redefinition of the situation in respect of historic crimes in ways that change what is understood to have happened. It is in this sense that the social control performed can be understood to be 'retroactive' as Hacking (1995: 249–50) conceptualizes it:

> That is why I say the past is revised retroactively. I do not mean only that we change our opinions about what was done, but that in a certain logical sense what was done itself is modified. As we change our understanding and sensibility, the past becomes filled with intentional actions that, in a certain sense, were not there when they were performed.

Retroactive social control is typically initiated by deliberate attempts to destabilize an official construction and labelling of a consequential past event, followed by the introduction and establishment of a new definition of the situation. This frequently involves having to subvert or circumvent denials issued by powerful agencies with a vested interest in maintaining things as they are. Such processes of retroactive social control can be detected, for instance, in the ways in which transitional states attempt to come to terms with past state crimes. This often entails, as Moon's (2008) work on 'truth and reconciliation' in South Africa illustrates, a re-narration of past events alloyed to justice attempts that address both victims and perpetrators of state crime.

In order to reflect and legitimize new moral orders, retroactive social control requires both a re-description and re-definition of the past. According to Innes and Clarke (2009), this involves the social control of memory and social control through memory. The former determines the contours of precisely what is remembered and how; the latter the mobilization of these collective memories to shape patterns of influence, compulsion, and compliance-seeking in the here and now. An important caveat to this is to be found in Moon's (2012) more recent work on the 'mothers of the disappeared' in Argentina and their refusal of reparations. Attempts at retroactive social control can be and frequently are contested.

Retroactive social control brings to the surface and condenses some of the complexities associated with the workings of control signals. For in the process of recovering a previously submerged and subterranean 'truth' about what happened in relation to a past crime, retroactive social control simultaneously signals the presence of control failure (in that the wrong outcome was originally reached), alongside a more positive control signal resulting from the correction to this that has taken place.

Algorithmic social control

Reaching back into the past, to place historical events under new descriptions and definitions, is not the only way in which the conduct of social control is changing. Indeed, a potentially even more consequential move relates to the development, across a number of domains, of what we might label algorithmic social control. That is, the encoding of social processes in data-processing algorithms, with the intention that these should be used to shape and steer human behaviour.

An obvious application of these techniques to the work of social control is to be found in the moves to develop predictive policing and crime forecasting methodologies. These involve the development of informatics-based approaches that fuse crime data with other available social datasets in an effort to anticipate future crimes, focusing specifically on: criminogenic locations; potential offenders; predicting offender identities; and profiling possible victims of crimes (Perry, et al., 2013). The idea is that via analysis of large datasets it is possible to put in place prognostic policing interventions that will interfere, in some way, with the social processes leading to crime. Albeit at the current time the accuracy and efficacy of such approaches is not settled, the point is that such ideas are exerting increasing influence over the organization and delivery of policing services.

In addition, however, data-mining algorithms are also having less obtrusive effects. They are, for instance, increasingly used by retailers to profile individual consumer preferences and personality types. In their most advanced forms these profiles direct certain forms of information towards customers, but are also used to guide interactions with them. Depending upon the profiled personality type, some people will be contacted and treated in particular ways, whilst other individuals will be subject to very different forms of interaction (Steiner, 2012). The point is that these mechanisms of persuasion and influence are sophisticated and they are subtle. Their power to control perceptions and behaviour resides in their veiled nature. Unlike many other forms of social control they are unobtrusive and seemingly innocuous.

At one level this sounds harmless enough and even potentially helpful. But these techniques and methods are filtering through into the conduct of social control. The majority of UK police forces now make use of MOSAIC, a demographic and lifestyle profiling tool, to inform how, when, and why they engage with different geographic communities (Ashby, 2005). This software package fuses demographic, crime, and individual level data about retail habits, to construct geodemographic community profiles, which in turn shapes the delivery of policing services to these areas.

One of the more interesting descriptions of algorithmic social control is to be found in O'Malley's (2010) notion of 'telemetric policing'. He refers to the ways in which certain forms of problematic behaviour are increasingly dealt with via virtual mechanisms, where both the offence is detected and the sanction executed through the auspices of computerized codes. So a speed camera will detect the number plate of the offending vehicle. This will then be relayed to a database that will connect the offence to the vehicle owner, which in turn will issue a notification of the offence and fine. Upon receipt of the notice, the offender will have the opportunity to pay the fine that has been issued online.

The proliferation of sensors through urban settings that relay data about emerging situations and problems is increasingly consequential for the conduct of social control. This is especially so as the potential to direct and task these sensors becomes more widespread:

> Facilitated by new technologies, the Sentient City talks back to its citizens . . . Real time information presented in machine readable format can be reprocessed, recombined and reflected upon, finding new purposes limited only by the imagination of the community. (MIT SENSEable City Lab, 2011: 92)

This discussion identifies two points of interface with the control signals construct. The earlier sections reference how algorithmic social control is shifting who is being exposed to what control signals and when, whereas the later examples focus upon how investment in these sensor-based systems is founded on the belief that they can be used to detect early warning signals of emergent problems.

Four archetypes

Taken together, what these examples point to is how the conduct of control is changing. Many social situations are now touched by overlapping instances of formal and informal, organic and manufactured controls. But in addition, the preceding discussion has foregrounded how these formations of social control routinely engage processes of communication. The combined consequence of this suggests a need to revise our base understandings of what social control is. This necessitates application of a deconstructive–reconstructive methodology that starts by breaking social control down into its elemental forms, before any attempt to make broader claims about more general trajectories and currents.

Threaded through the preceding empirical discussion, are four archetypes of social control:

- Persuasion—where the subject of control is influenced to voluntarily comply with norms and/or conventions. This can occur through both overt and covert forms, which determines how aware the subject is of the processes they are exposed to.

- Instruction—depends upon processes of obedience and acquiescence to authority. Whether a subject agrees with the content of the instruction is of little consequence to the accomplishment of control. There are two principal forms of instructive social control. The first involves directing behaviour, or telling the subject what to do. The second is based upon what Sennett (2008) describes, as 'showing not telling', that is, passing on the practical recipe knowledge of how to accomplish set ends in particular ways.
- Regulation—occurs when the explicit rules and shared conventions for conduct are established, and compliance is managed by non coercive penalties. The vital aspect of this as a form of social control is how it attends more to process than outcome. How something is undertaken, is of at least equal importance to any outcome. Regulation frequently involves interventions that are concerned with technical modifications of procedure, rather than explicit manifestations of overt power.
- Coercion—involves the application of physical or psychological force. In effect it is social control envisaged as the capacity and capability to require people to behave in ways other than those they would choose for themselves. As intimated in aspects of the previous discussion, coercive social control is often dependent upon the precepts of criminal law, but this is not a prerequisite.

These are the basic building blocks, the foundational materials, out of which other modalities of social control are rendered. Vitally, from the point of view of this essay, each of them can involve sending or transmitting signals. Although seeking to accomplish their ends in different ways, all of them are designed to achieve behavioural modification, getting people to think or act in ways other than those they might choose for themselves if not exposed to these signals. Under certain conditions and within certain settings these base elements are blended to produce particular control styles of the type highlighted by Black (1976). For example, therapeutic interventions routinely meld persuasion and instruction. The point of stripping our thinking back to these archetypes is that, in so doing, we are able to clarify just how, when, and why signalling processes are involved in the production of control.

The value of this emergent approach to understanding the conduct of social control is made evident by returning to examine some real life examples. For example, in a challenging housing estate in the North West of England it was observed how a group of local residents came together to try and arrest what they saw as the onset of a slow corrosive decline of standards of behaviour in the area. This involved them arranging meetings with any new tenants arriving on the estate, where they attempted to set out how the area worked and some semblance of a collective view about what acts and actions were tolerable, and what were deemed anti-social amongst local people. Framed in the terms of this essay, the residents were engaged in sending a mixture of regulatory, persuasive, and in-structive control signals to their compatriots.

The new architects of the soul

Casting symbolic communication as intrinsic to social control changes how it is understood to work across a range of settings and situations. Of particular value is how this approach keys into some of the increasingly subtle ways in which the work of social control is weaved through and permeates social relations. One final empirical case study will help to knit these themes together, to show how signalling processes are increasingly enmeshed in the conduct of contemporary social control.

Over the past five years there has been increasing interest shown by policy-makers in the sub-discipline of behavioural economics, that more colloquially has come to be dubbed 'Nudge Theory' (Thaler and Sunstein, 2008). In the UK this has become especially salient as a specialist unit to propagate and develop this agenda—the Behavioural Insights Team (BIT)—has been established within the UK Cabinet Office. This is significant inasmuch as it embeds a cross-cutting supra-departmental brief to operationalize behavioural economic methodolo-gies at the heart of government.

Albeit proponents of this approach would not conceive of what they are doing as social control, their precepts and working methods align closely to key elem-ents of Cohen's (1985) definition rehearsed previously. For nudging involves deliberate or programmed attempts to respond to behaviours that are, in some sense, deemed troublesome or problematic. Framed by the preceding discus-sion, behavioural economics blends persuasive, instructive, and regulatory modes of social control. Its defining logic is premised upon transmitting often fairly subtle control signals to shape people's patterns of affect and cognition to induce them to behave in particular ways. These individuals are often targeted on the grounds that they are making sub-optimal decisions, at least as adjudged by purely 'rational' criteria, that in effect cause harm to themselves, and by ex-tension the state, because they introduce a lack of efficiency in the use of social resources.

The promissory potential of such an approach is described in a report by the Cabinet Office and Institute for Government (Dolan et al., undated) in relation to Acceptable Behaviour Contracts (ABCs). ABCs were originally introduced to deal with anti-social behaviour of young people aged 10–17, but were subse-quently used increasingly regularly in the governance of adult misbehaviour. As regulatory instruments of social control, they established a set of control signals to individuals about how their behaviours were unacceptable and needed to be changed. A second example of how the behavioural modification techniques of nudge theory work in practice relates to a policy trial run by the Courts Service and BIT with the aim of increasing fine payments set by the courts. The trial in-volved sending differently worded text messages to individuals subject to a fine.

It was found that a third more paid the amount due when sent text messages addressed to them by name, compared with those sent the standard letter by the Courts Service. The BIT team estimate this would equate to an additional £3 million pounds in fines being paid annually (Haynes et al., 2012). In the terms developed over the course of this essay, what this involves is the strategic deployment of targeted control signals designed to persuade potential fine defaulters to comply with the instructions directed at them.

Nudge theory is often presented in relatively beneficent terms. It is deemed preferable to other modes of government intervention on the grounds that it eschews and provides an alternative to coercion and compulsion. Moreover, there is growing evidence that it is quite effective when it 'goes with the grain' of how people think they would like to act (Marteau et al., 2011). In this respect policy-makers and practitioners are urged to view their role as 'choice architects' (Dolan et al., undated). A choice architecture involves distributing alternative courses of action in ways that make it more likely that citizens electively select the option that those designing the policy view as being the optimum. The function of control signals in this context is to steer the subject's attention to the 'preferred' choice.

The embedded signals that seek to control peoples' choices in this way are comparatively weak, but work by refracting the cognitive biases and heuristics that routinely inform individual and group decision-making. A strong theme in this respect is habituation or the tendency for people to develop and act in accordance with fixed patterns of perception, cognition, and action (Kahneman, 2011). This is what Cialdini (2001) refers to as the 'click whir' effect. Confronted by particular risk and threat situations we tend to react in fairly automatic ways, and it takes considerable will and effort to respond other than in accordance with these patterns. This is highly relevant to understanding reactions to crime, disorder, and social control, which are some of the most routinely encountered risks and threats in contemporary societies. Another key influence upon decisions about how to act is what other people are believed to be doing (Cialdini, 2001). 'Social proof', especially under conditions of uncertainty, provides a powerful signal about how to act. In effect, the behaviours of others who are co-present in a setting can function as control signals that shape, pattern, and guide individual behaviour.

The integration of scientific research findings on the workings of affect and cognition into policy design is a critical component of the behavioural economics approach. It is part of the wider movement noted by Rose (1999) whereby the 'psy' disciplines of psychiatry and psychology have become increasingly influential across a number of domains. In his *Governing the Soul* Rose explains this expanding sphere of influence as part of an historical inversion of Foucault's modelling of disciplinary surveillance and social control. So where Foucault's historical examples document how behaviour modification was positioned as a mechanism for shaping people's subjectivities, Rose posits that since the 1960s onwards, many key modes of social control have come to pivot around the management of subjectivities as the principal route for shaping how people act and behave.

This is a trajectory that nudge theory and how it has been co-opted into the agenda of government seems to exemplify, with psychological research in particular, supplying much of the 'behavioural' understandings of the new doctrine for economics. Those designing policies using these techniques are assuming the mantle of acting as the new architects of the soul.[7] By placing subtle but effective control signals into situations where citizens are required to make choices between different options, the policy architects are engaged in deliberately formatting people's perceived desires, wants, and needs. Whilst securing compliance in this manner may ultimately be preferable to the invocation of compulsion and coercion, it remains fundamentally social control.

That this constitutes a modality of social control is implicitly recognized by the Institute of Government in their 'Mindspace' document.[8] This report is close to being a handbook for policy-makers in respect of how to operationalize and deploy nudges and 'tugs' within policy agendas. As the authors of the report describe it, 'Whether reluctantly, or enthusiastically, today's policy makers are in the business of influencing behaviour.' (Dolan et al., undated: 73)

Supporters of such approaches to developing and deploying choice architectures in this manner argue that they are important because they allow policy-makers to design more effective and socially efficient interventions. A more sceptical account would argue that those pursuing such a programme are akin to the new architects of the soul. They are instantiating particular aspirations and goals for people, on the premise that these would be more beneficial for them. The power of using nudges and choice architectures lies precisely in the ways that the expression of power is submerged.

Critically examining nudge theory as an approach that introduces an array of weak control signals into specific situations to modify behaviour, clarifies the extent to which signalling processes are not just focused upon the effectiveness of control measures, they are equally about efficiency. Propelled by greater knowledge about what drives human motivation, intention, and decision-making these interventions combine persuasive, instructive, and regulatory modes of social control, albeit in quite diluted forms. As such, advocates of nudging and tugging interventions like to claim they are, in many cases, more effective and efficient than those measures involving compulsion and coercion. This is oftentimes correct. But that doesn't mean that we should lose sight of the fact that they are nonetheless instances of social control.

---

[7] The somewhat arcane notion of 'the soul' is used here in the ways outlined by Hacking (1995) and Rose (1999). That is as a sense of 'oneself', and the influences that go to making up this ontological sense of selfhood. Taking the duality of 'body and soul', it comprises all those aspects of a person that are not related to the body.

[8] 'MINDSPACE' is presented as a 'checklist' of influences on behaviour for use when making policy. It includes: Messenger; Incentives; Norms; Defaults; Salience; Priming; Affect; Commitments; Ego (see Dolan et al., undated).

Conclusion: Signals of Control, Signals to Control

Control signals punctuate and permeate social orders. They are an integral part of how a whole range of social control acts and interventions persuade, instruct, regulate, and coerce individuals and groups to think and behave in particular ways. Informed by extensive empirical data on social controls as reactions to crime and disorder problems, as well as public reactions to these controls themselves, the discussion has mapped the presence of a number of principal types of control signal all inducing a variety of cognitive, affective, behavioural, and organizational effects.

Cutting across these various types of control signal, it can be seen that all of them function through two principal registers. This is a feature that has been tacit in many of the real life examples drawn upon in this essay, but so far has not been explicated conceptually. 'Signals of control' emanate from or are emitted by acts of social control. For the most part these are post-hoc, registering that an act or acts of social control have taken place, and seeking to project this to influence the thoughts, feelings, and actions of a wider audience. This contrasts with 'signals to control', which are more intentional and targeted in their purview, and largely prospectively and preventatively oriented. These are designed to signal to individuals or groups that some form of controlling presence is active, and so troublesome or problematic behaviours should not be engaged in.

This distinction between signals of control and signals to control is helpful in achieving more purchase upon how, when, and why particular control signals, either in isolation or concert, impact upon a situated social order. This is, after all, one of the main challenges for developing an innovative framework for interrogating the communicative properties and qualities of social control. For any meaningful analysis in this domain has to be able to disinter the unique effects of individual control signals, but also, the cumulative outcomes of the multiple control signals that can be identified within any given social situation. In this regard, being able to recognize that there can be organic and manufactured, anti-social and negative control signals all present at any one moment is vital for understanding how particular instances of social control do, or do not, send signals to a social audience.

Introducing this discussion with the historical account of the execution in Chichester provided a conceptual analepsis demonstrating that the transmission of signals and messages by acts of social control is not a new phenomenon. Rather, it is integral to how social control works. Intriguingly though, there may be lessons from history for the contemporary situation. For what the authorities in the eighteenth century sought to do was deliberately manipulate the power of their intervention to send a signal to the populace. In an era of public sector austerity, where it appears there is less appetite for expending public money on state-based social control, thinking seriously and creatively about how control signals can be designed to optimize levels of public safety and security would seem a worthwhile endeavour.

In some ways though, and in terms of contemporary social thought, it is not the visible instances of social control that we should worry about. Rather, it is the development of more insidious, almost invisible forms of social control that is of most concern. Charting a number of contemporary developments especially in respect of developments of surveillance and algorithmic social control, the discussion herein has shown how the power of these forms of social control resides in their relative invisibility. This is exemplified by the techniques of nudging, which arrange a cluster of weak control signals in carefully calibrated ways to steer the conduct of citizens.

This is important inasmuch as the accumulation of a multitude of weak signals may actually have greater consequences for the make-up of social order, than do a smaller number of powerful signals attached to a few high profile events. As Vic Gattrell (2008) once concluded:

A million disciplinary pinpricks deliver stronger effects than a single throttling.

Elevating the signalling dimensions of social control has implications for the ways that we think about how control is accomplished. It directs attention towards how social control acts and interventions are performed, in the very literal sense of the word. That is, how acts of social control project beyond the immediate concerns with which they are engaged, to influence the ways people think, feel, or act in relation to matters of safety and security.

An Afterword on Method
'Gonzo Research' and the Uses of Systematic and Unsystematic Social Observation

We are living through a moment where there is a general trend towards the formalization of method across the social sciences. This is most evident in relation to the increasingly technical nature of applications of quantitative method, but also in the profile being attained by advocates of randomized control trials for policy evaluation research. However, this increasingly formalized and disciplined approach to issues of methodology is also making its presence felt in relation to qualitative research, albeit in more subtle forms.

The accounting practices for reporting qualitative methodological research designs are increasingly conventionalized, ritualized, and adhered to in scholarly writings. In addition, the data collection instruments featuring in prominent studies are increasingly structured and systematic (for example, Sampson and Raudenbusch, 1999). Formalization can also be detected in respect of qualitative data analysis. Charles Ragin's (2008) excellent programme of work around qualitative comparative analysis (QCA), for instance, involves disciplined and structured data analysis in an effort to derive clear causality patterns from datasets whose particular value customarily lies in their messy, rich, and complex descriptions of social life.

In general this is a positive movement. It is a good and proper development if social science in all its forms is to be influential in public debates. Conducting research and reporting its results in ways that are clear and transparent, about both strengths and weaknesses, is intrinsic to the academic craft and what separates good scholarly work from the many other researches that one encounters from journalists, think-tanks, and the like. This notwithstanding though, we need to be honest, clear-eyed and precise about what such approaches can and cannot deliver.

Processing data more systematically affords more compelling accounts about social life, and enhances the validity and reliability of claims to particularly prescient insight. But this route does not intrinsically possess the capacity and capability to produce new theories and concepts that shift or subvert established paradigms. Given the pace with which the prevalent social order is currently evolving, and along with it new forms of deviance and social control emerging, this appears to be an important consideration. This is particularly so if criminological and sociological research is to shape and lead the contours of social deliberation about issues of crime, disorder, and control, rather than just follow or provide commentary upon ideas proposed by others.

How then should we proceed if we are to develop new concepts and theories that help us make sense of the contemporary social world? The essays that are collected together in this volume adopt a theme and variations approach in terms of their substantive orientations. The variations reflect the different issues and topic matters upon which they individually alight. At the same time, there is a shared commonality in terms of the ways in which these foci are unpicked, illuminated, and articulated. This conceptual bond is also a methodological bond though, in that these individual treatments further share a common methodological approach. It is a methodology that has sought to blend systematic and unsystematic observation.

The systematic aspects of the research have been present in the extensive and rigorous empirical fieldwork involved in testing and refining some of the new concepts and ideas that have been brought forward under the auspices of the signal crimes perspective. This is evident in the conduct of the large number of face-to-face in-depth interviews across 18 research sites, in order to appraise the extent to which the basic analytic framework was generalizable across a range of different contexts and situations in line with established notions of sample size and representativeness. This systematic style was also present in the work examining how fear travels in the aftermath of homicides, where the sample composition for the interviews was designed to allow the analysis to gauge the geographic and temporal decay patterns of high profile signal crimes.

But at the same time, the development of the ideas about signal crimes, signal disorders and control signals has been very much influenced by a less structured and 'ill-disciplined' conception of social observation. Whilst lacking the rigour of more formalized styles, this more creative and free-form approach has been vital to the 'discovery' of new ideas and concepts. In reflecting upon the extent to which methodology has been important in shaping the ideas set out in the preceding essays, it seems they are a product of navigating between forms of systematic and unsystematic social observation.

The details and considerations of the more systematic elements of the research programme will be dissected in more detail presently. But I shall start with the precepts of unsystematic social observation as this is the more unusual claim for contemporary social research. This use of unsystematically conducted observations of social processes and events, for want of a better term and for reasons elaborated later, can be dubbed 'gonzo research'. Borrowing from Hunter S. Thompson's (1971) articulation of 'gonzo journalism', it displays three principal commitments:

- Naturalism—an affinity for studying 'real' social situations and processes in their naturally occurring settings, rather than reducing them to isolated variables or intervening to manipulate them in some fashion in order that they be experimentally 'testable';
- Unsystematic social observation—a use of empirical data from a variety of forms and sources, rather than an insistence upon methodological 'purity'. This is in tandem with 'casual' comparative analysis across different sites and settings to enable the identification of the necessary and sufficient conditions that transcend defined situations, and thus aid robust conceptualization.
- Discovery and revelatory insight—this approach is proposed as a way of discovering new ideas and approaches, based upon an understanding that concepts and frames provide 'ways of seeing'. That is, new concepts can illuminate aspects of social life that were hitherto seen but unnoticed.

Of course, the critical question for this configuration is how the first two components seed the third, and what other ingredients are needed to endow the ability to perceive familiar scenes in unfamiliar ways? To stand at a slightly 'oblique angle' to the world and possess a sense of remoteness from what one is observing, seems to be helpful. But this should be conjoined with the kinds of working methods that C. Wright Mills (1959) drew attention to in his ruminations upon good intellectual craftsmanship, most notably being extremely well read in one's subject, and having a conceptual orientation derived from this that is continually parsing the social worlds that are in purview. It is in respect of this latter dimension in particular, that unsystematic social observation can help in terms of bringing to light unusual or unexpected analogues for that which is being formally studied.

Valuing Unsystematic Social Observation

The concept of unsystematic social observation originates in Philip Manning's (1992) incisive commentary on the working methods of Erving Goffman. Goffman is now widely celebrated as one of the preeminent innovators in ideas, albeit he did not furnish us with any macro-level grand theoretical statement of the sort associated with more celebrated thinkers. Instead, he provided a plethora of concepts that reveal crucial dimensions of the micro-politics of social life and as he termed it 'the interaction order'. Manning's point is that these ideas came from a style of research frequently unencumbered by many of the stylistic conventions that his contemporaries held to.

One of Goffman's (1961) best known and most influential works gravitates around the concept of the 'total institution'. In the book *Asylums* he documents the ways in which 'wrap around' modalities of control designed to envelop those subject to such regimes are devised and practised. But unlike several other analysts who have also attended to the problem of institutionalized social control (for example Foucauldian panopticism) Goffman is too acute an observer of human behaviour to equate the rhetoric and discourse of such establishments with what actually happens. Through careful empirical observation he details the 'underlife' of the institution and how, even in the most seemingly all encompassing of regulated environments, the inmates are able to subvert and 'bend' aspects of the control regimen. In so doing, and to make sense of these matters, he introduces a number of new and radical concepts—such as 'mortifications of the self' and 'social death'—that reveal common core patterns in how social control is conceived and conducted across very different social settings. At times these insights are engagingly provocative. For example, in the ways that he describes the routines and social order of a school as analogous to a prison.

Goffman's work on 'total institutions' has been described as constituting an 'ethnography of a concept' (Manning, 1992). This is important for picking up the methodological innovation that underpins how he is able to distil out empirical and subsequently theoretical patterns that others do not detect. This intertwining, interdependence and inter-play between theoretical and methodological innovation is a consistent theme in Goffman's work that has been highlighted by both Robin Williams (1988) and Philip Manning (1992). Williams emphasizes that Goffman's primary commitment was to the development of new ideas and concepts, and he refused to be constrained by a notion that his studies could only be based upon data collected via one method. Instead, he routinely integrated field observations, interview extracts, quotations from fiction, and press reports to develop and work through his ideas.[1] According to Williams, these different data performed different functions, enabling him not just to detect conceptual patterns, but also to test the limits of the legitimate conceptual 'reach' of the notion that is 'in play' at the time. It is this that Manning (1992) rather neatly labels 'unsystematic naturalistic observation'. In contemporary parlance it is a method we would probably refer to as 'bricolage'.

A further relevant contemporary resonance is Goffman's 'naturalism'. This is a methodological theme that has recently been revived by Sampson (2011) in his magisterial *Great American City*. Sampson contrasts his commitment to detailed study of places and how social forces and processes intersect and interact *in situ*, with the more orthodox focus upon the study of dependent and independent 'variables'. Such studies depend upon isolating a particular item of interest, stripping out layers of context and complexity, in order to try and say something certain about that facet of life. In many ways it is striking how Sampson's epistemological position echoes the kinds of defence that proponents of qualitative research have long been making. The value of naturalism is that its orienting disposition is towards situations in their organic richness and layered details, rather than manipulating artificially sequestered variables.

---

[1] This empirical eclecticism and compositional style is also a feature of the work of figures like Everett Hughes, W. Lloyd Warner and others within the Chicago School lineage who were a direct influence upon Goffman, and those subsequently who have been sympathetic to this tradition, such as Irwin Deutscher and Aaron Cicourel. I am grateful to Nigel Fielding for drawing this to my attention.

In terms of how Goffman translated his unsystematic and naturalistically collected data into new concepts and frameworks, it is of note that he frequently used multiple data streams. That is, it was comparing and contrasting between them that frequently gave him his most compelling and insightful ideas. Crucially, this was not done through the kinds of formal comparative case study designs increasingly common in the contemporary research literature, it was rather looser and unstructured. Nevertheless, it is worth acknowledging that such comparisons are a feature of how his concepts were constructed. In my own work, this casual comparative analysis has been an important feature of how the pivotal concepts associated with the signal crimes perspective have been developed. This approach is 'casually' comparative in the sense that it is not 'formal', but conducted in a more improvised, free-flowing way, where aspects of different situations and phenomena are informally brought together by the analyst to see if they might possess common affinities, features, or causes that are not immediately obvious.

I originally started to think about the power of single crime events and their influence over individual and collective perceptions of security in my ethnographic work on police murder investigations (Innes, 2003a). In this work I became interested in how certain murders could trigger significant public concern, where other ostensibly similar acts do not. In particular, I was interested in how police responses were calibrated in relation to their perceptions of the relative public harm of the act they were dealing with.

My thinking about such events was sharpened by the events of 9/11, which seemed to replicate the patterns observed in relation to homicides, both in terms of triggering public fear but also altering institutional responses. I then began to think about whether the processes of social perception and social reaction observed in relation to major 'high impact' crimes might be a more generic essential property of processes of social reaction to all crimes and disorder. These ideas were configured further when they were extended into empirical studies of community perceptions of anti-social behaviour and disorder.

This work seemed to confirm that some incidents matter more than others in shaping public sentiments and attitudes about crime, disorder, and control. Indeed, by looking at local crime and incivilities we can start to track in more fine-grained detail the ontology of social reactions to deviant behaviour, and how there is often considerable consensus about what the key signal crimes and disorders are in a neighbourhood. By scanning across terrorism, violent crime, and anti-social behaviour incidents, it became possible to suggest the presence of common 'reaction patterns'.

Introducing 'Gonzo Research' into the Conversation

In his now infamous and celebrated book *Fear and Loathing in Las Vegas*, Hunter S. Thompson outlined the basis of gonzo journalism. He did not provide a clear programmatic statement of this, but it is possible to infer that it is configured around several core precepts. First, it is opportunistic and situated, rather than programmed and systematic. The aim is not to make progress through a series of planned interviews or visits. Rather, it illuminates aspects of a particular issue that is being researched by plunging the researcher into the scene. At first glance this shares surface affinities with the ethics of ethnography, but whereas many accounts of ethnographic method tend to accent the need to retain suitable forms of distance, gonzo advocates immersion in the action. In an era of the research ethics committee, this is an aspect of field methods that has become increasingly rare. In effect, whereas formal ethnography has increasingly tended to valorize being an observer above a participant, the gonzo approach inverts this to favour being more a participant than detached observer.

However, the necessarily contingent and emergent approach via which issues are researched inherently contains implications for what is reported and how. A particular quality of gonzo journalism is its recognition of the importance of telling a good story. Given its situated nature, gonzo journalism attends to particular events and may accentuate aspects of them in order to illuminate key ideas and issues that are being pursued. This parallels Jack Katz's (2001) ideas about the power and value of 'luminescent' strips of data in ethnographic description. Katz maintains that within any qualitative data set there are always parts that are especially persuasive and compelling because of how they clarify and condense the issues in hand. This includes picking up on the myriad details and messiness that inheres in how real lives are lived. The danger for research, as opposed to journalism, is that this drifts towards 'never letting the truth stand in the way of a good story'. Conceptual saturation is helpful in this regard in terms of being able to determine the more (and less) valid elements in a good story.

The particular ethic of gonzo journalism is that there should be an element of subversion and of challenging received wisdom in terms of what is reported upon and how. The significance of challenging orthodox standpoints is also relevant to gonzo research and its accent upon generating conceptualizations that help to render visible aspects of social order and social life that were previously invisible. Here we can connect back to the value of Goffman's work on the intersections between social control and social identity. But in crafting a coherent research method—a gonzo research as opposed to gonzo journalism—there is inevitably a requirement to adapt and retune certain aspects of what can be derived from the source materials.

If unsystematic social observation combined with casual comparative analysis are the key ingredients of gonzo research, in practice they are augmented by the active use of what Paul Rock (2010) ironically defines as the 'detritus' of research. That is the messy, contingent complex aspects of research in action, rather than textbooks—the stuff that more traditional epistemological standpoints seek to minimize or downplay. This might include inspired leaps of logic, wild inferences based on limited data, and the acquisition of compelling observations of social life when not formally engaged in data collection that nevertheless shape one's thinking.

The argument traced out herein, is not that gonzo research should in any way serve as a substitute for carefully designed and systematic studies. Rather, it is specifically focused upon the moment in the research process concerned with generating new ideas and revelatory insights. What, to adopt Denzin's (2002) term, would count as a conceptual 'epiphany'.

The notion of approaching data collection and analysis in an unstructured and unsystematic fashion runs somewhat contrary to the standards and procedures that are increasingly used to assess the quality of research. But not all social problems can be subjected to the most rigorous research designs. This is relevant to considering the position of the signal crimes perspective, as it has achieved a certain amount of deployment by practitioner communities involved in neighourhood security work.

For practitioners and policy-makers who are charged to do something about often traumatic social situations, time and money are frequently in short supply. In addition then to facilitating paradigm disrupting criminological research, aspects of the gonzo research agenda might also have utility for those focused upon more avowedly policy and practice concerns.

The idea that public policy development should be evidence-based has proven to be increasingly enchanting and seductive. Across a range of policy domains, the claim that reform efforts are being crafted and led on the basis of the best available evidence has become increasingly prevalent (Hammersley, 2013). And yet, spend any time with researchers, policy-makers, and front-line public service providers, and it is not long before their sense of disenchantment with so called 'evidence-based' approaches surfaces. The complaint of researchers is that the realpolitik of policy formulation is always driven primarily by a blend of ideology and pragmatism. On this account, evidence can influence policy when it is coherent with the established ideologically motivated direction of travel, but will be ignored or marginalized when it does not. The counterpoint to this is that those who are charged to actually do something about pressing public and private issues claim that research takes too long, privileges rigour over informing action, and is frequently remote, abstract, and removed from the complexities of solving often contingent, intricate, and messy real-world problems. As a consequence, new policy ideas are often derived from think-tanks unencumbered by, and able to 'cut through', the constraints of empirical reality.

If we accept the viability of gonzo research's accent upon immersion and getting in 'where the action is', then the kinds of ideas previously set out might be deployed in invigorating new forms of exploratory study. In an era of austerity where significant disinvestment decisions are being made across the criminal justice sector, might we think about how those immersed in criminal justice delivery could be encouraged to use their experiences and data to drive innovative thinking?

Whilst this issue of the policy and practice relevance of gonzo research is potentially interesting, for the purposes of this afterword it is a diversion. For in terms of understanding the gestation and development of thinking about the signalling capacities of crime, disorder, and control, a 'gonzo' inflected approach has afforded ways of interpreting and reading social situations through different sets of optics than those afforded by more established positions. For example, some of the key insights into public reactions happened when I was immersed in fieldwork ostensibly focused upon very different issues. Relatedly, the opportunities to engage in forms of casual comparative analysis by thinking about the ways public responses to terrorist incidents were similar to, or different from, those recorded in relation to anti-social behaviour, helped to clarify some of the fundamental conceptual and methodological bases of the signal crimes perspective.

It would be highly misleading however, to say that all of the conceptual development work emanated from this more free-wheeling and creative approach. In terms of its overall contribution to the key ideas set out over the course of this volume, the influence of unsystematic social observation is at least matched by a far more rigorous and systematic style of collecting and analysing empirical data.

Systematically Observing Social Reactions

There were two particular data collection efforts that exemplify this more systematic and structured approach to generating qualitative data on social reactions to crime, disorder, and control. The first of these was especially relevant to, and is reported in some detail, in the investigation of how fear travels across social space and time in the aftermath of high profile homicides (Essay III). In each of the six individual case studies that inform that essay, the fieldwork involved starting with interviews close to the crime scene and then progressively increasing the levels of distance, both social and geographic, away from the originating incident. The objective was to examine how the influence of the signal event decays or changes the further away you get. However, because these methods are described in some detail in that essay, it is not necessary to rehearse such considerations again. The more important point is simply to record how the modelling of the harm footprints that lies at the core of the essay, required this systematic mode of investigation as much as creative, intuitive insight.

In terms of empirics, the other essays in this collection all draw wholly, or in part, from another attempt to conduct a complex, large-scale qualitative study. Data for this were collected in 18 areas of England between April 2002 and 2005 as part of a significant quasi-experimental police reform programme,[2] involving an initial small-scale pilot study, followed by two waves of in-depth interviews as

---

[2] The National Reassurance Policing Programme (NRPP) was established to develop and test the potential capacity of specific policing processes to reduce public fear of crime and increase levels of trust and confidence in the police. As part of these efforts an extensive programme of 'basic research' was commissioned in an attempt to establish data and methods that would produce detailed understanding of what the public's key neighbourhood security concerns were in each of the areas and how these might be explained (see Tuffin, Morris, and Poole, 2006).

part of the main study. The pilot study involving a total of 30 respondents was conducted in April 2002 in the towns of Guildford and Sutton (South London). It was designed to test the capacity of a qualitative interview instrument to collect the sorts of data necessary for developing an analytic framework capable of locating the presence of signals of different kinds. Whilst retaining the flexibility of semi-structured interview approaches in terms of the sequencing of questions, an important feature designed into the interview instrument was the principal of 'guided retrieval' and the four specific 'retrieval mnemonics' advocated by proponents of cognitive interviewing techniques (Geiselman et al., 1986). Fisher and Geiselman (1992) suggest that when asked to provide detailed accounts of complex and emotionally loaded past experiences and situations, peoples' memory retrieval can be enhanced if they are encouraged to: (1) mentally reinstate the context of the event; (2) report all available information whether they deem it relevant or not; (3) report the event in different sequences, particularly in reverse; (4) change their perspective in terms of their reporting of the event. There is certainly evidence from previous studies of the fear of crime, that respondents often struggle to articulate their complex thoughts and feelings about crime (Girling, Loader, and Sparks, 2000; Sasson, 1995).

Commencing with some fairly general questions about life in the local area, after about five minutes the interviewer then asked the respondents about 'any problems' in the neighbourhood and further afield that they were aware of, and they were encouraged to provide detailed descriptions of any pertinent issues or incidents. Depending upon how much detail the respondent provided, the interviewer might then intervene to try and encourage them to reinstate the context by asking questions such as: 'Can you describe to me precisely what it was that you saw?'; 'How did that make you feel?'; or 'What did you think about that at the time?' Typically in this phase of the interview interaction, respondents described a combination of first-hand experiences, tales told to them by other residents, and events that they had learnt about via mass media outlets.

Once this more open-ended phase of the interview seemed to be coming to an end in terms of the respondent having exhausted their descriptions, the interviewer provided three prompt cards to the interviewee. On these were listed a large number of crime, social disorder, and physical disorder problems. Introducing these cards often helped respondents to remember additional events that they would not otherwise have talked about. This was particularly helpful in eliciting data on 'minor disorders', which actually turned out to have salience to the respondents, but they would not have automatically talked about alongside other criminal matters as they seemed comparatively trivial. Thus in effect, the production of the prompt cards in the interview helped to encourage improved recall in terms of what people talked about in their neighbourhoods. In the main study, in the next phase of the interview, people were provided with a large A3 paper map of their neighbourhood and surrounding area and asked a sequence of questions. Firstly, the interviewer invited them to draw with a pen on the map 'anywhere they felt afraid of', 'anywhere they avoided', and 'any locations that particular problems tend to occur'. In essence, what was happening here was an attempt to reverse the accounting sequence, in that rather than starting with the crime or disorder event, the respondents were being asked to plot the effects that these were having upon their outlook. Having specified the problematic locations, the interviewer then asked the respondent to explain and describe what issues were occurring there. This frequently resulted in the interviewees returning to the incidents they had described in the opening phase of the interview and providing a location for these. On a number of occasions, by thinking in geographic terms, respondents started to identify incidents that they had not previously recalled. In effect, they had been encouraged to change their perspective on local problems.

The pilot study demonstrated that the instrument produced large amounts of highly detailed data that when subject to appropriate analytic treatments provided a rich and nuanced picture of local crime and disorder problems, and the impacts these were having locally. Consequently, with the introduction of the mapping component noted earlier, the instrument was adopted for the main study commencing August 2003. Following training, a team of six field interviewers conducted a total of 220 interviews in 16 electoral wards throughout Britain. Then between August 2004 and January 2005 a further 83 interviews were conducted in eight of the sites from the first wave. Sixty-three of these were re-interviews of the previous participants, plus an additional 20 new respondents. The significance of these second wave interviews is described in more detail in the analysis of 'scripting' later in this Afterward. All of the interviews were recorded on digital audio tape format and fully transcribed. The shortest of all the interviews was 42 minutes, the longest was two hours and seventeen minutes, and the average was about one hour and fifteen minutes.

In addition to the in-depth interviews, several other sources of data were available to the research team. Concurrent with the first wave of interviews, focus groups were convened with other residents, in some of the 16 sites where respondent recruitment for one-to-one interviews was proving difficult, where it was a particularly large research site, or where there were particular issues worth exploring. Additionally, police crime and incident data, and local authority administrative data were collated for each of the sites, although the quality of this varied markedly. The researchers in each site also attempted to keep a file of relevant news stories from local newspapers. Again the quality of this varied. Field observations were also conducted by the members of the research team in public spaces in the sites.

More importantly though, as part of the wider study, in each of the 16 sites a telephone survey with approximately 300 respondents per site was conducted. Although the purpose of the survey was principally evaluative, seeking to detect any police intervention impacts, a number of questions derived from the British Crime Survey were included within the schedule that were helpful in testing aspects of the validity and reliability of the signal crimes approach. For example, questions intended to capture levels of fear of crime and perceptions of disorder were used to gauge the extent to which the qualitative signal crimes analysis was producing valid insights into neighbourhood conditions and concerns.

Sampling

The two pilot and sixteen main study sites where data were collected were selected to provide a variety of contexts in which to investigate how certain incidents functioned as warning signals to people. So included in the sites were deprived, high crime neighbourhoods, areas with comparatively high numbers of minority ethnic residents, as well as more affluent, low crime ones.[3] Each of the sixteen sites was an electoral ward. At the time when the study commenced, electoral wards were the smallest administrative unit available in the English political system. Wards are not of a uniform size, and there was a significant difference evident in the number of residents in the largest and smallest wards included in the study. Nevertheless the advantage of using wards is that a range of administrative data are reported at this level and could thus be used to inform the research. Some summary and descriptive data for each of the sites is provided in Table A.1.

The column furthest to the left in the table lists the ward names and next to it, are the town, city, or county names where the wards are located. The third column provides the resident population for the ward according to the 2001 UK census. The 'deprivation' column is based upon the Index of Multiple Deprivation that is calculated for all wards by the UK Office for National Statistics. Based upon these scores, all 8301 electoral wards in England and Wales are ranked against each other with 'one' constituting the most deprived ward overall. As can be seen, a majority of the research sites were amongst the more deprived wards in the country, with five located in the top 10 per cent of most deprived wards and nine in the uppermost quartile. This is a factor that may have some bearing upon the generalizability of the findings reported. The two columns to the right-hand side of the table, record the number of interviews and focus groups conducted per site.

'Neighbourhood sentinels'

From the pilot study and early interviews for the main study, it became apparent that there were significant variations in the quantity and quality of data provided by individual respondents. Some were able to give 'high resolution' accounts, full of texture and 'thick description' about the problems in their neighbourhood and beyond. Whereas others living in the same area could say very little about what was going on near where they lived. The former group seemed to function as 'neighbourhood sentinels' who were especially watchful for, and attentive to, any actual or threatened breaches in the local social order.

---

[3] The only type of area not included was a rural one.

Table A.1 Summary of sites and data collected

Ward Name	Area	Resident pop.	Deprivation	Total no. interviews	Focus groups
Ash Wharf	Surrey	6073	N/a	13	0
Aston	Birmingham	27,000	27	39*	2
Brunswick	Blackpool	7353	1801	19*	2
Burghfield	Thames Valley	5894	7627	12	0
Colville	London	7909	1509	13	2
Failsworth West	Oldham	7827	1642	11	0
Falconwood & Welling	London	10,535	5882	25*	2
Greenham	Thames Valley	4843	4871	14*	0
Guildford (pilot)	Surrey	N/a	N/a	15	0
Ingol	Preston	7395	1487	14	2
New Parks	Leicester	16,022	410	17*	1
Walton North	Surrey	6650	4380	17*	0
St Helier	London	9000	2518	14	1
St Marys	Oldham	10,785	103	47*	0
Sutton (pilot)	London	n/a	n/a	15	0
Town centre	St Helens	8376	110(a)	22*	2
Upper Edmonton	London	14,923	n/a	13	0
West Park	St Helens	8953	809(a)	13	2

* denotes where re-interviews of some respondents are included.
(a) denotes approximation as these were new wards created after the 2001 census

Examining these differences, it appeared that those respondents possessing the neighbourhood sentinel traits tended to be, as a result of lifestyle factors and routine activities, connected to a comparatively broad and dense local social network, and to spend more time in public spaces. So, for example, mothers with children, those involved in voluntary community activities, together with people working in roles such as postal delivery workers, taxi drivers, and hairdressers all seemed to have a particular awareness of local problems that they heard about on the local 'grapevine'. There are important precedents within the literature for focusing upon 'high knowledge' individuals. For example, Gresham Sykes (1951) identified that if one is interested in the information about an area possessed by its residents, rather than the attitudes that they hold towards it, then there are socially structured patterns detectable between those groups who hold 'more' and 'less' neighbourhood information. Developing the implications of such a logic, Campbell (1955) systematically examined this 'asymmetry of knowledge'. In his test he differentiated between a randomly selected group of respondents who were surveyed and a smaller group of deliberately selected 'high knowledge' informants who were questioned using a semi-structured interview. He found that the data from the latter group was marginally more accurate than that derived from the far larger sample of randomly selected survey respondents.

In the present study, because the principal interest was in gauging the salience of actual crime and disorder events and the reactions to these in neighbourhoods, rather than more generic, abstract, attitudinal data, the interviews were purposively directed towards those key individuals thought to be performing a neighbourhood sentinel role. The success of this sampling strategy varied across the sites, proving more effective in some areas than others. Furthermore, the availability of the data derived from the telephone survey, with its far larger sample of randomly selected respondents, provided a mechanism whereby the likely generalizability of the more focused qualitative work could be assessed. Where the interview data was compared with that from the survey, albeit with a few exceptions, it did seem that the more focused signal crime interviews were identifying similar sorts of problems as those arising in the survey.[4] The advantage of the signal crimes analysis is it affords some unique insights into why these issues were being seen as problematic.

In the first wave of interviews, 61 per cent of the respondents were female (n=132) and 39 per cent (n=86) male. In the second wave, nineteen male and forty-four of the original female respondents were re-interviewed. The over-representation of female respondents seems to reflect a gender differential in terms of investment in their neighbourhoods, with them being more willing to commit the time to be interviewed and more likely to possess the neighbourhood sentinel qualities being sought. Relatedly, women may have been more likely to be available for interview at the time when the research teams were working.

Half of all those interviewed said they were aged between 30 and 60 with 25 per cent self-identifying as being less than 30 years of age and the same proportion saying they were aged over 60. Overall, 73 per cent of the respondents were white, 5 per cent black and 8 per cent Asian.[5] It is worth clarifying that there were distinct clusters of interviewees drawn from minority ethnicities in several particular sites where there were established minority communities. In total, 42 per cent of those questioned said they were owner-occupiers, with the vast majority of the rest saying they rented their house. Twenty-nine per cent of the interview respondents self-identified as disabled. Nearly one-third of the respondents

---

[4] It is of course to be expected that some differences will emerge given the influence we know that question formats exhibit over resulting data. Such methodological issues seem to account for most of the discrepancies between the qualitative and quantitative data. There were, however, some instances where the disjunctions were more substantive. For example, in Aston ward in Birmingham, 'gun crime' featured as a strong signal, but did not appear in the survey data.

[5] The remainder self-identified using other classifications or refused to provide this information.

reported having been a victim of a crime in the last 12 months and 80 per cent thought that, at the time of being questioned, there was more crime and anti-social behaviour now than two years ago. On average, respondents had lived for 18.4 years in their current area, but this figure masks marked variations, with a mean average of 4.2 years for Greenham, stretching up to 29.9 years in Falcon-wood and Welling.

Data analysis

Analysis of the data took place in two principal phases. The first focused upon analysing the individual interview accounts, and constructing and refining the conceptual framework for locating signal events in peoples' talk about their neighbourhoods and beyond. Thus in the early stages of this analysis, the focus was upon identifying all of the key components (expressions, contents, and effects) of different types of signal event. Analysis of the pilot study data and the early data from the main study suggested a total of five principal expression codes, six content codes and twelve possible effect types. Once this framework was established and confirmed, all of the interview transcripts that had been used in its development were re-analysed to ensure that they were compatible with the final version. From this point on, the procedure became more akin to a conventional coding exercise. Coding to locate all the signals across all of the interview and focus group transcripts took a team of six full-time researchers a period of about six months.

A particular challenge of deploying the linked expression, content, and effect constructs within the analysis was finding ways to maintain a record of the connections between these individual items of data within any interview transcript. Because of the dense ways in which people talk about crime and disorder problems, rapidly switching between personal experiences, mediated knowledge, conjecture, and general attitude, it was often quite challenging analytically to follow the threads of cognition and inference that connected expressions, to contents, to effects. It was certainly the case that the different parts of different signals were articulated in varied narrative sequences. So interviewees would sometimes start by describing an incident and the effect it had on them. But other times they would start by talking about a location that they were concerned about and only sometime later reveal the trigger for this concern. Further complexity was overlaid on such matters as a result of how multiple effects were frequently attributed to individual incident expressions by respondents. So for example, people described the ways an incident simultaneously triggered fear, behavioural avoidance of a location, and changes in how they perceived certain types of people.

A solution to these problems, which were compounded by the large volumes of interview data, was provided by the use of data management software. The package N.Vivo was used to assist in the coding process, providing a way of being able to connect the different bits of a signal together, whilst also enabling rapid searches through large amounts of data in order to locate different types of signal.

Each signal event located in interview was assigned a unique identifier through the software package, which recorded the type of signal it was and where it was located. This capacity to manage a comparatively intricate and layered coding frame, necessary for the identification of signals would have been far more difficult to accomplish with a manual coding system.

The second advantage of the use of this package was that it encouraged a disciplined approach to coding where a team of six researchers was involved (Fielding and Lee, 1998). Because codes had to be specifically introduced into the software it encouraged a systematic approach to the process. To deal with the inter-rater reliability issue, specific tests were conducted at the start, mid-point of the process, and at any point where new codes were introduced. Additionally, the software's audit-trail capacity enabled coder (and other analytic) decisions to be tracked and selectively revised when necessary.

The second phase of the analysis moved from an individual to a neighbourhood level. Having located all the signal events mentioned by individual respondents talking about their areas and neighbourhoods, the focus then shifted to using these to establish a rich picture of peoples' collective concerns in each of the sites. So in effect, the data from individual respondents were aggregated to establish where they were talking about the same crime and disorders, and the same troublesome locations. As part of this neighbourhood analysis, the qualitative data was compared with the results from analysis of the telephone survey. By comparing the two datasets it was possible to establish whether the qualitative data was identifying similar issues to that derived from the more extensive telephone survey data, and if so, what original insights application of the signal crimes framework provided. A comparative form of analysis was also then conducted to explore the similarities and differences in the signal profiles between the different areas.

This use of additional datasets is an important feature of several of the essays where more statistical and quantitative forms of data are introduced to validate or refine findings emanating from qualitative materials. This serves to clarify that this more systematic form of naturalistic social observation is not constrained to particular methods of collecting data, and can encompass both qualitative and quantitative approaches.

Conclusion

The principal focus of this note on method has been upon how to generate disruptive ideas, revelatory concepts, and theories with the power to fundamentally alter how we perceive issues of crime, disorder, and social control. What I have rather deprecatingly labelled 'gonzo research' is an attempt to think these matters through. My intention is not that such an approach could or should replace traditional research and its emphases on validity and reliability. Gonzo research cannot claim these qualities. But it can supplement them. What I have in mind is the sorts of techniques I have outlined being used to derive and devise new concepts and ideas. Once they have been formulated then they can be subject to more rigorous research designs to establish their wider relevance and general usability. It is this blended approach of conceptual innovation trailed by systematic testing that has underpinned each of the preceding essays in this collection.

References

Aaronovitch, D. (2010) *Voodoo Histories: How Conspiracy Theory Has Shaped Modern History*. London: Vintage.

Altheide, D. (2002) *Creating Fear: News and the Construction of Crisis*. New York: Aldine de Gruyter.

Allsop, C. (2013) 'Motivations, money and modern policing: Accounting for cold case reviews in an age of austerity' Policing and Society 23/3: 362–75.

Ashby, D. (2005) 'Policing neighbourhoods: Exploring the Geographies of crime, policing and performance assessment' Policing and Society 15/4: 413–47.

Becker, H. (1963) *Outsiders: studies in the sociology of deviance*. New York: The Free Press.

Best, J. and G. Honuichi (1985) 'The razor blade in the apple: The social construction of urban legends' Social Problems 32/5: 488–99.

Bittner, E. (1972) *The Functions of the Police in Modern Society: A Review of Background Factors, Current Practices, and Possible Role Models*. Washington, DC: National Institute of Mental Health.

Black, D. (1976) *The Behavior of Law*. New York: Academic Press.

Black, D. (2004) 'The geometry of terrorism' Sociological Theory 22(1): 14–25.

Blair, T. (2010) *A Journey*. London: Hutchison.

Bottoms, A. (2006) 'Incivilities, offence and social order in residential communities' in A. von Hirsch and A. Simester (eds) *Incivilities: Regulating Offensive Behaviour*. Oxford: Hart Publishing.

Bottoms, A. (2012) 'Developing socio-spatial Criminology' in M. Maguire, R. Morgan and R. Reiner (eds) *Oxford Handbook of Criminology* (5th edn). Oxford: Oxford University Press.

Bottoms, A. and J. Tankebe (2012) 'Beyond procedural justice: A dialogic approach to legitimacy in criminology' Journal of Criminal Law and Criminology 102: 119–70.

Brodeur, J-P. (2010) *The Policing Web*. Oxford: Oxford University Press.

Brookman, F. (2005) *Understanding Homicide*. London: Sage.

Burdge, R. and F. Vanclay (1996) 'Social impact assessment: A contribution to the state of the art series' Impact Assessment 14(1): 59–86.

Burke, J. (2011) *The 9/11 Wars*. London: Penguin.

Burke, K. (1954) *Permanence and Change: An Anatomy of Purpose* (2nd edn). Berkeley, Ca: University of California Press.

Cain, M. and A. Howe (2008) *Women, Crime and Social Harm: Towards a Criminology for the Global Era*. Oxford: Hart Publishing.

Campbell, D. (1955) 'The informant in quantitative research' American Journal of Sociology 60/4: 339–42.

Carr, P. (2005) *Clean Streets: Controlling Crime, Maintaining Order and Building Community Action*. New York: New York University Press.

Castells, M. (1997) *The Network Society*. Oxford: Blackwells.

Chancer, L. (2005) *High Profile Crimes: When Legal Cases Become Social Causes*. Chicago: University of Chicago Press.

Cialdini, R. (2001) *Influence: Science and Practice* (4th edn). Boston: Allyn and Bacon.

Cohen, S. (1985) *Visions of Social Control*. Cambridge: Polity Press.

Cohen, S. (1966/2002) *Folk Devils and Moral Panics: The Creation of the Mods and Rockers* (3rd edn). London: Routledge.

Cohen, S. (2005) *States of Denial: Knowing About Atrocities and Suffering*. Cambridge: Polity Press.

Collins, R. (2008) *Violence: A Micro-Sociological Theory*. Princeton NJ: Princeton University.

Condry R. (2007) *Families Shamed: The Consequences of Crime for the Relatives of Serious Offenders*. Cullompton: Willan.

Cooley, C. H. (1902) *Human Nature and the Social Order*. New York: Scribners.

Cronin, A. (2011) *How Terrorism Ends: Understanding the Decline and Demise of Terrorist Campaigns*. Princeton NJ: Princeton University Press.

Denzin, N. (1987) 'On semiotics and symbolic interactionism' Symbolic Interaction 10/1: 1–19.

Denzin, N. (2002) *Interpretive Interactionism* (2nd edn). London: Sage.

Ditton, J. and M. Innes (2005) 'Perceptual intervention and its role in the management of crime fear' in N. Tilley (ed) *The Handbook of Crime Prevention*. Cullompton: Willan.

Ditton, J., Bannister, J., Gilchrist, E., and S. Farrall (1999) 'Afraid or angry? Recalibrating the "fear" of crime' International Review of Victimology 6: 83–99.

Dolan, P., Hallsworth, M., Halpern, D., King, D., and V. Vlaev (undated) *MINDSPACE: Influencing Behaviour Through Public Policy*. London: Cabinet Office/Institute for Government.

Douglas, M. (1966) *Purity and Danger: An Analysis of Pollution and Taboo*. London: Routledge, Kegan and Paul.

Dunbar, R. (1996) *Grooming, Gossip and the Evolution of Language*. Cambridge, Ma: Harvard University Press.

Duneier, M. (1999) *Sidewalk*. New York: Farrar Straus Giroux.

Duneier, M. and H. Molotch (1999) 'Talking city trouble: Interactional vandalism, social inequality, and the urban interaction problem' American Journal of Sociology 104/4: 1263–95.

Eco, U. (1976) *A Theory of Semiotics*. Bloomington: Indiana University.

Elias, N. and Scotson, J. (1994) *The Established and the Outsiders: A Sociological Enquiry Into Community Problems* (2nd edn). London: Sage.

Elwood, S. and M.S. Cope (2009) *Qualitative GIS: A Mixed Methods Approach*. London: Sage.

Farrall, S., Jackson, J., and E. Gray (2009) *Social Order and the Fear of Crime in Contemporary Times*. Oxford: Clarendon Press.

Feinberg, J. (1987) *The Moral Limits of the Criminal Law Volume 1: Harm to Others*. Oxford: Oxford University Press.

Ferraro, K. (1995) *Fear of Crime: Interpreting Victimisation Risk*. Albany, NY: SUNY Press.

Fielding, N. (1995) *Community Policing*. Oxford: Clarendon Press.

Fielding, N. and R. Lee (1998) *Computer Analysis and Qualitative Research*. London: Sage.

Finckenaur, J. (1990) 'Legal socialization theory: A precursor to comparative research in the Soviet Union' Advances in Criminological Theory, Vol. 2.

Fine, G. (2001) *Difficult Reputations: Collective Memories of the Evil, Inept and Controversial*. Chicago: University of Chicago Press.

Fine, G. and B. Ellis (2010) *The Global Grapevine: Why Rumours of Terrorism, Immigration and Trade Matter*. New York: Oxford University Press.

Fisher, R.P. and R.E. Geiselman (1992) *Memory Enhancing Techniques for Investigative Interviewing: The Cognitive Interview*. Springfield II: Charles C. Thomas.

Florida, R. (2002) *The Rise of the Creative Class*. New York: Basic Books.

Fosher, K. (2009) *Under Construction: Making Homeland Security at the Local Level*. Chicago: University of Chicago Press.

Foucault, M. (1977) *Discipline and Punish*. New York: Vintage.

Garland, D. (2001) *The Culture of Control: Crime and Social Order in Contemporary Society*. Chicago: University of Chicago Press.

Garland, D. (2008) 'On the concept of moral panic' Crime, Media, Culture 4/1: 9–30.

Garland, D. (2010) *Peculiar Institution: America's Death Penalty in an Age of Abolition*. Oxford: Oxford University Press.

Gattrell, V. (2008) 'Inside stories' *The Guardian,* 30 August <http://www.theguardian.com/books/2008/aug/30/prisonsandprobation> (accessed 3 January 2014).

Geiselman, R., Fisher, R., Mackinnon, D., and H. Holland (1986) 'Enhancement of eyewitness memory with the cognitive interview' American Journal of Psychology 99/3: 385–401.

Girling, E., Loader, I., and R. Sparks (2000) *Crime and Social Change in Middle England*. London: Routledge.

Goffman, A. (2009) 'On the run: Wanted men in a Philadelphia ghetto' American Sociological Review 74: 339.

Goffman, E. (1961) *Asylums: Essays on the Social Situation of Mental Patients and Other Inmates*. New York: Anchor Books.

Goffman, E. (1972) *Relations in Public: Microstudies of the Public Order*. New York: Harper Colophon.

Hacking, I. (1983) *Representing and Intervening*. Cambridge: Cambridge University Press.

Hacking, I. (1995) *Re-writing the Soul: Multiple Personality and the Sciences of Memory*. Princeton NJ: Princeton University Press.

Hacking, I. (2011) 'Between Michel Foucault and Erving Goffman: Between discourse in the abstract and face-to-face interaction' Economy and Society 33/3: 277–302.

Hale, C. (1996) 'Fear of crime: A review of the literature' International Review of Victimology 4/2: 79–150.

Hammersley, M. (2013) *The Myth of Research Based Policy and Practice*. London: Sage.

Harcourt, B. (2001) *Illusion of Order: The False Promise of Broken Windows Policing*. Cambridge, Ma: Harvard University Press.

Harcourt, B. (1999) 'The collapse of the harm principle' Journal of Criminal Law and Criminology 90: 109–94.

Harfield, C. (2006) 'A paradigm shift in British policing' British Journal of Criminology 46, 4: 743–61.

Hawkins, K. (2002) *Law as Last Resort*. Oxford: Oxford University Press.

Haynes, L., Service, O., Goldacre, B., and D. Torgerson (2012) *Test, Learn, Adapt: Developing Public Policy With Randomised Control Trials*. London: Cabinet Office.

Her Majesty's Inspectorate of Constabulary (2011) *The Rules of Engagement: A Review of the August 2011 Disorders*. London: Home Office.

Hillsborough Independent Panel (2012) *The Report of the Hillsborough Independent Panel*. London: HMSO.

Hillyard, P., Pantazis, C., Tombs, S., and D. Gordon (2004) *Beyond Criminology: Taking Harm Seriously*. London: Pluto Press.

Home Office (2009) *Pursue, Prevent, Protect, Prepare: The United Kingdom's Strategy for Countering International Terrorism*. London: Home Office.

Horgan, J. (2005) *The Psychology of Terrorism*. London: Routledge.

Hunter, A. (1985) 'Private, parochial, and public school orders: The problem of crime and incivility in urban communities' in G. Suttles and M. N. Zald (eds) *The challenge of social control: Citizenship and institution building in modern society*, 230–42. Norwood NJ: Ablex.

Hutter, B. and S. Lloyd-Bostock (2013) 'Risk, interest groups and the definition of crisis: The case of volcanic ash' British Journal of Sociology 64(3): 383–404.

Hutter, B. and M. Power (2005) *Organizational encounters with risk: an introduction*. Cambridge: Cambridge University Press.

Inciardi, J. and L. Harrison (eds) (2000) *Harm Reduction: National and International Perspectives*. Thousand Oaks, Ca: Sage.

Innes, M. (2003a) 'Investigating murder: Detective work and the police response to Criminal Homicide. Oxford: Clarendon Press.

Innes, M. (2003b) *Understanding Social Control: Deviance, Crime and Social Order*. Open University Press.

Innes M. (2004) 'Signal crimes and signal disorders: Notes on deviance as communicative action' British Journal of Sociology 55/3: 335–50.

Innes, M. (2010) 'Criminal legacies: Community impact assessments and defining success and harm in police homicide investigations' Journal of Contemporary Criminal Justice 26/4: 367–81.

Innes, M., Abbott, L., Lowe, T., and C. Roberts (2007) *Hearts and Minds and Eyes and Ears: Reducing Radicalisation Risks Through Reassurance-Oriented Policing*. London: ACPO.

Innes, M. and A. Clarke (2009) 'Policing the past: Cold case studies, forensic evidence and retroactive social control' British Journal of Sociology 60/3: 543–63.

Innes, M. and N. Fielding (2002) 'From community to communicative policing: "Signal crimes" and the problem of public reassurance' Sociological Research Online (7/2) <http://socresonline.org.uk/7/2>.

Innes, M., Fielding, N., and N. Cope (2005) 'The appliance of science: the theory and practice of criminal intelligence analysis' British Journal of Criminology 45: 39–57.

Jackson, J. (2004) 'Experience and expression: Social and cultural significance in the fear of crime' British Journal of Criminology 44/6: 946–66.

Jackson, J., Bradford, B., Stanko, E., and K. Hohl (2012) *Just Authority?: Trust in the Police in England and Wales*. London: Routledge.

Jacobs, J. (1961) *The Death and Life of Great American Cities*. New York: Random House.

Jenkins, B. (1994) *Using Murder: The Social Construction of Serial Murder*. New York: Aldine de Gruyter.

Kahneman, D. (2011) *Thinking Fast and Slow*. London: Allen Lane.

Katz, J. (2001) 'From how to why: On luminous description and causal inference in ethnography (Part 1)' Ethnography 2/4: 443–73.

Kean, T. and L. Hamilton (2004) *The 9/11 Commission Report*. W.W. Norton: New York.

Keizer, K., Lindenberg, S., and L. Steg (2008) 'The spreading of disorder' Science, 12 December, 322(5908): 1681–5.

Kennedy, D. (2008) *Deterrence and Crime Prevention: Reconsidering the Prospect of Sanction*. London: Routledge.

Knorr-Cetina, K. (1999) *Epistemic Cultures: How the Sciences Make Knowledge*. Cambridge, Ma: Harvard University Press.

Kundani, A. (2009) *Spooked! How Not to Prevent Violent Extremism*. London: Institute of Race Relations.

Kury, H. (1994) 'The influence of the specific formulation of questions on the results of victim studies' European Journal of Criminal Policy and Research 2: 48–68.

Laqueur, W. (2001) *A History of Terrorism*. New York: Transaction.

Lambert, R. (2011) *Countering Al-Qaeda in London: Police and Muslims in Partnership*. London: Hurst.

Levi, M. (2008) *The Phantom Capitalists: The Organisation and Control of Long-Firm Fraud* (2nd edn). Aldershot: Ashgate.

Loader, I. (2006) 'Policing, recognition and belonging' Annals of the American Academy of Political and Social Science 605/1: 202–21.

Lofland, L. (1985) *A World of Strangers: Order and Action in Urban Public Space* (2nd edn). Illinois: Waveland Press.

Manning, P. (1987) *Semiotics and Fieldwork*. Thousand Oaks: Sage.

Manning, P. (1997) *Police Work: The Social Organization of Policing* (2nd edn). Illinois: Waveland Press.

Manning, P. (1992) *Erving Goffman and Modern Sociology*. Cambridge: Polity Press.

Manningham-Buller, E. (2007) 'The international terrorist threat to the United Kingdom' in P. Hennessy (ed) *The New Protective State: Government, Intelligence and Terrorism*. London: Continuum.

Marteau, T., Roland, M., Suhrcke, M., and M. Kelly (2011) 'Judging nudging: Can nudging improve population health?' British Medical Journal 342: 263–65.

Marwick, A. (2013) 'How your data are being deeply mined' New York Review of Books 61/1.

Maher, L. and D. Dixon (1999) 'Policing and Public Health' British Journal of Criminology 39/4: 488–512.

Meyrowitz, J. (1985) *No Sense of Place*. New York: Oxford University Press.

Mills, C. Wright (1959) *The Sociological Imagination*. Oxford: Oxford University Press.

MIT SENSEable City Lab (2011) 'Trash track' in M. Shepard (ed) *Sentient City: Ubiquitous Computing, Architecture and the Future of Urban Space*. Cambridge, Ma: MIT Press.

Molotch, H. (2012) *Against Security: How We Go Wrong at Airports, Subways, and Other Sites of Ambiguous Danger*. Princeton NJ: Princeton University Press.

Moon, C. (2008) *Narrating Political Reconciliation: South Africa's Truth and Reconciliation Commission*. Lanham, MD: Lexington Books/Rowman and Littlefield.

Moon, C. (2012) 'Who'll pay reparations on my soul? Compensation, social control and social suffering' Social and Legal Studies 21/2: 187–99.

Morris, C. (1964) *Signification and Significance: A Study of the Relation of Signs and Values*. Cambridge, Ma: MIT Press.

Muir, H. and R. Butt (2005) 'A rumour, outrage and then a riot. How tension in a Birmingham suburb erupted' *The Guardian*, 24 October.

NOP Social Research/Channel 4 (2006) *Attitudes to Living in Britain: A Survey of Muslim Opinion*.

175

O'Malley, P. (2010) 'Simulated justice: risk, money and telemetric policing' British Journal of Criminology 50: 795–807.

Neyland, D. (2009) 'Mundane terror and the threat of everyday objects' in Aas, K., Gundus, H., and H. Lovell (eds) *Technologies of Insecurity: The Surveillance of Everyday Life*. Abingdon: Routledge-Cavendish.

Pantazis, C. and S. Pemberton (2009) 'From the "old" to the "new" suspect community examining the impacts of recent UK counter-terrorist legislation' British Journal of Criminology 49: 646–66.

Park, R. (1916) 'The City: Suggestions for the investigation of human behaviour in an urban environment' American Journal of Sociology 20: 608–20.

Park, R. and E. Burgess (1925) *The City: suggestions for the investigation of human behavior in the urban environment*. Chicago: University of Chicago Press.

Pemberton, S. (2007) 'Social harm future(s): Exploring the potential of the social harm approach' Crime, Law and Social Change 48(1–2): 27–41.

Perry, W., McInnis, B., Price, C., Smith, S., and J. Hollywood (2013) *Predictive Policing: The Role of Crime Forecasting in Law Enforcement Operations*. Washington DC: National Institute of Justice.

Platt, R. (2011) *Smuggling in the British Isles: A History*. Stroud, Glouc: The History Press.

Polk, K. (1994) *When Men Kill*. Cambridge: Cambridge University Press.

Putnam, R. (2000) *Bowling Alone: The Collapse and Revival of American Community*. New York: Simon and Schuster.

Ragin, C. (2008) *Redesigning Social Inquiry: Fuzzy Sets and Beyond*. Chicago: University of Chicago Press.

Richardson, L. (2006) *What Terrorists Want: Understanding the Terrorist Threat*. London: John Murray.

Reiner, R. (2007) 'Media made criminality' in M. Maguire, R. Morgan, and R. Reiner (eds) *Oxford Handbook of Criminology* (4th edn). Oxford: Oxford University Press.

Rock, P. (1973) 'News as eternal recurrence' in S. Cohen and J. Young (eds) *The Manufacture of News: Deviance, Social Problems and the Mass Media*. London: Constable and Co.

Rock, P. (1998) *After Homicide: Practical and Political Responses to Bereavement*. Oxford: Clarendon Press.

Rock, P. (2004) *Constructing Victims' Rights: The Home Office, New Labour and Victims*. Oxford: Clarendon Press.

Rock, P. (2010) 'Comment on public criminologies' Criminology and Public Policy 9/4: 751–67.

Ross, E.A (1901) *Social Control: a survey of the foundations of order*. London: Macmillan.

Rose, N. (1999) *Governing the Soul: The Shaping of the Private Self* (2nd edn). London: Free Association Books.

Rose, N. and J. Abi-Rached (2013) *Neuro: The New Brain Sciences and the Management of the Mind*. Princeton NJ: Princeton University Press.

Rowe, M. (ed) (2007) *Policing Beyond Macpherson: Issues in Policing, Race and Society*. Cullompton: Willan.

Sacco, V. (2005) *When Crime Waves*. Thousand Oaks, Ca: Sage.

Sageman, M. (2004) *Understanding Terror Networks*. Philadelphia: University of Pennsylvania Press.

Sampson, R. (2009) 'Disparity and diversity in the contemporary city: Social (dis)order revisited' British Journal of Sociology 60/1: 1–31.

Sampson, R. (2011) *Great American City*. Chicago: University of Chicago Press.

Sampson, R. and S. Raudenbusch (1999) 'Systematic social observation of public spaces: A new look at disorder in urban neighbourhoods' American Journal of Sociology 105(3): 603–51.

Sampson, R. and S. Raudenbusch (2004) 'Seeing disorder: Neighbourhood stigma and the social construction of "broken windows"' Social Psychology Quarterly 67(4): 319–42.

Sasson, Theodore (1995) *Crime Talk: How Citizens Construct a Social Problem*. New York: Aldine de Gruyter.

Sennett, R. (1970) *The Uses of Disorder: Personal Identity and City Life*. New York: Knopf.

Sennett, R. (1990) *The Conscience of the Eye*. Norton: Knopf.

Sennett, R. (2008) *The Craftsman*. London: Allen Lane.

Sennett, R. (2012) *Together: The Rituals, Pleasures, and Politics of Cooperation*. New Haven: Yale University Press.

Shaw, M., Tunstall, H., and D. Dorling (2005) 'Increasing inequalities in risk of murder in Britain: Trends in the demographic and spatial distribution of murder, 1981–2000' Health and Place 11: 45–54.

Shibutani, T. (1966) *Improvised News: A Sociological Study of Rumour*. New York: Bobbs-Merrill.

Simmel, G. (1976) 'The metropolis and mental life' in K.H. Wolff (trans) *The Sociology of Georg Simmel*. New York: The Free Press.

Simon, J. (2007) *Governing Through Crime: How the War on Crime Transformed American Democracy and Created a Culture of Fear*. New York: Oxford University Press.

Skogan, W. (1990) *Disorder and Decline: Crime and the Spiral of Decay in American Neighbourhoods*. Berkeley: University of California Press.

Skogan, W. (2006) *Police and Community in Chicago: A Tale of Three Cities*. New York: Oxford University Press.

Slovic, P. (2000) *The Perception of Risk*. New York, NY: Earthscan.

Slucka, J. (1989) *Hearts and Minds, Water and Fish: Support for the IRA and INLA in a Northern Ireland Ghetto*. Connecticut: JAI Press.

Smelser, N. (2007) *The Faces of Terrorism: Social and Psychological Dimensions*. Princeton NJ: Princeton University Press.

Sparks, R., Bottoms, A., and W. Hay (1996) *Prisons and the Problem of Order*. Oxford: Oxford University Press.

Sparks, R., Genn, H., and D. Dodd (1977) *Surveying Victims: A Study of the Measurement of Criminal Victimisation*. Chichester: Wiley.

Sparrow, M.K. (2009) *The Character of Harms: Operational Challenges in Control*. Cambridge: Cambridge University Press.

Steiner, C. (2012) *Automate This: How Algorithms Came to Rule Our World*. London: Portfolio Penguin.

Sudnow, D. (1965) 'Normal crimes: Sociological features of the penal code in a public defender office' Social Problems I2 (Winter 1965): 255–74.

Sutherland, E.H. (1949) *White Collar Crime*, New York: Holt, Rinehart & Winston.

Suttles, G. (1970) *The Social Order of the Slum: Ethnicity and Territory in the Inner City*. Chicago: University of Chicago Press.

Sykes, Gresham (1951) 'The differential distribution of community knowledge' Social Forces 29: 376–82.

Taylor, K. (2004) *Brainwashing: The Science of Thought Control*. Oxford: Oxford University Press.

Taylor, R. (2001) *Breaking Away from Broken Windows*. Boulder, Co: Westview Press.

Thacher, D. (2005) 'The local role in Homeland Security' Law and Society Review 39(5): 635–76.

Thaler, R. and C. Sunstein (2008) *Nudge: Improving Decisions About Health, Wealth and Happiness*. New Haven: Yale University Press.

Thomas, W.I. (1928) *The Child in America: Behaviour, Problems and Prospects*. New York: Knopf.

Thompson, D. (2008) *Counterknowledge*. London: Atlantic Books.

Thompson, H. (1971) *Fear and Loathing in Las Vegas: A Savage Journey to the Heart of the American Dream*. London: Random House.

Tuffin, R., Morris, J., and A. Poole (2006) *An Evaluation of the Impact of the National Reassurance Policing Programme*. London: Home Office.

UK Drug Policy Commission (2009) *Safer Communities Special Issue: Law enforcement to reduce drug harms*. London: UKDPC.

Valverde, M. (2012) *Everyday Law on the Streets: City Governance in an Age of Diversity*. Chicago: University of Chicago Press.

Varese, F. (2011) *Mafias on the Move: How Organized Crime Conquers New Territories*. Princeton NJ: Princeton University Press.

Vulliamy, E. (2005) 'Rumours of a riot' *The Guardian*, 29 November.

Wacquant, L. (2007) *Urban Outcasts: A Comparative Sociology of Advanced Marginality*. Cambridge: Polity Press.

Warner, W. Lloyd (1959) *The Living and the Dead: A Study of the Symbolic Life of Americans*. New Haven: Yale University Press.

Warr, M. (1980) 'The accuracy of public beliefs about crime' Social Forces 59: 456–70.

Warr, M. (1982) 'The accuracy of public beliefs about crime: Further evidence' Criminology 20: 185–204.

Weston, N. and M. Innes (2010) *Re-thinking the Policing of Anti-Social Behaviour*. London. Her Majesty's Inspectorate of Constabulary.

Wilkins, L. (1964) *Social Deviance: Social Policy, Action and Research*. London: Routledge.

Wilkinson, P. (2000) *Terrorism vs Democracy: The Liberal State Response*. London: Routledge.

Williams, R. (1988) 'Understanding Goffman's methods' in P. Drew and A. Wootton (eds) *Erving Goffman: Exploring the Interaction Order*. Cambridge: Polity Press.

Wilson, J.Q. and G. Kelling (1982) 'Broken windows' The Atlantic Monthly, March: 29–38.

Wirth, L. (1938) 'Urbanism as a way of life' The American Journal of Sociology 44(1): 1–24.

Wolfgang, Marvin E. (1958) *Patterns in criminal homicide*. Philadelphia: University of Pennsylvania Press.

Wright, L. (2007) *The Looming Tower: Al-Qaeda's Road to 9/11*. London: Penguin.

Wilkinson, P. (2001) *Terrorism Versus Democracy: The Liberal State Response*. Abingdon: Frank Cass.

Young, J. (1999) *The Exclusive Society*. London: Sage.

Znaniecki, F. (1934) *The Method of Sociology*. New York: Farrar & Rinehart.

Subject Index

Author Index